ENCYCLOPAEDIA OF INDIAN GOVERNMENT: PROGRAMMES AND POLICIES

ENCYCLOPAEDIA
OF
INDIAN GOVERNMENT: PROGRAMMES AND POLICIES

Vol. 38

Scientific and Industrial Research

Edited by

Satish Tiwari

ANMOL PUBLICATIONS PVT. LTD.
NEW DELHI - 110 002 (INDIA)

ANMOL PUBLICATIONS PVT. LTD.
4374/4B, Ansari Road, Daryaganj
New Delhi - 110 002

Encyclopaedia of Indian Government: Programmes and Policies

First Edition, 2000
ISBN 81-261-0515-1 (Set)

PRINTED IN INDIA

Published by J.L. Kumar for Anmol Publications Pvt. Ltd., New Delhi - 110 002 and Printed at Mehra Offset Press, Delhi.

Contents

Preface

Encyclopaedia of Indian Government: Programmes and Policies contains authoritative information on about fifty departmental policies and their future developmental programmes.

Organised to be completed in 40 volumes, this gigantic work covers Agriculture; Atomic Energy; Chemicals and Fertilizers; Coal; Commerce; Communication; Culture; Defence; Education; Environment and Forests; External Affairs; Finance; Food & Consumer Affairs; Food Processing Industries; Health and Family Welfare; Home Affairs and Internal Security; Human Resources; Industry; Information and Broadcasting; Labour; Law, Justice and Company Affairs; Non-conventional Energy Sources; Ocean Development; Parliamentary Affairs; Personnel, Public Grievances and Pensions; Petroleum and Natural Gas; Planning and Programme Implementation; Planning and Statistics; Posts and Telegraphs; Power; Rural Development; Science and Technology; Social Justice and Empowerment; Space; States Affairs; Steel; Steel and Mines; Sugar and Edible Oils; Surface Transport; Textiles; Tourism; Urban Development; Water Resources; Women and Child development etc.

Based on the information derived from authoritative sources, this work contains authentic facts and figures. I am deeply beholden to all the scholars whose writings are cited or substantially made use of in the present work. I am also thankful to Anmol Publications Pvt. Ltd. for undertaking publication of this encyclopaedia. I am solely responsible for shortcomings in presentation of matter.

Encyclopaedic in nature, this will prove a dependable reference work for scholars and academics besides those appearing for different competitive examinations.

—Satish Tiwari

1
Introduction

The formation of the Ministry of Science and Technology was announced through a Presidential Notification dated January 4, 1985 (74/2/1/8. Cab.) contained in the 164th Amendment of the Government of India (Allocation of Business) Rules, 1961; the Department of Scientific and Industrial Research (DSIR) forms apart of this Ministry.

During 1998-99 the Minister In-charge is Dr. Murli Manohar Joshi, Union Minister for Ministry of Human Resource Development and Ministry of Science and Technology.

The Department of Scientific and Industrial Research (DSIR) comprises of the activities of the Council of Scientific and Industrial Research (CSIR), Departmental Schemes viz. Research and Development by Industry (RDI), Programme Aimed at Technological Self Reliance (PATSER), Scheme to Enhance the Efficacy of Transfer of Technology (SEETOT) and National Information System for Science and Technology (NISSAT) and two Public Enterprises viz. National Research Development Corporation (NRDQ and Central Electronics Limited (CEL).

Council of Scientific and Industrial Research

The CSIR is the national R&D organisation providing

scientific industrial research for India's economic growth and human welfare. It has a country-wide network of forty laboratories and eighty field centres covering fundamental and applied R&D in all areas -of science and technology barring atomic research, developing and nurturing S&T human resource for the country through extra mural support and promoting scientific talent through awards, fellowships etc.

As CSIR reorients itself to be market driven and move on the path of self-financing, its performance would be conditioned by the performance of the Indian industry and economy. Thus the rate of ECF generation from contract R&D and consultancy came down from 15 to 10%, the actual ECF going up from Rs. 190 crore to Rs. 209 crore. The contribution to creation of new knowledge was satisfactory, patent filings increased significantly, rising from 71 to 91 in the year for foreign patents and from 209 to 264 for Indian patents. The quality of papers contributed also showed a healthy upward trend although the number remained nearly static. CSIR's all round performance during the year was satisfactory. Most significant among its activities has been the winning initiative for revocation of US patent on turmeric, which besides confirming CSIR's pioneering efforts to successfully safeguard traditional Indian knowledge, created an unprecedented positive public goodwill for the CSIR. More importantly this success had some far-reaching effects viz: it demonstrated that CSIR and other Indian institutions were acquiring capabilities to fight the complex techno-legal issues of IPR, both defensively and aggressively, to meet the challenges under the WTO regime; it showed the importance of appropriate documentation and public availability of records of traditional knowledge base in a systematic manner, which can be provided as evidence of prior knowledge; it reassured the Indian people of the fair and transparent operations of the IPR system.

Some of the recent achievements of CSIR covering a wide spectrum are as follows:

The significant scientific achievements are:

In the field of bio-sciences including therapeutics: Regulation of cell growth, liposome, entrapped mite allergen, functional studies of lectins, tumor biology, brain cytochrome p450(s) enzymes, new approaches in chemotherapy of malaria, rapid screen for anti-TB drugs, molecular epidemiology of cholera, drug induced gastric hyperacidity, molecular studies on cytoplasmic male sterility, plant pathogens, DNA marker for papaya sex identification, somatic embryogenesis in mango, azadirachtin and limonoids in the Indian neem tree, antibacterial activity of Indian tree species and marine fouling & corrosion studies; *in the field of chemical sciences and technology*: liquid membrane modelling, pillaring of ion-exchanged clays, transition metal complexes with designed ligands, new chemical entities and Synthesis of N-protected precursors of synthetic sweetener Aspartame; *in the field of electronics and instrumentation*: electron cyclotron resonance source plasma, chemical composition of rainfall monitor and high performance CPU without secondary cache; in the field of Engineering: Control of Fly-rock due to blasting, Rural roads in Andhra Pradesh, Wind tunnel studies on structural models, Studies on vibration control of structures and foundations, Finite element analysis of large structures using parallel processing, Fatigue investigations of offshore structures, Creep damage and life assessment, Mining machinery Components and Industrial roofing system using cold forming steel section; *in the field of food processing*: Lipase catalysed esterification, Spices as nutraceuticals and Biofumigants for the control of insect pests; in the field of Information Products: Mathematical Models for Assessment of stability and Benchmarking the best practices of Research and Technology Organisations

(RTOs); *in the field of material sciences and technology:* RF-SQUID effect in boracarbide superconductors, Thermal modelling of DCC continuous casting and Foaming behaviour of FeO in slags during reduction; *in the field of physical sciences and earth Resources*: Modelling of Biogeochemical cycles of the Indian ocean, Crustal deformation using global positioning system, in situ stress measurement, Earthquake Studies and Oceanographic Studies and *in the field of societal and human welfare*: Neuroendocrine Regulation of Silk Protein biosynthesis.

The significant technological achievements are:

In the field of bio-sciences including therapeutics: Universal polymer support for synthesis of oligoribonucleotides, Diagnostic probe for leishmaniasis, Assay for Acute Lymphoblastic Leukemia (ALL), Human trial of a non-toxic cholrea vaccine, Novel usage of di-tert-butyl polycarbonate (DTBP), Isovitamin C by a genetically altered organism, Mini Chrysanthemum —CV. Mother Teresa, Application of chloro choline choride for bulb production of Tulips, Ocimum carnosum, a potential source of natural elemicin, New varieties of damask rose, Production technology for rose oil and rose water, Tissue Culture for Licorice & Ashwagandha, Plan transformation Technology, Biodegradation of endosulfan from contaminated soils and Wildlife management by genetic fingerprinting.

In the field of chemical sciences and technology: Foam as a reaction medium, Clay supported new reagents, Chiral template for enantiomers, Membrane/Adsorptive separation, Oxidative Coupling of Methane (OCM) to C_2-Hydrocarbons, Isomerization of O-dichlorobenzene to M-dichlorobenzene, CFC-113a technology for pyrethroids, Electro-chemical systems of naphthoquinone, Pyridine based chemicals, Cardanyl Acrylate and Poly Acrylate, Pervaporation Technology, Conversion of Methane to

Syngas, Conversion of NAtural Gas to Lower Olefins, MEnthol Manufacture, Soaker visbreaking technology, Conversion of Methane to Syngas, Conversion of Natural Gas to Lower Olefins, Menthol Manufacture, Soaker visbreaking technology, Mini Refinery, Reaction Engineering Laboratory and State-of-art system for chemical reaction studies; *in the field of electronics and instrumentation*: Electrical double layer capacitors (EDLC), Solid state room temperature gas sensor, Speed indicating and recording instrument for locomotives, Instrumentation for Microelectronics, RF Hyperthermia system for cancer therapy, Receivers for optical communication, Land based Digital Seismic Data Telemetry System, Inclinometer probe with digital indicator and PC based data acquisition system for thermo physical studies; *in the field of engineering*: Suprsonic combustor development, Development of powered hang glider, Wide Stall Mining Without Stowing, Multiblend cement, Natural rubber latex based cement concrete, Epoxy concrete for machine bed, Corrosion resistance of fly ash cements, Composition for Quick Setting of Cement, Flyash for highway embankment construction, Bio-energy for brick kilns, Cold forming of aluminium bicycle hubs, Improved iron removal for potable water, Decorticator for groundnut seeds, Remotely operated vehicle, Draft Tube (DT) Cone, Lignin from paper mill effluents, Bioremediation for Crude Oil contaminated soil and Eco-friendly coke-less cupola for Agra foundries; *in the field of food processing*: Modified atmospheric packaging. Technology protocols for mango export, Dehydrated green pepper, Dehydration of meat and Salt from the brines of Jambusar - quality improvement; *in the field of information products*: Software for fragment analysis, Software for electromagnetic design, Software for cathodic protection in off-shore platforms, software for the Analysis of Deflection Data, Engineering database on landslides, Multi-media database creation, CD-ROM Activities, Publication of research journals, Special Publications,

Popularisation of Science, Documentation centre for RGNDWM and Electoral Roll Database; *in the field of material sciences and technology*: High temperature superconducting wires/tapes and tube conductors, Carbon fibre epoxy prepregs, Ultra low expansion transparent glass-ceramic, Radiation Shielding Windows (RSW) glass, Flotation column for industrial applications.

Tiles from ferro-chrome and other industrial wastes, Improvement in efficiency of ferro-chromium process, Masonry cement from industrial wastes and Transmittance Standards for the infrared; in the field of Physical Sciences & Earth Resources: Green house gas inventory, Laser Heterodyne System in Antartica, Identification of deep seated weak zones, Gravity anomaly map and Comparative assessment of clean coal technologies; Studies and *in the field of societal and human welfare*: Leather Technology (LTM), Rehabilitation of tannery wastes, Ethnobotanical investigations of Kangra Valley in Himachal Pradesh, Improvement in rose oil distillation unit, Mechanisation of tea plucking, New propagation technology for tea, Banana Fibre, Fresh water prawn cultivars, Habilitation of the mentally challenged people and Floriculture Industry in H.P.

The major programmes of Department of Scientific and Industrial Research (other than CSIR) have been grouped as under:

I. Research and Development by Industry (RDI) consisting of:

   (a) In-house R&D by corporate/commercial sector of Industry.

   (b) R&D by Scientific and Industrial Research Organisation SIROs).

   (c) Fiscal Incentives for Scientific Research.

II. Programme Aimed at Technological Self-Reliance (PATSER) consisting of:
   (a) Development of new or improved technologies.
   (b) Development of special/custom built capital Goods.
   (c) Absorption and Adaptation of imported technology.
   (d) Studies and interactions concerning Technology Evaluation and pre-industry feasibility of major sectors/products.

III. Scheme to Enhance the Efficacy of Transfer of Technology (SEETOT) consisting of:
   (a) National Register of Foreign Collaborations (NRFC).
   (b) Industrial Technology
   (c) Transfer and Trading in Technology (TATT).
   (d) Promotion and Support to Consultancy Services (PSCS) which also include the Consultancy Development Centre (CDC).

IV. Linkages with International Organisations

V. National Information System for Science and Technology (NISSAT).

VI. Public Enterprises viz.
   (a) National Research Development Corporation (NRDC).
   (b) Central Electronics Limited (CEL).

Research and Development by Industry (RDI)

DSIR is the nodal department for granting recognition to In-house Research and Development centres; there were 1222 units having valid recognition as on 31 December 1998. 250 In-house R&D centres incurred an annual expenditure of over Rs. 1 crore and above. During the year,

59 in-house R&D centres incurred an annual expenditure of over Rs. 1 crore and above. During the year 1998, Twelfth National Conference on In-house R&D in industry was organised; DSIR National Awards were presented to 6 industrial units; Compendium on in-house R&D Centres (1998), Outstanding in-house R&D Achievements (1998) and 4 issues of In-house R&D in Industry Update were brought out.

Scientific research foundations in the area of medical, agriculture, natural and applied sciences and social sciences seek DSIR approval as Scientific and Industrial Research Organisations (SIROs) under the DSIR scheme of granting recognition to Scientific Industrial Research Organisations notification under 35(1)(ii)/(iii) of I.T. Act 1961 and for availing customs duty exemption on import of equipment and excise duty assumption on the purchase of essential scientific and technical instruments, apparatus, equipment (including computers), accessories and spare parts thereof and consumables required fro research and development activities and programmes. During the year, 19 new SIROs have been accorded DSIR recognition and 165 SIROs have been accorded renewal.

Government has introduced a few incentives to encourage investments in R&D by industry. These include depreciation allowance on plant and machinery set up based on indigenous technology. Customs duty exemption on goods imported for use in Government funded R&D projects, Customs & Excise duty exemption to recognised SIROs. During the year 1998, 11 certificates involving Rs. 2744 lakhs on cost of plant and machinery, 18 certificates for import of capital equipment and consumables/ materials for R&D projects supported by DSIR, 700 essentiality certificates for claiming customs duty exemption amounting Rs. 35 crores, 53 essential certificates for claiming excise duty exemptions amounting Rs. 153.63 lakhs were issued by DSIR.

DSIR is nodal department for registration of Public funded research institutions/universities /IITs/IISc., Bangalore/RECs other than a hospital for availing Customs Duty Exemption in terms of Notification No. 51/96 dated 23, July 1996. During the year, 175 such institutions were registered with DSIR.

Programme Aimed at Technological Self Reliances (PATSER)

Under the "Programme Aimed at Technological Self Reliance" (PATSER) the Department has so far supported about 85 R&D projects of Industrial units. These projects cover products and processes in various important industries such as metallurgy, electrical, electronics, instrumentation, mechanical engineering, earth moving and industrial machinery, chemicals and explosives. The projects in progress include those of M/s Semiconductor Complex Limited, (SCL), Chandigarh and C-DAC, Pune for development of ASIC (Application Specific Integrated Circuit) for Indian languages computing system GIST-II and the related card; M/s Semiconductor Complex Ltd. (SCL), Chandigarh and M/s Bharat Heavy Electricals Ltd. (BHEL), Bangalore for development of the ASIC and ASIC based 3 Phase multifunctional electronic energy meter for industrial applications; M/s Turbotech Precision Engineering Pvt. Ltd. Bangalore for the development of low cost gas turbine (LCGT) generator set of 500 KW power class, with multi fuel capability (biogas, piped natural gas and diesel fuel); M/s Andrew Yule & Co. Ltd., Calcutta for development of rough top rubber conveyer belting; M/s Bharat Earth Movers Ltd. (BEML), Bangalore for the design and development of 460 HP Wheel Dozer; M/s ACE Designers Ltd. and CMTI, Bangalore for development of PC Based CNC System.

The completed technology development projects supported under PATSER Scheme have resulted in significant technological and commercial returns to the industries concerned such as cost reduction, higher quality, improved products and processes as well as foreign exchange savings, while building up the R&D capabilities of the industrial units.

The on-going projects are expected to result in high commercial/societal impact and will lead to commercialisation and utilisation of 'state-of-the-art' technologies.

A new programme called 'Technopreneur Promotion Programme' (TePP) which aims to support individual innovators be they be housewives, artisans, farmers, students etc., in their attempts to commercialise their innovations has been introduced by PATSER alongwith 'Home Grown Technology Programme' of TIFAC(DST). 5 proposals have been financially supported so far and the others are in process.

Scheme to Enhance the Efficacy of Transfer of Technology (SEETOT)

The Department continued its activities relating to the scheme on National Register of Foreign Collaborations & Technology Management (NRFC & TM). A compilation of primary data on FCs for the year 1997 was brought out. Computerisation of data collected on foreign collaborations for 1997 has been completed. During the year, reports on Market and Development prospects of Fruits and Vegetable Processing industry in the Eastern and North Eastern Regions was finalised. A status study covering the performance, of the DSIR national award winning technologies and companies is also being completed. With a view to enhance capabilities in the area of Technology Management, a number of programmes have been initiated and ate in progress. These include case studies on Technology Management, bringing out bibliographies-oh various areas of technology management and othets. Interaction meets were organised covering interalia awateness programes on Intellectual Property System, technology acquisition and other related issues.

Under the Scheme on Transfer and Trading in Technology, activities carried out include: setting up of a Technology Exports Pavilion at India International Trade Fair' 1998 (IITF '98), in Pragati Maidan, New Delhi in which 12 organisations including industrial companies and research laboratories participated and displayed their technological capabilities; organisation of a "Seminar on Technologies from India" covering 3 sectors, viz. Drugs & Pharmaceuticals, Chemicals & Petrochemicals and Food Processing & Packaging; release of 3 quarterly issues of a Newsletter on Technology Exports; printing and release of a publication on Non- Conventional Technology Based Services- Capabilities & Export Opportunities; printing of a Compendium of Technology Exports from India covering data on technologies and services exports during 1995-96; printing of a brochure on Transfer and Trading in Technology Scheme; and launching of "Technology Exports Development Organisation", an institutional mechanism to promote technology exports, as recommended by the Task Force on Technology Exports.

The scheme relating to promotion and support to consultancy services essentially aims to strengthen consultancy capabilities for domestic and export markets. During the period under review the main activities have been towards setting Up of design and engineering service centre for Food Processing Industry at Kanpur and a Consultancy Clinic for Textile Industry at Bhilwara primarily to help small and medium industries. Besides, Studies on. (i) Status of Consultancy services in India, and (ii) Policies and Incentives for Consultants in various countries were carried out, and institutional and programme support to Consultancy Development Centre (CDC) was provided.

CDC was promoted in January 1986 as a non-profit society, primarily with a view to implement some of the programmes of DSIR. CDC is implementing 4 programme on Consultancy Development, Promotion & Assistance (CDPA) scheme, maintains a computerised database of consultants, organises training particularly on ISO-9000 and ISO-14000 and Human Resources development Programmes for promoting consultancy, conducts programmes sponsored by other agencies. DSIR is providing recurring and non recurring support to CDC. First National Consultancy Congress was conceptualised and organised on 15 January 1998, the foundation day of CDC and National Awards for Excellence in Consultancy were given away. Second Conference was organised on 151 January 1999, with the theme of "Project Management & Financing". To enhance technological and managerial capabilities of consultants as well as export capabilities, interactions with international organisations such as World Bank, APCTT, ITC and ESCAP were organised by CDC. Under the post graduate degree (MS) programme in Consultancy Management in association with BITS, Pilani 17 trainees of the 4" batch were undergoing training.

Linkages with International Organisations

During the year, the Department continued to participate in the activities of various international organisations such as UNCTAD, WIPO, UNIDO, ESCAP and APCTT at various levels and forums on issues related to Technology Development and Technology Transfer in coordination with other concerned Ministries.

DSIR participated in We Fourteenth Technical Advisory Committee meeting of Asian Pacific Centre for Transfer of Technology (APCTT) and the Thirteenth session of the Governing Board of APCTT held in Manila, Philippines.

National Information System for Science & Technology (NISSAT)

National Information System for Science &Technology

(NISSAT) promotes and supports the development of a compatible set of information systems on science and technology and interlinks these into a network to facilitate the effective transfer of latest information to users in all parts of the country.

NISSAT programme continued support to information Centres to meet information needs of scientists, technologists and decision makers. The activities of the NISSAT centres were augmented and their services and revenue generation improved. The NISSAT Access Centres on International Databases Services continued services on full cost recovery basis. Five metropolitan library networks in Calcutta, Bombay, Pune, Ahmedabad and Mysore continued their services related to interlinking of information resources in a metropolitan area. NISSAT established Value Added Patent Information System (VAPIS) at NCL, Pune and CMTI, Bangalore to offer specialised value added information services. Selective Dissemination of Information (SDI) is provided by institutions by using databases like ADONIS, BIOSIS, BNB, BOOKFMD, COMPENDEX, CHEMBANK, DISCOVER, IRS, INSPEC, NTIS, TTD, World Research Database and ISDS, Library automation software programmes viz. SANJAY and TRISHNA were maintained. The quarterly NISSAT Newsletter viz. Information Today & Tomorrow (1717) is produced in cooperation with NISSAT centre at CLRI, Madras for dissemination of information related activities.

Public enterprises

Two public enterprises namely. National Research Development Corporation (NRDC) and Central Electronics Limited (CEL) attached to the DSIR were engaged in important activities of development and commercialisation of indigenously developed technologies.

Some of the major technologies licensed by NRDC

during 1997-98 include Biodegradable plastic, Liposomal Amphotericine-B, Vijetha (Silkworm bed Disinfectant), Silver Impregnated Graphite, Rice Husk Particle Board, NIM76 -A Spermicidal formulation from neem oil, Dental varnish etc. The Corporation has successfully completed the preparation of 40 project profiles for industrial projects and services for Industrial Project Services, Etheopia.

Central Electronics Limited (CEL) holds a unique position among the family of Public Sector Enterprises in electronics, with its emphasis on indigenous technology inducted both from its in-house developments and from the National Laboratories, for its production programme in diverse high-technology areas of national importance. The activities of CEL are sharply focused in three thrust areas:

(i) Solar photovoltaic cells, modules and systems for a variety of applications.

(ii) Selected Electronic Systems Equipment for Railway Signaling and Safety, Cathodic Protection Equipment for Oil Pipelines, Switching Systems and Very Small Aperture Terminals (VSATs).

(iii) Selected Electronic components-professional (Soft) Ferrites, Electronic Cerarmics, Piezo Electric Elements and Microwave Components.

CEL has been the pioneer in the country in the areas of solar photovoltaics, ferrites and piezo ceramics. Today, it enjoys the international status of being among the top producers of single crystalline silicon solar cells in the world.

During the year 1997-98, there was an all-round progress and growth in the activities under different programmes of DSIR.

2

Council of Scientific and Industrial Research (SCIR)

The CSIR is the national R&D organisation providing scientific industrial research for India's economic growth and human welfare. It has a country-wide network of forty laboratories and eighty field centres covering fundamental and applied R&D in all areas of science and technology barring atomic research, developing and nurturing S&T human resource for the country through extra mural support and promoting scientific talent through awards, fellowships etc.

As CSIR reorients itself to be market driven and move on the path of self-financing, its performance would be conditioned by the performance of the Indian industry and economy. Thus the rate of ECF generation from contract R&D and consultancy came down from 15 to 10%, the actual ECF going up from Rs. 190 crore to Rs. 209 crore. The contribution to creation of new knowledge was satisfactory, patent filings increased significantly, rising from 71 to 91 in the year for foreign patents and from 209 to 264 for Indian patents. The quality of papers contributed also showed a healthy upward trend although the number remained nearly static. CSIR's all round performance during the year was satisfactory. Most significant among its activities has been the winning initiative for revocation of US patent on turmeric, which besides confirming CSIR's pioneering efforts to successfully safeguard traditional Indian knowledge, created an unprecedented positive public goodwill for the CSIR. More importantly this success had some far-reaching effects viz: it demonstrated that CSIR and other Indian institutions were acquiring capabilities to fight the complex techno-legal issues of IPR, both defensively and aggressively, to meet the challenges under the WTO regime; it showed the importance of appropriate documentation and public availability of records of traditional knowledgebase in a systematic manner, which can be provided as evidence of prior knowledge; it reassured the Indian people of the fair and transparent operations of the IPR system.

Scientific and technological achievements

The S&T Contributions from CSIR are of value to almost all socio-economic sectors. CSIR carries out R&D and provides services of value not only industry but also to other sectors of the economy e.g. agriculture, health, energy, rural development, transport and defence. CSIR's help to domestic industry is not only by way of relevant/ competitive technologies but also through search of raw materials and components, pollution control, productivity enhancement etc. A few of the more significant achievements during the year are reported through the charts and write-up given herein

Bio-sciences Including Therapeutics

Scientific achievements

Regulation of cell growth

In studies on the cell cycle regulated protein tyrosine phosphatases, CCMB has reported that over expression of PTP-S2 shortens the duration of S-phase (DNA replication) suggesting thereby that the duration of DNA replication is being reduced in these cells. It was also seen that over expression of PTP-S2 in Cos 1 cells resulted in cell death by apoptosis in about 30% of transfected cells after 48 hours.

Liposome entrapped mite allergen

Liposomes, which are non-toxic biodegrdable and biocompatible lipid vesicles are known to act as adjuvant and antigen materials and can be attached to the outer surface or encapsulated within the internal aqueous spaces. CBT studies aimed at further evaluating liposomes containing mite (Dermatophagoids farinae) in different strain of mice, confirm the immuno-adjuvant effect of liposome for immunotherapy in allergic disorders. These studies lead to the conclusion that increase in formation of protecting antibodies IgG and at the same time decrease in specific IgE. Using Liposome Entrapped Allergen (LEA) reduces the risk of systemic reaction associated with conventional allergy immunotherapy.

Functional studies of lectins

In symbiosis, soil microbes (Genus, Rhizobium) infect leguminous plants to form root nodules where bacteria inhabit and fix atmospheric nitrogen for the plant, and in return the plants supply food (sugar) to bacteria. The first step for this pleasant dwelling together is the selection of right partner. It has been proposed by many groups, including CBT that bacterial polysaccharides interact with root lectins specificaNy and that is the basis for recognition of correct partners. CBT has now experimentally demonstrated how the root lectin (PRA II) interacts with specific rhizobial polysaccharides.

Tumour biology

CCMB is studying the mechanisms involved in the spontaneous regression of a rat histiocytoma, AK-5 in syngeneic hosts. The tumor rejection antigen from the cDNA library developed from the tumor was cloned. The fusion protein from this clone is immunogenic and renders the animals partially resistant to tumor challenges. The nature of this antigen is being studied further to understand its immunological behaviour and to study the physiological function of the protein.

Brain cytochrome P450(s) enzymes

Studies conducted at ITRC have shown evidence of multiple forms of cytochrome P450 using specific antibodies and enzyme activity in different parts of rat brain. A commonly used pesticide, deltamethrin in coils and mats for mosquito control was found to enhance the activity of brain 7-pentoxyresorufin O-dealkylase (PROD). Prolonged exposure to the pesticide resulted in a significant increase in the activity of brain (EROD 1.3 fold) as well. The addition of anti-P450 antibody in 2B 1/2132 in vitro to the reaction mixture inhibited the enzyme activity of PROD upto 80%, whereas no inhibition was observed in EROD activity when compared to the control where pre-immune IgG was added. The results suggest that deltamethrin preferentially induces isoenzymes involved in the metabolism of deltamethrin and the role of P450 2B I/ 2B2 mediated metabolism in the neurotoxicity of pesticide.

New approaches in chemotherapy of malaria

It is known that intra-erythrocytic proliferation of malaria parasite is mainly responsible for pathogenesis and pathology of malaria infection. Recent studies at CDRI have demonstrated two distinct biochemical targets for antimalarial drug action:

a) The process of heme polymerisation whereby the malaria parasite converts hemoglobin to free toxic heme and finally to a polymeric detoxified product called hemozoin which is necessary for growth and survival of the parasite. A novel reaction initiated by blood schizontocidal antimalarials causing depolymerisation of hemozoin has been identified, as a result compounds specifically inhibiting this process may provide novel effective antimalarials.

b) Stage specific increase in polyamine levels (spermine, spermidine and putrescine), present only in traces in normal erythrocytes, was observed during growth and multiplication of malaria parasite in intraerythrocytic schizogony. Parasite induced putrescine transport system was highly specific and was inhibited by compounds interfering with polyamine biosynthesis. This provides an effective strategy for development of new chemotherapeutic molecules against malaria.

Rapid screen for anti-TB drugs

Recombinant Mycobacterium aurum A+, a fast growing non-pathogenic strain, expressing Escherichia coli lacZ gene has been constructed at CDRI, with -galactosidase as the reporter system. A good correlation was observed between inhibition in -galactosidase production and growth of recombinant strain by anti-TB drugs. The assay is highly predictive of activity against M. tuberculosis.

Molecular epidemiology of Cholera

In the study on molecular epidemiology of cholera IMT in collaboration with NICED, Calcutta has been able to empirically establish that the clones of V cholerae 01 or 0139 emerge, purge the existing clones and then spread spatially in waves and that the genetic flux in the V cholerae aids in the process. It also showed that the new clone of V. cholerae which appeared in Calcutta in September 1993 migrated to Guinea-Bissau within a year and was responsible for the epidemic which began in 1994 there.

Drug induced gastric hyperacidity

IICB had earlier shown that mercaptomethylimidazone (MMI) an anti thyroid drug of thiomide group, is a potent inducer of gastric acid secretion. While studying the mechanism it was observed that the system of isolated parietal cell activate the for acid secretion. H_2O_2, generated by inactivation of the H_2O_2, degrading enzymes can also stimulate acid secretion in the isolated gastric mucosal and gastric gland preparations. The plausible role of H_2O_2 acting like a second messenger to activate the parietal cell has thus been suggested.

Molecular studies on Cytoplasmic Male Sterility

The cytoplasmic male sterility (CMS) in plants has been exploited in the seed industry for the production of improved hybrid seeds. A rice mitochondrial gene orfl 55, characterised at NBRI showed altered transcript size between CMS and maintainer lines. The nucleotide sequence of the gene cloned from mitochondrial genome was compared with that of cDNA of the corresponding transcript. The orfl 55 posseses 7 editing sites in both the CMS and the maintainer lines.

Plant pathogens

(i) Bacterial infection of rice: CCMB continued the studies on the interaction between the rice plant and the bacterial pathogen Xanthomonas oryzae pv. Oryzae (Xoo), and reports that incorporation of both the xa-13 and xa-21 resistance genes into susceptible rice cultivars might provide broad-based protection against Xoo.

(ii) Microbial resistance to-plant antibiotics: studies on the response of Dictyostelium to isoflavonoid phytoalexins has enabled CCMB to propose a novel plant-microbe interaction between leguminous plants and cellular slime moulds. The leguminous plant uses isoflavonoid compounds to manipulate the foraging behaviour of amoebae so as to get rid of potentially pathogenic rhizosphere bacteria from the vicinity of root lesions,

DNA marker for papaya sex identification

In papaya, where male and female plants are separate, a method has been developed to identify sex at seedling stage. The method involved identification of male specific DNA marker using microsatellites as well as RAPD primers.

Somatic embryogenesis in Mango

NCL has succeeded in achieving direct somatic embryogenesis and plantlet regeneration in economically important monoembryonic mango varieties viz. Alphonso,

Mundan and Baneshan. The plants have been transferred to field. Long term repetitive somatic embryogenesis have also been obtained which is an important step towards scaling up of protocols. The achievement is significant as complete plantlet have been obtained and field planted.

Azadirachtin and limonoids in the Indian neem tree

A detailed investigation was carried out by CIMAP to document the variation in azadirachtin, nimbin, nimbidin and salanin contents during growth of neem seeds in different agro-climatic zones of India depending upon temperature, humidity and altitude. It has been observed that the percentage of all these limonoids in the seeds keep on increasing right from the formation of fruit fill the maturity of the seeds and biosynthesis of these limonoids is very fast while the fruit is being converted from green to the ripe, thereafter the increase is slow, and slightly declines when the fruit is about to fall or has just fallen from the tree suggesting that harvesting at the time of maturity is beneficial.

Antibacterial activity of Indian tree species

CIMAP evaluated the fruits and seeds of three-tree species namely Indian walnut (Albizia lebbeck), drum stick (Moringa oleifera), and Indian beech (Pongamia pinnata) using tissue discs or fragments directly for antibacterial activity against three bacteria: Salmonella typhimurium, Pseudomonas aeruginosa and Mycobacterium smegmatis (non-pathogenic soil saprophyte spp.). The results indicate the presence of a highly potential anti-mycobacterial compound in the extracts of Moringa (drumstick) fruit.

Marine fouling and corrosion studies

Extracts of two terrestrial plants belonging to the family Leguminoceae and Lecythidaceae studied by NIO were found to exhibit potent antifouling activity against some important fouling organisms.

Technological achievements

Universal polymer support for synthesis of oligoribonucleotides

Solid phase synthesis of DNA and RNA requires at least eight different prederivatised polymer supports. The commercial availability of base labile synthons for DNA and RNA synthesis has necessitated the need to prepare a large number (50-60) of such pre-derivatised polymer supports making DNA and RNA synthesis a time consuming task. CBT has developed a versatile universal polymer support devoid of nucleotidic material and compatible to the existing methods of synthesis and deprotection of oligodeoxyribo and oligobionucleotides. The universal support obviates the need to prepare a large number of pre-derivatised polymer supports. Patent has been applied for the development in India and USA.

Diagnostic probe for leishmaniasis

A probe for early detection of visceral leishmaniasis has been developed at CDRI, by using a pair of oligonucleotide primers constructed from predominant sequence class of kinetoplast DNA minicircle of leishmania donovani. An Indian patent has been filed for the development.

Assay for Acute Lymphoblastic Leukemia (ALL)

Childhood acute lymphoblastic leukemia or 'ALL' requires prolonged maintenance therapy for eliminating residual leukemic blast cells which cannot be detected by standard morphological methods. These persisting cells are responsible for relapse and is called 'Minimal Residual Disease' (MRD). Employing a unique 9-0-acetylated sialic acid binding lectin (ATNH), two 9-0 acetyl sialoglyconjugates (9-OacSGs) on lymphoblasts have been identified by IICB. 'A lymphoproliferative assay which is selective for PBMC of 'ALL' and not of other blood disorders has been developed.

Human trial of a non-toxic cholera vaccine

CSIR developed indigenous and genetically engineered

oral cholera vaccine named Val -3 has been cleared for human trials by the Drug Controller. This development has been the result of a collaborative project between IMT, IICB and NICED, Calcutta and is based on a non-reactogenic natural isolate of V cholerae 01.

Novel usage of di-tert-butyl polycarbonate (DTBP)

IICT has been successful in utilizing DTBP for cyclodehydration of n-acylamino acids to substituted oxazoles and enantiopure synthesis of bioactive alkyl amino benzoxazinones which are effective protease inhibitors. Currently, DTBP is used for introduction of acid labile BOC protecting group in amino acids, peptides and proteins.

Isovitamin C by a genetically altered organism

A fermentation process for the production of 2-keto-gluconate - a penultimate intermediate of isoascorbic acid (Isovitamin C) used as antioxidant for the preservation of food products has been developed by RRL -Jammu. The laboratory has demonstrated the process at 500 litre scale to a firm in Hyderabad. The Chemostat studies on the genetically modified Pseudomonas clone revealed 40% increase in the productivity of 2-keto-gluconate. The organism mediating the glucose oxidation process has been improved by cloning another set of glucose dehydrogenase derived from Acinetobacter calcoaceticus.

Mini Chrysanthemum—CV. Mother Teresa

A new chrysanthemum cultivar, selected from open pollinated seedlings, named "Mother Teresa" was released by NBRI. It is a small flowered, white Anemone type mini chrysanthemum which has all the qualities to occupy a high position in floriculture trade. It requires neither 'Pinching' nor 'Staking'. It can easily be transported in small containers due to its mini habit.

Application of chloro choline chloride for bulb production of Tulips

IHBT has shown that chloro choline Chloride treatment at the early stage of flower emergence increases the bulb yield per plant by nearly 50%, bulb weight by over 100%, bulb size (circumference) about 20%, bulblet production by 30% and weight of bulblets over 50% as compared to the untreated plants.

Ocimum carnosum, a potential source of natural elemicin

Elemicin is highly valued in the pharmaceutical industry besides being an important flavouring agent. It is the base material for the production of 3,4,5 trime thoxy benzaldehyde and is also a starting material for the synthesis of trimethoprim, an ingredient used in the formulation of anti-bacterial drugs. A valuable elemicin source is the herb Ocimum carnosum, which RRL-Jammu has established and developed for commercial cultivation.

New varieties of damask rose

IHBT has released two new cultivars of Damask Rose designated as IHBT, Gulab-I (Jwala) and IHBT Gulab-II (Himroz) during the year. Jwala is suitable for sub-tropical plains and mid hills upto 1400 in altitude while Himroz is suitable for temperate zone upto 2500 in altitude.

Production technology for rose oil and rose water

CIMAP has developed a low cost and efficient technology for the production of rose oil and water. A directly fired type rose oil distillation plant of 150 kg flower capacity was designed, fabricated and installed at village Devnagar in Ajmer (Rajasthan). The composition of the major constituents of the rose oil produced with Pushkar (Rajasthan) rose as determined by the GLC has been found to be at par with the composition of the rose oil produced from the flowers of Rosa damascena grown by CIMAP in Kashmir.

Tissue Culture for Licorice and Ashwagandha

Tissue culture studies were under taken by NCL for

propogation of Neem (Azadirachta indica) and Licorce *(Glycyrrhiza glabra), Ashwagandha (Withania somnifera)* using different pathways like micropropogation, direct and indirect induction of somatic embryogenesis and induction of secondary metabolites from callus cultures, Protocols for mass production were developed for Licorice and Ashwagandha. The technique has tremendous potential for selection of variants adoptable to extreme conditions.

Plant transformation technology

NCL developed plant transformation technology for improved chickpea and pigeonpea and also standardized protocols on regeneration of whole plants from various explants via somatic embryogenesis and organogenesis.

Biodegradation of endosulfan from contaminated sons

A two-member bacterial coculture has been isolated at ITRC from contaminated soil that biodegrades alpha and beta isomers of endosulfan. Degradation of alpha and beta-endosulfan was 18% and 27% respectively in uninoculated conditions and by inclusion this was enhanced to nearly 75% for both the isomers. Biodegradation also caused substantial reduction in the toxicity of endosulfan as tested by ecotoxicity protocols. Another bacterial strain ITRC- I degraded all four isomers of HCH in flooded conditions, showing formation of 2,5-dichlorophenol by thin layer chromatography technique.

Wildlife management by genetic fingerprinting

(1) Genetic diversity in Indian big cats: studies at CCMB have led to the identification of Asiatic lions and tigers with high genetic variability which could be used for front line breeding. Also, observations of the Indian big cat species suggest that low genetic variability may be a characteristic feature rather than the result of intensive inbreeding as commonly thought.

(2) Fertility status of lions, tigers and leopards in India:

CCMB has established the fertility status of the male cats based on the semen profiles and hormonal levels. Lions (8), tigers (2 1) and leopards (15) from the Nehru Zoological Park, Hyderabad, the Sakkarbaug Zoo, Junnagadh and the Nandankanan Zoo, Bhubaneshwar have been successfully electroejaculated and the semen characteristics such as motility, viability, sperm number and morphology among others, were evaluated.

Chemical sciences and technology

Scientific achievements

Liquid Membrane Modelling

RRL-Jorhat in association with C-MMACS developed a mathematical model incorporating external mass transfer across the aqueous boundary layer and interfacial chemical reaction and diffusion in the emulsion globule. The model has been validated through a computer simulation exercise describing the experimental extraction kinetics of various cephalosporin antibiotics in an optimised liquid membrane system.

Pillaring of ion-exchanged clays

NCL has employed a novel, ultrasonic technique to regulate and accelerate the pillaring process. In this method, the process of pillaring of alumina and zirconia is complete within a matter of few hours with minimum or no elimination of the partent clay. The conditions, the concentration of pillaring species and the frequency of ultra-sonication have been optimised to achieve alumina and zirconid pillared clays (montmorillonite) which also showed much better thermal and hydrothermal stabilities than reported before.

Transition metal complexes with designed ligands

CSMCRI in continuation of the ongoing effort to design transition metal complexes with specific properties synthesised and characterised the following:

a) Polypyridyl complexes to study energy transfer processes: hetero bi and tri-nuclear metal complexes of Ru (III)/(II) and Fe (II) incorporating the ligands, pyridyl derivatives of ferrocene, polycarboxylic acids (edta) and 2,2' - bipyridyl were synthesised. All these new complexes showed a moderate to weak electrochemical interaction between the redox centre. A series of mono nuclear ru. (3)-polypyridyl triazine) complex synthesised showed excellent catalytic property towards electrocatalytic reduction of carbon dioxide to formic acid.

b) Coordination polymer for adsorption: a series of polymeric Co(II) and Cu(II) complexes using adipic acid as bridging ligand and 2,2' -bipyridyl as terminal ligand were synthesised and characterised crystallographically. Analysis of the structures show strong intra and inter molecular H-bonding interactions forming two-dimensional network structures.

c) Biomimitic molecular models: dinuclear Cu(II) complexes of diethylenetriamine, using dicarboxylato and substituted imidazolato ligands as spacer between the metal centres and also some schiff base complexes were synthesised as model systems.

d) Thermochromic materials: a number of Ni(II) and Cu(II) complexes with the ligands dialkyl-/tetraalkyl-ethylenediamine and diazaclothep-tane with various anions have been synthesised and characterised crystallographically. These complexes exhibit thermochromic transitions (reversible colour change) at liquid nitrogen temperature. The variable temperature single crystal X-ray studies of some samples and the latice energy computations for the molecular motions involved in the crystal during transition were carried out in collaboration with IICT.

New chemical entities

IICT has focussed research efforts on development of novel synthetic molecules with significant level of biological activity for possible applications in drugs/ pharmaceuticals, agrochemicals and performance products. Notable among the molecules taken up are Gonio furfurones, Epothilines/ amphidinolides, Azamacrolides [optically active], Macrocyclic lactones, Glycopeptides, Sugar aminoacids, 2-Tetra zolyl-3-aryl propanols.

Synthesis of N-protected precursors of synthetic sweetener aspartame

N-protected derivatives of L-aspartyl-L-phenylalanine methyl ester are useful as precursors of synthetic sweetener : Aspartame which is 200 times sweeter than sugar and used in industry as artificial sweetener in beverages and food additives. Enzyme assisted reaction of N-[benzyloxy carbonyl]-L-aspartic acid [ZASP] or N-[phenylacetyl]-Laspartyl acid [PASP] with L-phenylalanine methyl ester [PME] was achieved by IICT to produce N-[benzyloxycarbonyl]-L-aspartyl-L-phenylalanine methyl ester [Z-aspartame] or N-[phenylacetyl]-L-aspartyl-L-phenylalanine methyl ester [Phaspartame].

Technological achievements

Foam as a reaction medium

The IICT-CCMB joint efforts, have led to the development of foam as an environment friendly reaction medium for enzyme mediated organic reactions. The typical example is lipase catalyzed transformations of aliphatic acids/ alcohols to corresponding esters. The specific advantages of employing foam are, reduced hydrolysis of products and absence of organic solvents. There are good prospects of applying this option for chemical synthesis.

Clay supported new reagents

Clay supported new reagents preparation and their applications in functional group transformations especially under microwaves was an important area of research at IICT. A general method for the synthesis of iso-thiocyanates from dithiocarbamates has been developed using 'clay-cop'. The method is applicable for the preparation of a variety of iso-thiocyanates, including aminoacids. The method avoids the use of toxic chemicals like thio-phosgene and lead nitrate.

Chiral template for enantiomers

Amino acids are of paramount importance in asymmetric synthesis and are used extensively in both the 'chiral substrate' and 'chiral auxiliary' based versions of stereoselective reactions. Under the research programme directed towards the synthesis of enantiopure compounds of biological interest, IICT has developed methods to synthesize a number of bioactive molecules utilizing the easily available amino acids as 'chiral template' to obtain enantiomerically pure compounds of contemporary interest.

Membrane/adsorptive separation

RRL-Jorhat developed liquid membrane process for selective separation of cephalosporin-C from its mixture with de-acetyl cephalosporin-C generated in the fermentation broth of Cephalosporin acremonim.

Oxidative Coupling of Methane (OCM) to C2-Hydrocarbons

A highly stable and active, selective catalyst comprising of alkaline and rare earth oxides supported on low surface area microporous catalysts carriers has been developed at NCL. An energy efficient process for the oxidative coupling of methane to C2-Hydrocarbons over this catalyst using a concept of catalyst dilution by inert solids for exothermic oxidative conversion and endothermic thermal cracking reactions to avoid the hot spot formation and heat removal problems has been developed. The novelty of the process is its reduced hazardous nature.

Isomerization of O-dichlorobenzene to M-dichlorobenzene

The isomerization of O-dichlorobenzene is usually carried out with homogenous catalysts ($FeCl_3$, etc.) which have detrimental effect on the environment with problems of separation. M-dichlorobenzene is a value-added chemical intermediate. NCL has developed a suitable zeolite based catalyst for the isomerization and fixed bed operation. The reaction parameters have been optimized to achieve maximum conversion of odcb and selectivity to mdcb. The novelty in this development is a regenerable catalyst, patented and not reported earlier for such application. The development for an Indian Industry, planning to put up a semi-commercial (pilot) plant of 1000 tons per annum capacity with its own engineering inputs. This will be a non-polluting chemical plant. The development paves way for developing suitable heterogeneous catalysts for isomerization of other organic substrates.

CFC-113a technology for pyrethroids

1,1,1-Trichloro-trifuoroethane [CFC-113a] is a eommercially important synthone for the introduction of a two carbon functionality terminating in trifluoromethyl group in bioactive molecules. The CFC-l13a is a key raw material for producing highly potent and less toxic pyrethroid class of insecticides like lamdacyhalothrin. Its commercial production has become the monopoly of those agencies having access to CFC- 113a. The recent restrictions on the use of CFCs under Montreal Protocol has made its availability difficult for the Indian industry.

IICT has entered into an agreement with a private sector company in Mumbai for development of lamdacyhalothrin and CFC-113a The CFC-113a is made by the catalytic isomerization of CFC-1 13 followed by fractional distillation. The development of process for CFC-113a on pilot scale has been successfully demonstrated on a 3 kg/batch. The requisite catalyst has also been developed by the laboratory.

Electrochemical systems of naphthoquinone

Naphthoquinone (NQ) and its substituted derivatives are

industrially significant as intermediates in the synthesis of anthroquinone, dyes and pharmaceuticals. The current process for the production of NQ and its substituted derivatives is by oxidation of Naphthalene. The yield of NQ in this process is less than 40%. CECRI has developed an electro mediated synthesis route where the purity and yield of NQ are high. Further the process enables the synthesis of number of versatility of industrially important compounds like aldehydes, as well. Electro organic synthesis of NQ is mote convenient, economical and environmental friendly.

Pyridine based chemicals

CFRI successfully demonstrated the process to convert 3-picoline to 3-cyanopyridine and the conversion of 4-cyanopyridine to INH. The maximum yield of 3-cyanopyridine achieved so far is 85% by weight. Zeolite and pillared clay based vanadia catalyst have been prepared and tested for the reaction. Construction of a plant to produce 1 1000 kg per day nicotinamide from 3-cynopyridine is in progress.

Cardanyl Acrylate and Poly Acrylate

RRL-Tvm has standardised process know-how for the laboratory scale production of cardanyl acrylate and poly acrylate. The technology was transferred to a small scale firm.

Pervaporation technology

IICT has acquired specialised expertise in pervaporation technology. It is devising an economically attractive pervaporation process for the separation of paraffins and olefins to upgrade commercial propylene for a company in Visakhapatnam.

Conversion of methane to syngas

An energy efficient and safe to operate process for the methane to syngas (CO and H_2) based on simultaneous partial oxidation, steam reforming and CO_2 reforming of methane over a novel supported nickel catalyst has been developed at NCL. Because of the simultaneously occuring exothermic oxidative conversion and endothermic steam and CO_2 reforming reactions, the process occurs in a most energy efficient and safe manner, requiring little or no external energy. NCL is trying to operate this process in an adiabatic reactor, as the process can be made almost thermoneutral.

Conversion of natural gas to lower olefins

Natural gas contains methane with appreciable amount of C_2-C_4 alkanes. It is practically important to convert the C_{2+} hydrocarbons without their separation from natural gas into ethylene and C_3-C_4 olefines. For this purpose two different processes, one based on the catalytic oxidative conversion of all the hydrocarbons in the presence of a limited oxygen, and the second based on the non-catalytic oxypyrolysis of natural gas in the presence of limited oxygen, have been developed at NCL. In both processes, the exothermic oxidative conversion and endothermic thermal cracking reactions, which are occurring simultaneously, are coupled to make these processes most energy efficient.

Menthol manufacture

A novel technology for the manufacture of menthol from menthol oil has been developed at IIP which gives product of a very high quality at lower processing costs. The technology offers special features of distillation of mentha oil through a more efficient column enabling the higher yield of menthol of high purity meeting international specifications and chemical transformation of menthone to menthol and the isomerisation of undesired to desired isomers of menthol.

Soaker visbreaking technology

IIP has developed a state-of-art indigenous technology for

soaker visbreaking, an improved version of the coil visbreaking, for processing of petroleum residues into more value added products. The technology has been developed in collaboration with EIL and optimised at the pilot level. The technology offers advantages of lower operating temperatures and higher residence time leading to nearly 15% savings in fuel consumption in comparison to the coil visbreaking. Almost all the coil visbreakers in the Indian refineries have been revamped based on the data generated at the IIP pilot plant, besides two grass roots plants being put up.

Mini refinery

IIP has been pioneering the concept of mini refineries for the country. In this direction it has prepared several techno-economic reports for various clients for mini refineries with capacities varying from 0.5 to 2.0 MMTPA. These mini refineries are self contained, skid mounted, low cost and low maintenance units congenial for installation in any location.

Reaction engineering laboratory

The IICT has recently established sophisticated experimental facilities for the development of eivirocatalyzed chemical processes for the speciality chemical sector. Laboratory is equipped with a unique bench scale facility for the standardization of catalyst preparation, full range of physicochemical test facilities for characterization of catalysts [heterogeneous], micro and mini flow reactor with online GO HPLC facilities, reaction calorimeter for standardization of batch processes, accelerated rate calorimeter for assessing the thermal hazards of chemical processes and bench and pilot scale fixed bed reactors with downstream processing facilities.

State-of-art system for chemical reaction studies

IIP has procured a versatile computer controlled general

purpose facility comprising micro reactor and pilot plant system used for conducting scale-up studies of chemical processes. The facility is specially useful for reaction studies in liquid/gas phase over fixed catalyst bed at micro level and as well as at pilot scale at temperatures upto 500°C and upto 50 bar pressure.

Electronics and Instrumentationn

Scientific achievements

Electron cyclotron resonance source plasma

CSIO has developed an electron cyclotron resonance (ECR) system for studying microwave plasma in argon, oxygen, carbon tetrafloride and in a mixture of oxygen and carbon tetrafloride. A cylindrical Langmuir probe was used to measure the current and its variation with respect to input power (50 - 1000W), flow rates, probe position in the reactor and pressure. These measurements give optimum operational parameters. It has been observed that ion current increases linearly with microwave power.

Chemical composition of rainfall: monitor

CSIO studied the rainwater composition at event temporal resolution, over a 6- month period, at a site in south east England. The data were used to assess the overall levels of acidic deposition at the site and to identify functional relationships between wet deposition and casual meteorological processes. It was seen that a power-law relationship existed between wet deposition and rainfall amount. A microprocessor based acid rain monitor designed for the study not only fulfilled requirements of various international bodies but also emerged as basic research tool in the field of acid precipitation studies.

High performance CPU without secondary cache

While undertaking the mammoth project to port and parallelise the T-80 weather prediction code on NAL's parallel computer, Flosolver, it was found that there was a large discrepancy between the advertised peak speed and the realised sustained speed on the intel 1860 processor—a discrepancy which appeared to be general to all RISC processors. Scientists in NAL supported by the CSIR's New Idea Fund (NIF) undertook the project to design a high performance CPU without secondary cache. The basic methodology used was to design the CPU card and RAM interface, develop logical equations, fabricate the printed circuit board, and finally develop, test and analyse the board. The board has now been designed and tested and proved to be functionally working.

Technological achievements

Electrical double layer capacitors (edlc)

Usually non-aqueous solvents are used as electrolytes in edic to achieve voltage windows higher than 1.25V For the first time edic using aqueous alkaline electrolyte with carbon and/or Ni/NiO as electrodes have been fabricated, by CECRI, Button type, coin type and cylindrical type capacitors and capacitor banks have been fabricated and tested.

Solid state room temperature gas sensor

CEERI is using the properties of high Tc cuprate superconductor to detect NH_3 and NO_x gases at room temperature. A Capacitively-Coupled Field Effect Transistor (CCFET) has been developed as a sensor for the purpose which gives a 10mV output for a 5 ppm NH 3 concentration.

Speed indicating and recording instrument for locomotives

A PC-based speed indicating and recording instrument has been developed by CEERI for diesel and electric locomotives in collaboration with a private industry. The performance of the prototype model has been tested on an electric locomotive of Indian Railways. The salient features of the instruments are: non-contact inductive DC type proximity sensor with IP-6 standards, 6 digit odometer with bright LED display, speed indication, full-function key board for initial data entry, data retrieval and data transfer interface/ switch and interactive selection of conditional data for display and analysis. The instrument is useful for indicating and recording relevant train data such as loco speed, time, date etc. in NVROM. The system provides valuable information for locomotive movement and analysis of causes in case of accidents.

Instrumentation for microelectronics

CSIO with the assistance from UNDP and Government counterpart funding from the CSIR and the DoE has successfully developed the following:

a) *Molecular Beam Epitaxy (MBE) System* used for growth of semiconductor epitaxial layers, monolithic microwave integrated circuits (MMICs), very high speed integrated circuits (VHSICs) etc.

b) *Stepper Optical Lithography (SOL)* facility essential for the fabrication of LSI/VLSI devices and ASICs in all microelectronic foundries.

c) *Reactive Ion Beam Etching (RIBE) System* based on ECR source used for etching fine anisotropic patterns for fabricating microelectronic (VLSI/ VHSIC) devices as well as for micromachining and making fine optical gratings.

d) *Reactive Ion Etching (RUE) System* necessary for etching a variety of materials like Silicon, Polysilicon, Silicon Dioxide, Nitrides, Silicides, Group III-V Compound Semiconductors, etc. for fabrication of microelectronic and photonic devices. This system also finds applications in the areas of microfabrication and micromechanics.

e) *RF/DC Sputtering System* which has applications for deposition of thin films in semiconductor industries, optical industries, integrated optics, industrial hard and decorative coatings, etc.

f) *Electron Beam Controlled Evaporation (EBCE)* system for growth/deposition of high quality thin films of different solid materials. It finds wide applications in areas of microelectronics, optics, superconductors, etc.

g) *LSI/VLSI Testing System* for general purpose programmable testing of LSI/VLSI devices as well as for sorting of devices having particular specifications.

RF Hyperthermia system for cancer therapy

Hyperthermia is a new emerging technique for treatment of localised cancers. CSIO has designed and developed a Hyperthermia System at 27 MHz for intracavitary applications in uterine cervix using capacitive type of non-invasive applicator system. A specific control algorithm has been developed for control of temperature measurement.

Receivers for optical communication

CEERI has developed Need Specific Detectors and Receivers for Optical Communication System comprising hybrid optical fron-end module and integrated optical receiver module.

Land based Digital Seismic Data Telemetry System

CSIO in collaboration with NGRI has developed an eight-channel Digital Seismic Data Telemetry System based on state-of-art technology. The system is meant to monitor and analyse micro-earthquakes/earthquakes data telemetered from a network of seismic remote stations via digital ground telemetry down to a central recording and analysis base station. At the base station, the seismic data can immediately be processed and analysed for the purpose of research in the field of earthquake prediction.

Inclinometer probe with digital indicator

CSIO has developed a portable and light weight inclinometer which incorporates special features of high accuracy and ruggedness; excellent stability; water proof stainless steel housing; digital data indicator with 4 1/2 -

digit large LCD display, dust proof enclosure and rechargeable battery.

PC based data acquisition system for thermo physical studies

NAL has successfully developed a PC based data acquisition system for thermophysical studies. The system, built around a temperature controlled furnace with attachments for studying several thermo physical phenomena is available both in the PC based and manual models. The PC based system offers software control of temperature, temperature gradient and the computation of different physical activities.

Engineering

Scientific achievements

Control of Fly-rock due to blasting

A blast mat was indigenously designed, manually weaved and used by CMRI to control fly-rock at a limestone mine. The use of bottom bole initiation, adequate stemming equal to burden and hole to hole delay pattern helped in total control of fly-rock and production of an ideal muck profile. Each blast mat was of 6×6m in dimension and the ropes were interlocked with each other. Elimination of fly-rock using blast mats at the peripherial areas of this mine generated scope of cost reduction by minimising ripping and dozing operations which accounted for 20-25 percent of the total cost of production as it was extensively used in these areas to prevent environmental hazard.

Rural roads in Andhra Pradesh

CRRI has been entrusted the task of preparing a project report for the rural roads component of the Andhra Pradesh Economic Restructuring Project (APERP) funded by the World Bank. The study interalia includes the preparation of master plans, review of design standards, development of policy framework, identification of project scope. Three pilot districts were selected for the purpose to study the upgradation of a selected core network to all weather standards and building up of technical, institutional and financial capacity for sustainable maintenance and management of the core network. This study has proved that the core network identified by CRRI is cost effective and at the same time ensures 100% village accessibility.

Wind tunnel studies on structural models

SERC-M is now developing experimental techniques for testing of models of dynamically sensitive structures in the atmospheric boundary layer wind tunnel (BLWT) with the aim of improving the analytical tools for analysis of wind sensitive structures. Wind tunnel tests on 1:300 scale model of a coal storage shed without gable walls have been carried out. This enabled the optimisation of structure design to be done by a good bracing system connecting the frames in the front and rear.

Studies on vibration control of structures and foundations

SERC-M has taken up a project to study the dynamic characteristics of selected types of vibration isolators for developing standard criteria for analysis, design and evaluation of isolator supported machine foundations and investigate relative efficiency of base isolation techniques. A test facility for evaluating the dynamic stiffness and damping characteristics of vibration isolators under direct compression has been set up at the centre and trial tests have been carried out on a typical isolator having wide industrial application.

Finite element analysis of large structure using parallel processing

SERC-M has been working on development of parallel processing approaches for finite element analysis of large structures. Efficient mesh partitioning algorithms and a method of domain decompositions were developed for parallel processing. A portable Graphic User Interface (GUI) for the domain decomposition algorithms has been developed using X windows and Motif routines on workstation platforms. The expertise developed has enabled SERC-M to bag several grant-in-aid projects on specific aspects in the field.

Fatigue investigations of offshore structure

Corrosion fatigue behaviour of welded steel tubular joints of offshore structure has been experimentally investigated at SERC-M to formulate guidelines for fatigue-resistant design of offshore platform structures. The effect of cathodic protection on fatigue life of these joints was studied, both under constant amplitude and random loading. A life reduction factor by about 2 to 2.5 times was observed under free corrosion environment as compared to air environment. Adequate cathodic protection is found to help in restoring the in-air fatigue strength of tubular joints, both under constant amplitude and random loading conditions.

Creep damage and life assessment

A method for obtaining the oxidation rate constant under creep conditions has been suggested by NML. This is based on an analysis of the shape of the creep strain time plot. A new concept of a shape factor has been introduced for generating geometry independent master creep curves. The model has been validated with experimental data on Incone IX-750 and CrMoV steel. A finite Element Method based software has been developed to implement the model developed for specimen to the design of components.

Mining machinery components

In engineering components design apart material related factors like microstructural features, composition and engineering properties determines performance of a component. These parameters can be manipulated through appropriate metallurgical treatments, to ensure efficient working. RRL-Bhopal has taken up investigations on mining machinery components with a view to improve their life. Systematic metallurgical and tribological studies showed that life of indigenous shovel teeth could be enhanced to be at par with imported teeth.

Industrial roofing system using cold forming steel section

Use of Cold Forming Steel Section (CFSS) in structural construction, such as beams, columns etc. is yet to take off in any noticeable way in India. SERC-M took up a project to develop industrial roofing system using CFSS. Software was developed for determining the allowable axial load capacity and the bending strength of CFSS members as per IS: 8011975. Comparison of experimental result with applicable BS, AISI & IS codal provision brought to light the inadequacies of the present Indian code.

Technological achievements

Supersonic combustor development

DRDL, Hyderabad, is developing a hydrogen fuelled supersonic combustion ramjet for the hyperplane, which will be a fully reusable, single stage, hypersonic vehicle. As a part of this programme, NAL has developed the technology for the design of supersonic combustors. A direct connect supersonic combustor test facility, which is suitable for simulation of flight at six times the speed of sound and an altitude of 30 km altitude has been successfully set up and experimentally validated.

Development of powered hang glider

Probably for the first time in the world, a powered hang glider was flown with a rotary Wankel engine. The engine, an air-cooled 35 hp engine, was modified for this application in a project supported by AR&DB at NAL. NAL's flight activities involving the powered hang glider encourage the hope that the great potential of the Wankel engine may eventually be tapped.

Wide stall mining without stowing

Wide stall mining, an eco-friendly mining method without

stowing, has been developed by CMRI for optimal recovery of coal in developed pillars as well as for improvement in productivity and safety of workers for workings underneath delicate surfaces. The method was tried on experimental basis at Chirimiri mine of SECL for extraction of a 8.4m thick seam underneath a hill. The method is especially useful for regions where stowing materials are not available for packing of the mined-out areas.

Multiblend cement

CBRI has optimised four promising multiblend cement (MBC) formulations using portland cement clinkers and industrial by product wastes such as blast furnance slag, flyash and gypsum. These exhibit better strength, durability, impermeability and resistance to aggressive environments as compared to ordinary cements.

Natural rubber latex based cement concrete

SERC-M has developed a process for production of natural rubber latex based cement concrete (NR-LMCC), overcoming the problem of coagulation of the matrix which hinders the workability of concrete. The process has been utilised to develop mixed having higher strength, greater stiffness and more energy absorption compared to control concrete of M20 grade. The product exhibits quality of good adhesion to cementitious substrates, higher durability, impermeability to water, chlorides and carbon dioxide, resistance to salt water exposure and reduced drying shrinkage. The development is the subject matter of a patent application filed in India.

Epoxy concrete for machine bed

Epoxy concrete, a cold curing mixture of a reactable epoxy resin and hardener system (binder) and a carefully selected and graded aggregate system (filter), has potential in replacing cast iron and mild steel structural elements for machine tools. CMERI has taken up the development of epoxy concrete or epcon technology for manufacturing beds of grinding machines and other precision machine tools complete with inserts, including pre-machined metallic inserts, by in-situ casting methods. The technology has also been utilised for the manufacture of grinding machine beds with finished or semi-finished guideways, which can be moulded in with the main structure, bolted on to mould-in plates or cast with special formulation.

Corrosion resistance of fly ash cements

It has been reported that fly ash cement in general is less corrosion resistant compared to ordinary portland cement and hence large-scale blending of such cement in reinforced concrete construction is on the decline. CECRI has developed inhibitor admixture that will impart adequate corrosion resistance to flyash dust and facilitate its use in reinforced concrete.

Composition for quick Setting of cement

An inorganic chemical composition has been developed by CMRI for use in cement capsules to get instant grip, high strength and better performance compared to capsules available in the market. The know-how of the composition has been transferred to CIL. For effective use, the dry chemical is encapsulated in polythene capsules with closely spaced perforation. These capsules are immersed in water for few minutes before putting them into the holes. It has shown an anchorage strength of 2.5 to 3 tonnes after half-hour of installation.

Flyash for highway embankment construction

CRRI has successfully demonstrated the use of flyash for construction of highway embankments for the 6 to 9 meters high, 1.9 km long approach embankment for the Indo-Japan Friendship Bridge at Nizamuddin in New Delhi. Flyash has been used as a core material in floodzone area for the embankment.

Bio-energy for brick kilns

R&D efforts of CBRI to utilize high caloric value biomass as a partial or total substitute for coal & other fossil fuels for burning of bricks have yielded very encouraging results. Successful commercial trials utilizing agricultural by products and forest residues have been conducted at conventional Bull's trench kilns and other small scale intermittent kilns obtaining nearly 950 to 1000°C. The technique has been employed for commercial burning of bricks in Western UP, Haryana, Punjab and Gujarat where these bio-masses are available in plenty and also in other brick kilns situated far way from coal mine pits.

Cold forming of aluminium bicycle hubs

Cold forming is a process in which a near-net shape product with better mechanical properties can be achieved by forming a material at room temperature. CMERI has developed a suitable cold forming technology for aluminium alloy bicycle hub. The total hub was divided into two parts that were manufactured separately by cold forming process and were joined by friction welding to constitute the complete hub.

Improved iron removal for potable water

CMERI based on the inputs derived from evaluation and monitoring of iron removal plants installed under the RGNDWM has developed an improved version of iron removal plant. Better aeration by CMERI design features double aeration chambers and proper air flow; presettling chamber along with the settling chamber; optimum settling and filtration area that give significantly improved performance.

Decorticator for groundnut seeds

Decortification, a vital step in the production of edible oils from seeds is a candidate area requiring technological upgradation for optimisation of oil yield and quality. To bridge the existing gaps in technology. The MERADO,

Pune centre of CMERI under took the development of an efficient single roll decorticator for groundnut seeds. The design developed is versatile and enables decortication of groundnut as well as other seeds by changing the operating variables.

Remotely operated vehicle

CMERI has taken up the design and development of an upgraded version of a Remotely Operated Vehicle (ROV) to operate at a depth of 250 m, as an extension of the earlier sponsored programme of the DOD. The ROV will have application in marine geological survey, photography and collection of samples from the Exclusive Economic Zone.

Draft Tube (DT) Cone

BHEL Bhopal, manufactures hydroturbines of various capacities which presently employ DT cones imported from Japan and Russia. RRL-Bho developed and demonstrated seamless casting of acrylic polymer to make large thickness DT cones which also eliminated some of the design deficiencies. A prototype cone has been developed for BHEL for their model hydroturbine.

Lignin from paper mill effluents

India has a large number of pulp and paper mills based on agrowastes. These mills have capacity to produce 25-50 tons per day of paper, generate about 150 cubic meter of wastewater per ton of paper produced. The currently practiced processes do not have capability to separate the lignin and other components contributing to the high COD and BOD values to the effluent water.

NCL has developed a process for the treatment of the effluent water to separate the lignin. This process uses a material named as "ECONCL" developed at NCL (Indian Patent application filed). The effluent water when treated with ECONCL separates out the lignin and other Organic impurities as precipitate that settles down fast. The clarified water can be recycled in the pulp making plant. The process has been successfully demonstrated in the laboratory and pilot scale units at NCL.

Bioremediation for crude oil contaminated soil

RRL-Jorhat completed bench scale studies on 'bioremediation of crude oil contaminated soil of Borhola oil field' of ONGC. It lead to site characterisation and developing a bioremediation protocol for crude oil contaminated oil fields. The technique developed is expected to help restore the soil health of crude oil contaminated soils.

Eco-friendly coke-less cupola for Agra foundries

A tripartite agreement was signed between Tata-Korf, the Agra Iron Foundries Association (having nearly 250 foundries) and NNE for transfer of the coke-less cupola technology involving installation, commissioning, demonstration and diffusion in the Agra region. NML developed environment friendly coke-less cupola technology using liquid fuel or almost sulphur free natural gas will be engineered by Tata-Korf to commercial level for Agra foundries.

Food Processing

Scientific achievements

Lipase catalysed esterification

CFTRI has studied in detail the role of water of reaction and the micro-aqeous enzyme-water-solvent interphase on the esterification reaction catalysed by lipase. The studies score over usual chemical synthesis and other enzymatic process due to milder reaction conditions, low water environment, lesser concentrations of enzyme, less strenuous reaction conditions as compared to chemical synthesis and clean products. The investigations have generated information on these esterification equillibria useful in developing newer techniques for large scale applications. These studies have also resulted in the development of novel experimental designs for the synthesis of the esters on a bench scale level.

Spices as nutraceuticals

Spices and herbs are extensively used in Ayurvedic system of medicine. Investigations at CFTRI on dietary curcumin (from turmeric) and capsaicin (from chillies) have helped to establish the antiarthritic and antinflammatory properties of these spices as also explain the mechanisms by which these act on the pathological conditions. CFTRI has demonstrated the prophylactic and therapeutic effects of dietary curcumin and capsaicin in adjuvant induced arthritis model in rats. Studies showed that these spice principles delayed the onset of the disease, decreased inflammation of joints and reduced paw oedema in arthritic animals.

Biofumigants for the control of insect pests

CFTRI has discovered the potent biofumigant activity of a compound FPIC-CO01, present in foods conventionally used as a flavouring agent and also synthetically manufactured. FPIC-CO01 is listed as safe by the Flavour and Essence manufactures Association, USA. The insecticidal activity exhibited by the compound is seen to be the most potent as compared to other biofumigants being investigated elsewhere, thus having good potential for exploitation against mosquito mats, coils, vapourisers and use as a biofumigant for the protection of stored grain from insect infestation. The fumigant assumes importance in view of the phasing out of allethrin, phosphine and methyl bromide.

Technological achievements

Modified atmospheric packaging

Modified atmospheric packaging (MAP) wherein the atmosphere surrounding the commodity is rendered different from normal through manipulation of CO_2,O_2 and N_2 levels in suitable polymeric film packages of desired permeability is one of the effective methods for extending storage life of fruits. Active modification involves creating slight vacuum inside the package and replacing it with a desired mixture of gases to establish an optimum equilibrated modified atmosphere (EMA). The MAP offers potential for long distance transportation including export of commercially important fruits such as mango, banana, lichi, pomogranate and strawberry as well as important vegetables.

Technology protocols for mango export

Mango, considered the king of tropical fruits is a universal delicacy and has high potential for exports. CFTRI has developed specific pre-and post harvest technology packages for export of the famous alphonso and bangalpalli varieties of Indian mangoes by ship in reefer containers. The appropriate pre-harvest technology protocols include orchard management, treatments to control spoilage, optimum stage of maturity for harvest, desapping, grading, and washing followed by post-harvest dip treatments to minimise spoilage, ripening, low temperature storage in containers and packing in specially designed CFB boxes. The process capable of handling one tone mango per hour, helps in increasing shelf life of the produce to 35 days with desirable and acceptable ripening characteristics.

Dehydrated green pepper

Dehydrated green pepper (DGP) has a good potential for export. CFTRI has developed an improved process for dehydration of green pepper which avoids the use of chemicals for the retention of the green colour, a significant breakthrough in the technology development. Fresh tender green berries are subjected to high temperature in short time (HTST) treatment and then dried to a desired level under controlled conditions. The DGP thus obtained has a good flavour with a rehydration ratio of 1: 3, and a piperine content of about 5 %. A patent has been filed on this method for production of DGP.

Dehydration of meat

Dehydrated meat is a shelf-stable product and storable without refrigeration at ambient temperatures. It is a ready-to-use processed material which can be available at all times for preparation of meat dishes. CFTRI has developed a process for making the convenient ready-to-use meat and lends itself convenient to transportation.

Salt from the brines of Jambusar-quality improvement

Salt produced from subsoil brine available in Jambusar (Bharuch) is reported to be of inferior and inconsistent quality, CSMCRI developed a method which involved external additives and gives acceptable and consistent quality of salt.

National centre for food safety

The food related safety standards are now followed strictly by most of the countries. The health concerns for infants, children and elderly has made it necessary to put in place special regulations applicable to Infant and other foods. CFTRI under funding from DBT is setting up a National Centre for Food Safety. The Centre would house modern facilities for various food safety evaluations.

Information products

Scientific achievements

Mathematical models for assessment of stability

CMRI has developed mathematical comprehensive analysis models for assessment of stability criterion of wedges formed by four and five joint planes. The graphic software is used to determine rock pressure and optimum support design paratmeters of underground openings, tunnels and caverns. It also deals with the orientation of the drivage of excavation. The stability of abandoned mines, tunnels and caverns can also be assessed with the help of this package.

Benchmarking the best practice of Research and Technology Organisations (RTOs)

In the new environment of globalisation and liberalisation the RTOs are seeking to restructure but have little experience in organising their activities for the new environment. NISTADS after carefully studying RTOs the world over undertook a project aimed at addressing this question by setting up benchmarks and establishing a methodology. An information package has been developed on the methodology and best practices derived from the study.

Technological achievements

Software for fragment analysis

A fragment image analysis software package -FRAGALYST for post blast fragmentation has been developed by CMRI in collaboration with a private sector software company. This software accepts the digitized image of a pile of fragments and analyses the image for vital size and shape related information of visible fragments in the image. It offers variety of features, which help in visualizing scientific, statistical and geometric analysis of an image.

Software for electromagnetic design

NAL has developed a comprehensive software package, 'Aavrita' for EM design and analysis of radomes, both ground based and airborne. Aavrita aims at providing design solutions from the EM perspective incorporating variation in the material properties and the fabrication tolerances. Given a radome design, Aavrita is also capable of analysing it with respect to the EM performance parameters such as transmitted power, reflected power, voltage standing wave ratio (VSWR), insertion phase delay (IPD) etc.

Software for cathodic protection in off-shore platforms

The software is the first of its kind in India and has been developed for ONGC, subsequent to denial of the international software from the Norwegian consortium. Offshore platforms are expensive metallic structures for oil & gas exploration, the longivity of these structures thus depends critically on the extent of cathodic protection provided to them. CECRI has developed an highly useful indigenous software called CPSEA++ which facilitates early recognition of corrosion and areas prone to corrosion, thereby providing timely protection of off-shore structures.

Software for the analysis of deflection data

Under a joint study with C-MMACS, CRRI has developed a Mathematical Model for Multilayer Road System, Types prevalent in India and a software analysis of Falling Weight Deflectometer deflection data. Validation of the software is being carried out.

Engineering database on landslides

CRRI has developed a user friendly engineering database on landslides (EDBLSD) comprising all important factors influencing landslides and the associated impacts. The database would be useful towards developing national policies on mitigation and management of landslides and also assist highway engineers working on hilly regions in preparing at operational strategic plans.

Mufti-media database creation

INSDOC has been making endeavours to develop expertise in the area of multimedia databases. It has developed the following multi-media products:

a) *Multi media Encyclopedia on Carnatic Music:* The database is of hypermedia documents which are linked to each other through hyperlinks. It has been authored in ICON AUTHOR software, provides detailed information in the form of text, picture or sound on the various aspects of Carnatic music.

b) *Multi media Photo I-card Preparation:* INSDOC has developed a high efficiency system for the preparation which enables online delivery of photo I-cards. It continued the preparation of photo I-cards for electors of 50 assembly constituencies in the National Capital Territory of Delhi.

CD-ROM activities

INSDOC has published two databases on CD-ROM using in house facilities these are:

a) National Union Catalogue of Scientific Serials in India (NUCSSI) Database: It is a valuable user friendly menu-driven retrieval information product which helps in locating the availability of S&T serials in the country. The database covers nearly two lakh holdings in over 400 S&T libraries in the country.

b) Indian Patents (INPAT) Database can be searched by different parameters. It contains nearly 50,000 records on patents granted in India from 1972 to December 1997.

Publication of research journals

NISCOM, continued the publication of the thirteen research journals covering all the major disciplines of science. In all nearly 1400 papers were published in these journals during the year. Some Special issues of these journals brought out during the year were on:

a) Organic Synthesis-Growing Interface with Adjacent Sciences proceedings of an Indo-German Symposium (Indian Journal of Chemistry, Sections A&B June, 1997);

b) Condensed matter Physics (Indian Journal of Pure and Applied Physics, November 1997) ;

c) Role of Eukaryotic Cell Surface Macromolecules (Indian Journal of Biochemistry and Biophysics, February & April 1998 combined issue);

d) Satellite Oceanographic Modelling (Indian Journal of Marine Sciences, march 1998);

e) Recent Advances in Technical Textiles (Indian Journal of Fibre and Textile Research, December 1997) ;

f) The publication of the Chinese editions of Indian Journal of Chemistry, Sections A&B was continued in collaboration with the Shanghai World Publishing Corporation, Shanghai.

Special publications

NISCOM published two reference proceedings, viz; Advances in High Pressure Research in Condensed Matter Physics, Proceedings of International Conference on Condensed matter under High. Pressure held at BARC during Nov. 1996, the Physics of Disordered Materials, Proceedings of the International Conference held at Jaipur in January 1997. All the twenty-four issues of the fortnightly newsletter CSIR News for the year were published on schedule.

Popularisation of science

The Golden Jubilee series of popular science books initiated at NISOM during 1992 have been in great demand, a new title brought out was on 'Holography' by M.G. Joshi. In the Sci-Fun Series of books targeted for children in the age group of 8-10, a new title on 'Bubble Bubble by HS Ray was published and the manuscripts of two other books, 'Strange Plants' by Parul Sheth and 'Deserts' by Vineeta Singhal, are press ready. Besides this two lavishly illustrated books 'How?' and 'Why?' each containing 100 mind boggling questions (with their answers) in was released under the Q-Series.

Documentation centre for RGNDWM

INSDOC has been approached by Rajiv Gandhi National Drinking Water Mission (RGNDWM) for establishment of its Documentation and Information Centre on a turn key basis. The project phase involving setting up of infrastructural facilities is nearing completion which will be followed by an operational phase of one year. 'The resource collection for the centre is being built up concurrently. The first issue of the quarterly R&D newsletter entitled "MISSION NVATS AN" has been published. The centre is scheduled to be inaugurated shortly.

Electoral roll database

INSDOC was assigned by Chief Electoral Officer (CEO), Delhi a project on computerisation of electoral rolls of the National Capital Territory of Delhi. The work involved creation of a database of nearly 45 lakh electors of 40 Assembly constituencies in English and Hindi. The software has been developed in 'Windows' and database design provides improved storage efficiency by introducing dictionary concept. It facilitates conversion of English data into Hindi automatically. The database will simplify the process of updating electoral rolls and bring about overall improvement in the management of electoral rolls data.

Material sciences and technology

Scientific achievements

RF-SQUID effect in borocarbide superconductors

NPL has observed, for the first time, rf-SQUID effect due to natural grain boundary weak links in a bulk sample of YNi_2B_2C superconductor at 4.2 K, confirming that the superconducting grains are coupled at the grain boundaries through Josephson effect.

Thermal modelling of DC continuous casting

NML has developed an efficient numerical simulation method for the steady-state Direct-Chill continuous casting of aluminium-magnesium (AI-Mg) alloy cylindrical ingots, results from which show excellent agreement with the published experimental data.

Foaming behaviour of FeO in slags during reduction

RRL-Bhu conducted a number of experiments in a plasma reactor of 50 kW capacity to investigate the influence of

FeO content in slag on the foaming taking place in hearth portion of the blast furnace in steel making. It was seen that the maximum foam height increased with decrease of temperature, initial FeO content of slag and initial slag height.

Technological achievements

High temperature superconducting wires/tapes and tube conductors

Keeping the possibility of use of high temperature superconductors as current carrying conductor in mind, NPL has been developing technology for fabrication of silver clad superconducting wires using high temperature superconducting BPSCCO conductors on:

a) Fabrication of long length silver clad BPSCCO mono-filamentary;

b) Fabrication of multi-filamentary silver clad BPSCCO tapes and;

c) Fabrication of high current tube conductors.

It appears that high current leads featuring rods or tubes would be the first applications of ceramic superconductors in electrical power engineering as they offer a major advantage of reduction of heat load at 41K by more than a factor of 10 with a current of 500-1000 A for various applications. NPL has prepared 10,20 and 43 cms long tube conductors capable of carrying more than 120-200 A at 771K in the superconducting state. These can be used as current leads for conventional superconducting magnets, particularly suitable for operation with cryo-coolers.

Carbon ore epoxy prepregs

By virtue of the numerous advantages they offer prepregs are the most popular 'building blocks' in composite product development. Currently most prepregs used in India are imported. NAL, with support from TIFAC and ADA has developed aerospace grade carbon fibre prepregs know how which has been transferred to IPCL, Vadodara.

Ultra low expansion transparent glass-ceramic

Ultra low expansion transparent glass-ceramic is a strategic material used as a mirror substrate mount for astronomical telescopes, reflector in radiometer of satellites and as standard reference material for dimension control in engineering industry. CGCRI carried out extensive work on the development of the ceramic (equivalent to 'ZERODUR') and has been successful in producing 5 kg of the strategic material and moulded glass blanks of different sizes. Scale up to a 100 litre melting capacity plant is now contemplated.

Radiation Shielding Windows (RSW) glass

CGCRI has been successful in developing a high density (>=5.0 g/cm^3) RSW glass (both unstabilised and Ce-stabilized in lab-scale (2kg) under the sponsorship of Board of Research in Nuclear Sciences (BRNS), Department of Atomic Energy (DAE). Efforts are on to upscale the melting parameters for the preparation of large size (150×150×100 mm) blanks for further evaluation.

Flotation column for industrial applications

A 75mm diameter automated flotation column designed by NML Madras Centre was fabricated and supplied to National Mineral Development Corporation Ltd., Hyderabad. The column incorporates many salient features like precise feed/discharge controls and level controls and is highly automated.

Encouraged by the success and the excellent metallurgical results obtained using this column, NML recently designed and developed a semi-commercial column of 50 mm, diameter with a capacity to treat 2-4 tonnes of ores per hour. This column has complete instrumentation for level control, wash water control, automatic sampling etc. It incorporates a special sparger designed and developed at the Centre. The column has been successfully tested for Bharat Gold Mines Ltd., at

Kolar Goldfields for their gold ores and for Gujarat Mineral Development Corporation, at Kadipani for fluorspar.

Tiles from ferro-chrome and other industrial wastes

The mixing and grinding for various compositions were chosen and carried out in pot mill to get the desired fineness and the parameters were optimised. The tiles were then fired in an electric furnace at a sintering temperature in the range of 1050-1150^{0}C. The properties of these tiles were evaluated with reference to the European Nation (EN) Standards of ceramic tiles and were found to confirm to the standards in most aspects.

Improvement in efficiency of ferro-chromium, process

NML has developed a thermochemical model of the production of FeCr in the Submerged Arc Furnace to predict the quantity of metal that could be produced. An excellent correlation was observed between the quantity predicted by the model and the amount actually produced in a 150 TPA plant. It is estimated that an industrial unit could secure about Rs. 100 lakh per annum from productivity improvement by implementing the process modifications arising from the model.

Masonry cement from industrial wastes

CBRI has taken up work on utilising mining and industrial wastes for production of masonry cement. Performance evaluation of a number of preliminary mixes of desired fineness prepared by varying proportions of wastes as binary and tertiary systems was done and mix proportions optimised with respect to percentage wastes. The product is cheaper than portland cement and found to be equally good for plastering and mortar purposes.

Transmittance standards for the infrared

Infrared radiation standards are not readily available from any of the standards laboratories in the world. The currently available standards provided by the National Institute of Standards & Technology (NIST), USA, operate in the uv, visible, and near infrared spectral region up to 2.5 m only. Now, NIST has established wavelength scale for the calibration of FTIR instruments. NPL has worked on the development transmittance standards at normal as well as oblique angles (10 to 70 degree) of incidence in the infrared (2.5 to 25 m) spectral region. The materials employed are silicon germanium, potassium bromide, zinc sulphide, zinc selenide and calcium fluoride. The transmittance/reflectance values of these standards have been intercompared with those measured at NIST and have been found to be in good agreement. These standards are used for the calibration of infrared spectrophotometers/radiometers which are an important tool for analysing the product quality in various industries i.e. chemical, pharmaceutical, food, tobacco etc. and for the evaluation of the performance of infrared scanners, night vision, thermo-vision and remote sensing systems by measuring the true transmittance of their window materials and filters.

Physical sciences and earth resources

Scientific achievements

Modelling of biogeochemical cycles of the Indian ocean

The study of biogeochemical cycles of the Indian Ocean are important for the estimation of carbon flux and marine fishery potential. A nonlinear dynamical system model developed by C-MMAC consisting of twenty seven parameters has been applied to the Indian Ocean. The model includes the effect of upwelling velocity, photosynthetically active radiation, nonlinear closure terms and grazing threshold. The model tuning is being carried out to capture the chlorophyll seasonal variation in the upper ocean, as obtained from CZCS data.

Crustal deformation using global positioning system

C-MMACS analysed the Global Positioning System

measurements data collected in the last 3 years, to estimate the convergence rate of the observation points in North India with respect to observation point in IISc to assess the stability of the South Indian peninsula using the International GPS Service (IGS) estimated orbits and pole parameters and International Terrestrial Reference Frame (ITRF 96). The results suggest that the point in Delhi has not moved much with respect to Bangalore in the last two and half years, implying that the Indian plate between Delhi and Bangalore is relatively stable. However two points in Garhwal Himalaya, one is Chamba (CHAM) just north of Main Boundary thrust and the Sukhi (SUKI) point north of Chamba, are converging towards the Indian plate at the rate of 14 rum and 18 mm/ per year. Analysis of four South Indian points with respect to Bangalore point yielded average linear strain rate of 0.001 microstrain/year, establishing the stability of South Indian peninsula and least possibility of occurrence of big earthquakes. There is also an indication of volumetric strain of the South Indian peninsula.

Insitu stress measurement

Insitu stress measurements have been carried out by NGRI upto ~600m depth in a very small diameter core-drilled borehole in the meizoseismal area of Latur earthquake for the first time in the world using a miniaturized hydroffacture packer assembly. The results demonstrate that the near-surface principal horizontal stresses are higher than the overburden pressure, indicating that they are of tectonic origin.

Earthquake studies

NGRI carried out a number of earthquake studies, leading to significant findings, some of these are given here under:

a) At Koyna the 3-13 velocity image suggests that this zone is marked by high velocity in upper crust as well as in deep lithosphere. Hypocentral locations revealed two NNE-SSW trending active faults at a depths of 11 km. The moderate earthquakes were found to nucleate near the surface, but propagating northward and downward, within planar rupture areas of 70-80sq. km. The depth range of 0-1 and 5-11 km were found to give higher magnitude and higher stress drop events.

b) At Jabalpur study of fault plane solution, isoseismals and aftershocks indicates overthrusting of southern block, of the ENE-WSW trending south Narmada fault at a depth of 35 km. The fault length is estimated to be about 5.7 km. Gravity profiles across epicentral zone of this earthquake delineated a horst structure between north and south Narmada faults which is related to the epicentre. Inferred structure across the Narmada-Son lineament obtained from MT studies could be related to seismogenic fault related to Jabalpur earthquake.

c) At Latur site amplification and coda Q_c attenuation evaluated by using after shock digital data showed that the maximum amplitude of site amplification was at villages around Killari. The fault length for the Latur earthquake is found to he 4.8 km. Teleseismic broadband data of Latur and Jabalpur earthquakes reveals that for these earthquakes the corner frequency estimate are relatively consistent. The Latur earthquakes indicates a stress drop and apparent stress which are 5 times more compared to the Jabalpur earthquake.

Oceanographic studies

i) Coastal studies

a) Under the Coastal Ocean Monitoring and Prediction System (COMAPS) extensive chemical and biological observations were made by NIO during pre and post monsoon seasons along Ratnagiri-Mangalore coastal stretch. The studies indicated that the region is free from contamination. Higher values of standing stock and densities of zooplankton were observed during premonsoon than postmonsoon season.

b) Cycling of combined nitrogen in sediment and water column of mangroves were studied. It was observed that nitrate dominated in the water column while nitrate as well as ammonium occurred in high concentrations in the sediments. Experiments on uptake and assimilation of nitrogenous nutrients by phytoplankton of sediment and water column indicated that ammonium was the most preferred nutrient to be taken up by the autotrophs with high specific rates in the month of May.

c) Studies on littoral drift and sink along the Indian coast indicated an active removal of sediments in the Gulf of Kachchh, Gulf of Khambhat, Gulf of Maṇnar, Palk Bay and Sandheads. Strong currents and wave energy concentrations are the causative factors resulting in coastal erosion.

d) Hydrographic data collected during the pre and post southwest monsoon seasons in Gauthami Godavari estuary were utilised to estimate residual fluxes of water salt and vertical diffusivity. The residual flux of salt due to tidal pumping appears to be the main factor controlling the salt balance of the estuary.

ii) Offshore processes

a) Magnetic survey along a transect running from 1^0S, 81^0 24′E to 7^0N, 87^0 WE has led to the identification of a cretaceous Magnetic Quiet Zone (CMQ) in the distal Bengal Fan. This has established a continuous evolutionary record of the Bay of Bengal since India's break up from the eastern Gondwana continent. Bathymetric and magnetic studies in the distal Bengal Fan reveal the presence of -seamounts, which are possible locations of polymetallic encrustations.

b) Under the Joint Global Ocean Flux Study (JGOFS India) programme, the spatial and temporal variability in air-sea fluxes of carbon dioxide was studied and found that higher biological production results in higher respiration rates. The surface waters of the central Arabian Sea are supersaturated, with respect to pCO_2 in atmosphere.

c) High resolution seismic reflection profiting along the western continental margin of India revealed the presence of characteristic acoustic maskings in the form of wipeouts, reflector terminations and seeps in the inner shelf. These maskings are considered to be methane-rich. Seismic profiles also revealed the presence of bottom simulating reflectors (BSRs) in the mid-lower slope-rise regions, presumably suggesting the presence of gas hydrates.

Central Indian ocean basin studies

In the first phase programme on Environmental impact Assessment at NIO for nodule mining, studies for evaluating the baseline (undisturbed) conditions have been completed in the test and reference areas. Wailed analyses of the seafloor features, nodule distribution, bathymetry, sediment characteristics and composition, as well as macro, meiobenthic and micro-biological assemblages, have been carried out to understand the present status of the benthic environment. In the second phase, a simulated "Disturbance" was conducted at a pre-selected test site.

The result showed that the changes, were the greatest within the disturbance zone, whereas the resedimentation from the plume generated by the disturber, was concentrated mainly in the southern and southwestern directions of the zone, which corresponds to the mean direction of currents during that period.

Technological achievements

Green house gave inventory

The NPL in association with other sister CSIR laboratories has developed the greenhouse gas inventory (GHG) for India since 1991. The 1998 report from NPL is the most comprehensive report to dates. The base-year considered for calculations in this report is 1990. The various sectors for which emission estimates have been made are: (i) Energy which includes emissions from Industry and Transport; (ii) the Agriculture sector (rice paddy fields and enteric fermentation from animals and manure, emissions due to burning of agricultural crop residue and emissions from Wetlands); (iii) Land use changes and forestry sector includes emissions from grassland conversion, change in forests and other woody biomass stock, abandonment of managed lands and finally the net emission from forestry and land use sector; (iv) the Waste sector includes emissions from municipal land filled areas and area in which fruit and vegetable waste are dumped. (v) waste water emissions.

Laser heterodyne system in Antartica

A highly sophisticated and High-Tech laser heterodyne system using a tunable CO_2 laser as a local oscillator and sun as a source with one GHz acousto-optic spectrometer (AOS) as back end has been designed and developed at NPL. I was deployed at Maitri station (70^0 46' S, $11^0$44'E) in Antarctica during 161 Indian Scientific Antarctica expedition (1996-97) to measure the vertical profiles of minor constituents in the stratosphere and troposphere.

The observations for ozone line profiles were continued during 1997-98 on all clear blue sky/ cloudless sunny days. The ozone line profiled thus obtained are in turn used to get vertical height profiles of ozone using inversion technique developed again at NPL for Antarctic conditions. This is the firm time that this system has been deployed for Antarctic winter time and data were collected successfully during spring i.e, September-October to study ozone bole.

Identification of deep seated weak zones

Multi-parametric geophysical studies by NGRI in thick sand covered areas of the Thar desert near Jaisalmer have succeeded in identifying deep seated weak zones, oriented broadly in the NNW-SSE and NE direction. These zones, that have played a significant role in the emplacement of dykes during earlier magnetic episodes, are important for assessing groundwater circulation.

Gravity anomaly map

Based on zero free air values, NGRI prepared a new gravity anomaly map for South India. This map can be directly interpreted in terms of subsurface mass in homogeneities and has brought into focus new anomalies which were not identified earlier from the Bouguer anomaly map due to negative bias.

Comparative assessment of clean coal technologies

CFRI commissioned an exercise to assess the relative merits of thermally efficient technologies for coal conversion to assess their applicability for Indian coals using ASPEN simulator. Eight technologies, four based on gasification and four based on combustion including conventional pulverized coal system were chosen for the study. Conversion efficiency as a function of varying quality of coal with respect to pure coal heat value and ash content and unit cost of power generation in relation to pulverized coal combustion has been worked out.

Societal and huuman welfare

Scientific achievements

Neuroendocrine regulation of silk Protein biosynthesis

The neurosecretory system of the Muga silkworm with particular emphasis of neurosecretory cells (NEC) at different regions of the brain and their positional arrangements according to the age of the silkworm was studied at RRL-Jorhat. The ultrastructure of the silk gland and brain during developmental stages showed qualitative and quantitative variations in their secretory products which clearly suggests direct control of the neuroendocrine system over silk gland development and silk protein biosynthesis.

Technological achievements

Leather Technology (LTM)

LTM made a tangible impact on the national scenario, through nearly 160 activities initiated in 17 States, of these 90 activities were completed. The highlights of achievements during the year are as follows:

a) Twelve carcass utilisation benefiting 300 families.

b) Field implementation viz. enzyme assisted dehairing, chrome recovery/ reuse, chrome management etc. were carried out in several locations.

c) A demonstration common effluent treatment plant (CETP) was commissioned at Madhavaram. Process control systems and cleaner tannery wet operations were demonstrated at four tanneries in UP and Haryana.

d) Human resource development activities viz. Programmes for artisanal development, training of shop floor management personnel for leather industry, training of trainers, training of women were carried out at several locations. Twenty cobblers from Chennai and Guntur were trained in modern methods of foot ware manufacture. Two hundred artisans from Athani have been trained in improved tanning of sole leather.

Rehabilitation of tanners in Tamil Nadu

The project aptly named 'Operation Greenstar' was luanched on a warfooting as a tripartite arrangement between CLRI, NEERI and AISHTMA. Each of the partners was assigned a designated role and responsibility; CLRI for technology for inplant control, NEERI for end of the pipe treatment and AISHTMA for implementation of the technology.

CLRI carried out an intensive survey of nearly 500 tanneries to identify and establish process information and operational data of each tannery. As a result 36 cluster groups were formed for implementation of the technology intervention packages comprising green technologies for beam-house operations, clearner tanning techniques and effluent treatment systems. NEERI carried out surveys on estimation of quantity and characteristics of the Waste Waters, based on which designs of new and redesign of existing common effluent treatment plants (CETPs) was undertaken to enable cenfermance with satutory norms. The design involved high rate transpiration & sludge management system. This enabled about 500 tanneries to be rehabilitated and made up for the loss of employment of the disadvantaged section of the society.

Value added products from tannery wastes

Tannery fleshings and chicken intestines, the two major wastes from tannery and poultry industries pose disposal problems. CLRI has studied the enzymatic hydrolysis of tannery fleshings using chicken intestine protease. The protein hydrolysate obtained could be used in poultry or fish feed formulations. In investigations on chicken intestines as a source of proteolytic and autolytic enzymes for hydrolysis of tannery fleshings, it was seen that about 75% of the total protease activity of the chicken intestines was in the mucosal layer.

Ethnobotanical investigations of Kangra Valley in Himachal Pradesh

NBRI carried out an extensive ethnobotanical investigation in Kangra valley. It has provided new knowledge on the traditional uses of several plant species which can be utilized in tribal development programmes. The inventory provides very useful data for establishing plant based cottage industries in the tribal tracts, especially for herbal drugs, food processing, fibre products and gum resin etc.

Improvement in rose oil distillation unit

IHBT improved upon an existing rose oil distillation unit (400kg capacity per batch) by integrating a compatible cohobation column designed by it with the oil distillation unit resulting in 30% increase in oil recovery.

Mechanisation of tea plucking

IHBT has standardised the mechanical plucking of china hybrid tea by machines keeping in view the two leaves and a bud plucking standard. This will greatly help the tea industry in Himachal Pradesh, which is currently facing the problem of labour shortage.

New propagation technology for tea

IHBT has succeeded in propagation of tea by 4 to 8 node cuttings as against conventional method of single node cutting by treating the node cuttings with different auxins and phenols resulting in 85-90% success in rooting and transfer to field within 9 months as against conventional methods needing nearly 2 years.

Banana fibre

RRL, Jorhat undertook study on the utilisation of wild banana plants for producing fibres and other useful materials. The main objective was to develop an appropriate technology to extract fibres from the sheaths of banana plants and then convert the fibres into twines and fabrics in conventional jute processing machinery for making eco-friendly products. Based on this work the Government of Sri Lanka has requested RRL, Jorhat to extend technical assistance to develop industries based on banana fibre in Sri Lanka and to impart training to Sri Lankan entrepreneurs.

Fresh water prawn cultivars

The suitability of freshwater prawn Macrobrachium rosenbergii for commercial production- was tested by NIO with minor modifications of the hatchery for rearing the larvae. Water quality management, feed formulation and feeding schedule for different larval stages and maintenance of hygiene in the hatchery are the factors which control the growth of larvae. Commercial production of larvae with this technique was achieved.

Habilitation at the mentally challenged people

NISTADS conceived and executed a field experiment called SAKSHAM (meaning empowered or enabling) for habilitating the mentally challenged adults to become partially/fully economically independent. A reconnaissance study was conducted by NISTADS to understand the actual condition of the mentally challenged adult after they leave the special schools or vocational centres followed by another study of employing appropriate select technologies which they could pursue as a vocational career to move on the path of economic independence. The technology of mushroom cultivation was selected for field testing the concept. Though mushroom cultivation technology is well known, application of this environment sensitive technology by a group of mentally challenged people made the experiment unique. Ibis was a departure from routine repetitive tasks used for training such people. It proved that mentally challenged were capable of performing more complex functions than is usually believed. The Project has since been selected as on the innovative projects having societal impact potential by Third World Network of Scientific Organisations (TWNSO), Trieste, and the United Nations Development Programme (UNDP) of sharing of experience among developing countries.

Floricultuure industry in H.P.

Floriculture was most non-existing in Himachal Pradesh (HP) a decade back. Arising from the training imparted to 150 growers of HP by IHBT on commercial floriculture sponsored by the Govt. of Hp, DRDA and HIMCON. 150 ha have been brought under commercial floriculture.

3

Research Development by Industry (RDI)

The EFC Memorandum for the plan scheme, Research and Development by Industry, for the Eighth Plan Period (1992-97) was approved in 1992 with an allocation of Rs. 4 crores. The Scheme is continued in the Ninth Five-year plan period. The broad objectives of the scheme are to:

- bring in-house R&D into sharper focus,
- strengthen R&D infrastructure in industry and SIROs,
- promote R&D initiatives of the industry and SIROs;
- ensure that the contributions made by the in-house R&D Centres and SIROs& dovetail adequately in the overall context of technological and industrial development.

The scheme on Research and Development by Industry covers the following areas:

A) In-house R&D by corporate/ commercial sector of Industry

B) R&D by Scientific and Industrial Research Organisations (SIROs)

C) Fiscal Incentives for Scientific Research

Activities and achievements in each of above non commercial areas are presented below:

In-house R&D by corporate/commercial sector of industry

Recognition of in-house R&D units

A strong S&T infrastructure has been created in the country. This covers a chain of national laboratories, specialised R&D centres, various academic institutions, training centres, which continuously provide expertise, technically trained manpower and technological support to the industry. Various policy measures have been introduced from time to time, to meet the changing industrial and technological requirements of the industry. The Government has been giving special attention to promotion and support to industrial research in industry. Several tax incentives have also been provided which encourage and make it financially attractive for industrial units to establish their own in-house R&D units.

A scheme for granting recognition to in-house R&D units in Industry is operated by the Department of Scientific & Industrial Research. The incentives and support measures presently available to recognised in-house R&D units include: income tax relief on R&D expenditure as per IT Act; weighted tax deduction for sponsored research programs in approved national laboratories, universities and IITs; weighted tax deduction on R&D expenditure in drugs, pharmaceutical, electronic equipment, computers, telecommunication equipment and chemicals, accelerated depreciation allowance on new plant and machinery set up based on indigenous technology, custom duty exemption on goods imported for use in Government funded R&D projects; excise duty was for 3 years on goods designed and developed by a wholly Indian owned company and duly patented in any two countries out of India, USA, Japan, and many country of the European Union; exemption from price control for bulk drugs produced based on indigenous technology, 5 years tax holiday to commercial R&D companies; financial support for R&D projects; National Awards for outstanding in-house R&D achievements and commercialisation of results of public funded R&D and other indirect benefits.

The in-house R&D units qualifying for recognition are expected to be engaged in research and development activities related to the line of business of the firm, such as development of new technologies, design and engineering, process/ product/ design improvements, developing new methods of analysis and testing; research for increased efficiency in use of resources such as capital equipment, materials, fuel, pollution control, effluent treatment and recycling of waste products.

The R&D activities are expected to be separate from routine activities of the firm such as production and quality control. The in-house R&D units should have at least some staff exclusively engaged in R&D beaded by a full-time R&D manager who would-have, direct access to the Chief Executive or to the Board of Directors depending upon the, size of the unit.

Number of in-house R&D units recognised by DSIR has increased steadily from about 100 in 1973 to about 275 by 1975, to, over 700 by 1980, around 925 by 1985, over 1100 in 1990 over 1200 in 1995 and 1222 as on December 1998. Of these 1222 units, around 135 units are in public sector, 35 in joint sector, and the remaining in private sector. A revised and updated 'Directory of Recognised in-house R&D Units' was brought out during November 1998.

For the purpose of recognition, the R&D units have to apply to DSIR as per a standard profarma. The proforma and other details about the scheme are available in the-DSIR publication "Promotion and support to

Indigenous Technology". The applications after scrutiny in the DSIR are circulated for comments to various other Departments/ Agencies, such as, concerned administrative Ministries, DCSSI, CSIR, ICAR, ICMR, DBT, DCPC, DOE, DOT, DRDO and NRDC. The units seeking recognition are visited if need be, by expert teams comprising of representatives of DSIR as well as outside agencies like administrative ministries, CSIR, NRDC, ICAR, ICMR, DRDO, DOE, DOT, IITs and local educational and Research Institutions before they are taken up for consideration. The applications along with comments from outside agencies, visit reports, along with the Department's evaluation are considered by an Inter-Departmental Screening Committee constituted by the Secretary DSIR. The Committee meets every month to consider the applications and makes recommendations to the Secretary, DSIR based on its evaluation of R&D infrastructure and R&D activity of the applicant firms.

During the year 1998 the Screening Committee met 12 times and considered 81 applications for recognition; 59 R&D units were granted recognition and 22 applications were rejected.

128 In-house R&D units were visited till the end of December 1998 by expert teams for a first hand assessment of the R&D work, infrastructural facilities and other claims made by the in-house R&D units. Also, nearly 300 discussions/meetings were held with heads of in-house R&D units.

Renewal of recognition

Recognition to R&D units is granted for a period ranging from 1 to 3 years. The R&D units are advised to apply for renewal of recognition well in advance (3 months) of the date of expiry of the recognition. Applications received for renewal of recognition are circulated to CSIR, NRDC and/ or the concerned Administrative Department of

Government of India for comments. The applications are examined in the Department taking into account the inputs received from other agencies for taking suitable decision on their renewal. During 1998, 528 in-house R&D units were due for renewal of recognition beyond 31 March 1998; of which 463 applications were received. Based on the evaluation of the performance of the R&D units, renewal of recognition was granted to 447 R&D units. Recognition granted to 16 Companies could not be renewed because their R&D performance was not upto the mark.

Zonal distribution of in-house R&D units

The in-house R&D units are distributed throughout the country. There are around 200 units in the Northern Zone (Delhi, Haryana, Punjab, Uttar Pradesh, Jammu & Kashmir), around 100 units in Western Zone (Rajasthan and Gujarat), around 450 units in the Central Zone (Maharashtra, Madhya Pradesh and Orissa), around 350 units in the Southern Zone (Andhra Pradesh, Karnataka, Kerala and Tamil Nadu) and around 125 units in the Eastern Zone covering Bihar, West Bengal, Assam and other north eastern states.

R&D expenditure

The expenditure incurred by in-house R&D units in industry has steadily increased. During 1980-81 it was of the order of Rs. 300 crores. In 1985-86, it was of the order of Rs. 500 crores. It is estimated that the present R&D expenditure of the 1222 recognised R&D units is of the order of Rs. 1800 crores. The share of public and joint sector is about 35 % and that of private sectors about 65%. 250 in-house R&D units spend over Rs. 1 crore each on R&D, 340 in-house R&D units spend between Rs. 25 lakhs to Rs. I crore each per annum on R&D.

R&D infracture

The in-house R&D Centres have created impressive

infrastructural facilities for R&D including sophisticated testing facilities, laboratory equipment and pilot plant facilities. Analytical facilities such as HPLCs, IR spectrophotometers, UV-Vis spectrophotometers, NMR spectrometers, electron microscope, high temperature test and evaluation facilities, CAD-CAM facilities, and EDM's are available with many in-house R&D units.

R&D Manpower

There has been a steady increase in R&D manpower employed by the in-house R&D units. By 1975-76 about 12,000 R&D personnel were employed by recognised in house units; by 1981-82 the figure was over 30,000. The present estimated manpower for the 1,222 in-house R&D units is around 50,000 out of which around 17,500 R&D personnel are employed in public sector in- house R&D units and around 32,500 R&D personnel are employed in the private sector in house R&D units. Of the total 50,000 R&D personnel, around 2700 are Ph.D's, 16,500 Post Graduates, 14,000 graduates and the rest are technicians and support staff.

Sectorwise Break-up of in-house R&D units

A broad sectorwise breakup of the recognised in-house R&D units is as below:

i)	Chemical and Allied industries	-425
ii)	Electrical and Electronics industries	-325
iii)	Mechanical Engineering industries -	-240
iv)	Process industries (Metallurgical, Refractories, Cement, Ceramics, Paper, Leather and others)	-180
v)	Agro and food processing industries and others	-50

In-house R&D units: output

Some of the R&D achievements reported by the recognised in-house R&D units are listed below:

Chemical and allied industries

Development of process for the manufacture of sparfloxacin, anti fungal-terbinafine hydrochloride, anti-histamine-lorotadine, anti-physcotic-resperidone and anti inflammatory-nimesulide.

- Development of HIV Elisa test kit, HIV rapid test kits.
- Development of ayurvedic drug formulation for anti Parkinson's disease.
- Development of processes for, amlodipine besylate (anti-anginal), azithromycin (anti-bacterial), cefixime cefuroxime axetil and clarithromycin.
- Development of Livoplus/Hepafyt, targeted specifically at alcohol induced bepatotoxicity.

- Development of process for extraction of humic acid from lignite.
- Development of process for the manufacture of amyl meta cresol and 2, 4 dichloro benzyl alcohol.
- Development of process for para hydroxy phenol glycerine, 3,4,5 -trimethoxy benzoic acid methyl ester.
- Development of process for continuous tow dyeing of acrylic fibre.
- Development of epoxy preweld primer for naval ships and epoxy polyurathane for fertilizer plants.
- Development and commercialisation of gear oil for transmission and rear axle.
- Development of process to prepare high grade pectin from lemon and papaya fruits.
- Development of a process for high quality yeast extract 'tryptoni'.
- Development and commercialisation of paraffins

dehydrogenation catalyst and multi-metallic reforming catalysts.

Electrical and electronic industries

- Development of an advanced land navigation system.
- Design and development of Doppler Very high frequency Omni Range equipment with Remote Monitoring & Maintenance facility (DVOR with RMM).
- Development of Omni directional antenna (collinear array), grided paraboloid antenna, co-axial resonator and microwave band pass filter.
- Development of Hull Mounted Sonar Advanced (HUMSA), very low frequency receiver (CLF Rx), Secure telephone (SECTEL), Artillery Combat Command & Control System (ACCCS) and Automatic Electronic Switch (AES) Mk II.
- Development of LCD based cockpit display system for LCA, integrated fish finder radar cum navigational guidance system, APARNA radar for navy; electronics for gunners main sight for indigenous battle tank Arjun, night driving goggles.
- Development of mathematical models for simulating a fighter aircraft of Indian defence services.
- Development of batteries for Nag missiles, electric locomotive batteries.
- Development of tactical fibre optic link for Indian army, optical fibre end polishing machine.
- Development of torpedo simulator and video surveillance system.
- Development of Micro barograph.
- Development of 130 MW air cooled turbo generator suitable for rail transportation.
- Development of solar powered automatic light emitting diode (LED) for traffic signal system.

- Development of multiaxis blood collection monitor, composcale and plasma expressor, R.F. tube sealer and blood bank management software.
- Development of Compact Fluorescent Lamps; 11W, 3W, 10W, 13W, 4 in electronic ballast for 10W, 14W, electronic converter gears.
- Development of laser based systems for non -contact diameter gauging, positioning, laser line marking, Surgical microscope for ENT application, NAVAL command and control system.
- Development of laser based contact lens guage and alignment measurement system (LGMS-1) for railway track recording.
- Development of vertical gyro and altitude encoder.
- Development of point of sales terminal using smart card, automated teller machine and express money transfer systems.
- Development of multi function console (MFC) for INDRA-II, TV demodulator.
- Development of 8 MB optical line terminal equipment.
- Development of upgraded superfledermaus radar (USFM), naval fire control system, CFM-SCPC flyaway terminals & hub -station and VHF Trans receiver.
- Development of textile design CAD software for woven and jackuard system.
- Development of computerised braille transcription system.
- Development of cordic chip based portable ultra sonography meter.

Mechanical engineering industries

- Development of Advanced Light Helicopter,

- Development and indigenous manufacture of 6 seater aircraft.
- Development of CNC Double Disc Grinder, Twin Spindle CNC Chucker, Dual Spindle CNC Chucker, Vertical Machining Centre.
- Design and Development of CNC control system for injection moulding machines and passenger car/light commercial vehicle radial tyre building m/c.
- Design and development of a new compact floor washing machine.
- Development of 350 diameter clutch for Leyland Hino engines.
- Development of roof mounted packed AC in all stainless steel structure for railway passenger coach.
- Design and development of 44 ton rear dumper, 70 ton rear dumper and 300 HP wheel loader.
- Development of computerised gear rolling tester.
- Development of axial piston pump technology for truck hydraulics, 3 way tipping system for trucks.
- Development of cooking gasifiers.
- Development and execution of off shore and mobile flare systems and a waste incinerator system, low Nox burners and efficient combustion system.
- Development of Tilting Disk Heart Valve Prosthesis.
- Development of rice husk gasification unit and solid biomass gasifier.
- Design and development of environment control system & equipment, hydraulic system components & undercarriage door actuators, wheels & brakes system and engine fuel control system components.
- Development of automated carding engine.
- Development of CFC free centrifugal chiller.

- Development of clutch testing machine for automobile clutch assembly coaches; 1.5 ton vertical slip on stainless steel body and copper fins on condenser and evaporator for defence mobile shelter applications.

Processing industries

- Development of doped tungsten powder, swaged tungsten bars and tungsten wire for lamp filament application.
- Development of process for Electro refining of crude gold.
- Development of Fe-Co-V soft magnetic alloy with high saturation flux density and curing temperature for space application.
- Development of process for manufacture of glass fibre reinforced plastic containers for Prithvi Missile programme of DRDO.
- Process for development of recovery of lead & silver from lead sulphate and manganese, lead and silver from anode mud.
- Development of partially stabilized zirconium oxide ceramics.
- Processing of cold rolled non-oriented electrical steel coil through continuous casting route.
- Recovery of Palladium from spent gold electrolyte & process intermediates.
- Development of "Interstitial Free Steel" for automobile sector.
- Development of process for manufacture of chewing gum warp with tatoo; odourless PET laminate for snack food and gold coloured cigarette foil with menthol resistant ink.

– Development of process for manufacture of 44 GSM Newsprint in wider range of quality and grade., low cost good quality economy/standard grade newsprint from waste paper; superior grade writing, printing paper.

Agro and food processing industries

– Development of probiotic feed supplement for poultry & cattle; vermi culture; compost culture; seed coating technique and enzymes as feed supplement.

– Development of CMS lines for hybrid seed production in onions and cabbage.

– Development of high oil content & yield in varieties of Indian mustard.

– Development of digested organic supplement enriched with micro nutrients.

– Development of process for manufacture of cold soluble instant tea.

– Development of BRASSINOSTEROIDS—New generation plant growth promoters for enhancing crop productivity.

– Development of a new bio-fertilizer strain for sugarcane crop. A diazotrophicus and mixed Bio fertilizer.

– Development of a process for manufacture of Azadirachtin Tech (neern based pesticide).

Imports made by R&D units

The recognised in-house R&D units have imported a variety of equipment, raw materials and samples for their R&D activities. These include: Laser based particle size, analyzer, digital distortion analyzer, dielectric loss analyzer, schering bridge, scanning spectrometer, computerised organic carbon analyser with high performance liquid chromatograph, atomic absorption spectrophotometer, X-ray spectrophotometer, virtual digital circuits, ASIC development system, CAD and UNIX work stations, oscilloscope with instant plotter, and automatic dew point meter and analyser and Stereo Zoom Microscope, single beam UV-VIS-NIR Fibre-Optic spectrophotometer for absorbance, transmittance, reflectance, Karl Fischer Titrator, UV-VIS Dual Beam Spectrophotometer, film casting unit, cryptometer colour computer for colour matching, NMR, GLC, IR, HPTLC, high speed centrifugal counter current and droplet counter current chromatographs, Beta Scope, Perkin-Elmer GC-FTIR system, FT-NMR spectrometer, inverted phase contrast fluorescence microscope, 4 channel 100 MHz Oscilloscope, Microsheen Digital Opacity reflectometer Colour image analysis system, CO Sensor and Filter, portable digital pneumatic calibrator, vacuum coating unit with electronic beam gun, rapid prototype machine, EDM, microprocessor double ended inertia dynamometer, dual channel FFT sound analyser, static / dynamic seat strength testing system and impact testing equipment, computer controlled eddy current dynamometer, CAD system logic analyser, fibre optics evaluation kit, intelligent universal programmer, development system for micro controllers, Laser Power meter, DIN Abrasion testing machine.

Certificate of indigenous development of technology/ knowwhow for bulk drugs

Bulk drugs manufactured through process know-how developed through in-house R&D are eligible for exemption from the Price Control for a period of five years after their introduction in the market. The Department examines the requests of the in-house R&D Units for issuance of a certificate of indigenous technology development for seeking price control exemption. The examination is through detailed discussions, inputs and views of experts in the field of drug development and discovery, and visits by expert teams. Taking into account the various inputs and also considering the novelty and innovativeness of the process, the certificate of indigenous development of process know-how is issued for seeking price control exemption to deserving cases. No request for price control exemption for drugs based on indigenous technology was received during the year.

Other benefits availed by the recoggnised R&D units

The Department provides assistance to recognised in house R&D units in a number of ways, such as cases of industrial R&D units requiring remittance of foreign exchange for deputing experts to attend international symposia and seminars, exhibitions, trade fairs, international R&D collaborations, engagement of foreign experts for R&D and for maintenance/ commissioning of imported R&D equipment requiring such expertise, allotment of special controlled materials for R&D, permission to export of specialised products reserved for small scale industries by medium scale industries for test marketing in other countries are examined for making suitable recommendations to concerned agencies.

A number of cases regarding locational clearance with respect to expansion of R&D have been dealt with. A number of applications regarding disposal of R&D equipment and also, pilot plant produce and permission to export of specialised products reserved for small scale industries by medium scale industries for test marketing in other countries were examined and the decisions of the Department conveyed.

Computerisation of data on in-house R&D units

Names, addresses and also location of in-house R&D units as well as validity of recognition of all the recognised in-house R&D units are computerised and updated. As on 3 1. December 1998, there were 1222 in-house R&D units recognised by DSIR and whose data are entered in the computer.

Conferences, awards, project support and publications

Twelfth national conference on in-house R&D in industry

Department of Scientific and Industrial Research (DSIR) organised the Twelfth National Conference on in-house R&D in Industry in association with the Federation of Indian Chambers of Commerce and Industry (FICCI) on 2223 December 1998 in New Delhi. Attended by nearly 500 delegates from industry, National Laboratories, IITs and Universities, Scientific and Industrial Research Organisations (SIROs), Consultancy Organisations, Government Departments, the Conference was inaugurated by Union Minister for HRD and S&T in the FICCI Golden Jubilee Auditorium, New Delhi. The Union Minister for HRD and S&T gave away the 1998 DSIR National Awards for Outstanding in-house R&D achievements to six industrial units and released the DSIR special publications "Compendium on in-house R&D Centres (1998)" and "Outstanding in-house R&D achievements (1998)". The valedictory address was delivered by Prof. M.M. Sharma.

b) National awards for R&D efforts in industry

In order to provide recognition to the efforts of the industry towards innovative research and technological development, the DSIR had instituted National Awards for R&D Efforts in Industry in 1987. These awards are in the form of shields made of sterling silver and are presented along with citations at the inaugural session of the Annual National Conference on in-house R&D in Industry. During 1988, National Awards were presented to 7 firms; in 1989 to 9 firms; in 1990 to 12 firms; in 1991 to 8 firms; in 1992 to 9 firms; in 1993 to 9 firms, in 1994 to 12 firms, in 1995 to 15 firms, in 1996 to 7 firms, in 1997 to 6 firms and in 1998 to 6 firms for outstanding R&D achievements.

Following is the list of the award winners in 1998:

Chemical and Allied Industries

Indian Petrochemicals Corporation Ltd., Vadodara

Drugs and Pharmaceuticals Industries

Ranbaxy Laboratories Ltd., New Delhi

Bio - tech Industries

Shantha Biotechnics Pvt. Ltd., Hyderabad

Mechanical Engineering Industries

Hindustan Aeronautics Ltd. (RWRDC), Bangalore

Processing Industries

Avasarala Tungsten Ltd., Mysore

Successful Commercialisation of Public Funded R&D

Bharat Electronics Ltd., Bangalore

Compendium on in-house R&D centres—1998

Efforts have been initiated to assess the contributions made by the in-house R&D units. Since 1985, DSIR has brought out publications highlighting the achievements claimed by the in-house R&D Centres in order to generate awareness of these developments. The first publication of "Compendium on in-house R&D Centres" was brought out during 1985 covering 193 in-house R&D Centres, second in 1986 covering 132 Centres, third in 1987 covering 209 Centres, fourth in 1988 in 4 volumes covering 589 Centres, fifth in 1989 covering 188 Centres, sixth in 1990 in two volumes covering 448 Centres, seventh in 1991 in two volumes covering 439 Centres, eighth in 1992 in two volumes covering 384 Centres, ninth in 1993 covering 291 Centres, tenth in 1994 in two volumes covering 491 Centres, the eleventh in 1995 in two volumes covering 376 Centres, the twelfth in 1996 covering 283 Centres and the thirteenth in 1997 in two volumes covering 391 Centres.

The Compendium on in-house R&D Centres - 1998 was compiled by DSIR based on the information and material received from 376 in-house R&D Centres along with their applications for renewal of recognition beyond 31 March 1998. This publication is in two volumes.

d) Outstanding in-house R&D achievements—1998

DSIR had brought out a special publication "Outstanding in-house R&D Achievements (1988-1991) during December 1991 covering the award winning achievements of 36 companies. A second publication "Outstanding in-house R&D Achievements (1992 & 1993)" was brought out during November 1993, covering the award winning achievements of 18 companies. A third publication "Outstanding in-house R&D Achievements (1994 & 1995)" was brought out during November 1995, covering the award winning achievements of 27 companies. A fourth publication "Outstanding in-house R&D Achievements - 1996" was brought out during December 1996, covering award winning achievements of 7 companies. A fifth publication "Outstanding in-house R&D Achievements - 1997" covering the award winning achievements of 6 companies was brought out during October 1997. The sixth publication "Outstanding in-house R&D Achievements - 1998", covering the award winning achievements of 6 companies was released during the inaugural session of the Twelfth National Conference on in-house R&D in Industry on 22 December 1998.

e) In-house R&D in Industry

As the number of in-house R&D Centres has increased while the activities of DSIR have also diversified significantly with respect to in-house R&D units, it was felt appropriate to devise a communication system between DSIR and in-house R&D units. Accordingly, the DSIR started bringing out a quarterly Information Update on in-house R&D in Industry on a regular basis since April 1988. The Information Update is intended to provide a communication link between DSIR, in-house R&D units and SIROs and serve to disseminate useful and important information relevant to R&D in Industry.

During 1998-99, four issues of in-house Update on R&D in Industry were brought out in April, July, October

1998 and January 1999. These have been widely disseminated to industry, SIROs, Government Departments, missions abroad and others and are well received.

Scientific and industrial research organisations

Scientific Research Association, Institutions, Universities and Colleges which undertake research in the area of Medical, Agricultural, Natural and Applied Sciences and Social Sciences seek approval under section 35 (1) (ii) or (iii) of the Income Tax Act 1961 if they wish to obtain donations from industry or other sources. The institutions notified under the section obtain benefit to the effect that any sum obtained by them for research purposes is wholly exempted from the levy of Income Tax. The donors who pay sum to such notified institutions are allowed deductions from their income to the extent of donations given for scientific research.

Prior to I June 1982, ICAR, ICMR or ICSSR were the Prescribed Authorities for approving research foundations for notification by the Ministry of Finance in the areas of Agricultural Sciences, Medical Sciences and Social Sciences respectively. With effect from 1 June 1982, Secretary, Department of Science & Technology was designated as the single Prescribed Authority to deal with approval of all the above areas. Consequent to the creation of Department of Scientific and Industrial Research, Secretary, DSIR has been designated as the single Prescribed Authority for approval u/s 35 (1)(ii)/(iii) of I.T. Act 1961.

Through an amendment by the Direct Tax Laws (Amendment) Act, 1987, effective from I April 1988, certain provisions under section 35 inter-alia were deleted. Government however, reintroduced the provisions withdrawn earlier under section 35 of the; Income Tax Act with modifications by Direct Tax Laws (Amendment) Act 1989 w.e.f. I April 1989. The, Prescribed Authority for

Section 35 is the Director General (Income Tax Exemptions) in concurrence with Secretary, Department of Scientific & Industrial Research.

Recognition of scientific and industrial research organisations (SIROs)

The DSIR has launched a scheme of granting recognition to Scientific and Industrial Research Organisations (SIROs) in 1988. SIROs recognised by DSIR are eligible for Customs Duty Exemption and Excise Duty Waiver in terms of notification Nos. 51/96-Customs dated 23.7.1996 and 10/97 - Central Excise dated 1.3.1997 respectively.

The DSIR has brought out Guidelines for Recognition of Scientific and Industrial Research Organisations (SIROs) and Approval Under Section 35(1)(ii)/(iii) of Income Tax Act, 1961, which gives procedural details and application proforma for seeking recognition under the SIRO Scheme. Functional Scientific and Industrial Research Organisations (SIROs) having broad based Governing Council, Research Advisory Committee, Research Personnel, Infrastructural facilities for research, well defined research programmes and clearly stated objectives of undertaking scientific research are considered eligible for recognition by DSIR

Applications for seeking recognition under the SIRO scheme are considered in DSIR by an inter Departmental Screening Committee with members from Council of Scientific and Industrial Research (CSIR), Indian Council of Medical Research (ICMR), Indian Council of Agricultural Research (ICAR), Indian Council of Social Sciences Research (ICSSR), University Grants, Commission, and Central Board of Direct Taxes (CBDT)/Director-Gencral-Income Tax (Exemptions). The recommendations of the Screening Committee are put up for approval of Secretary, DSIR

During the period January, 1998 to December 1"8, the Screening Committee met 6 times and recommended 18 cases for recognition as Scientific and Industrial Research Organisations and notification U/s 35(1)(ii)/(iii) of IT Act, 1961.

Recognition granted to SIROs is for duration ranging from I to 3 years. The SIROs are advised to apply for renewal of recognition well in advance (3 months prior to the date of expiry of recognition). Such Vocations received for renewal of recognition are examined by Research Review Groups by involving representatives from ICAR, ICMR, CSIR and ICSSR depending cc the area. Based on the evaluation made by the. Research Review Groups, renewal of recognition is granted to SIROs and concurrence of Secretary DSIR is communicated to DG (ITE), Calcutta for notification of SIROs u/s 350)00/04) of IT Act, 1961.

At present there am 534 SIROs duly recognised by DSIR. Of these, 188 are in the am of Natural & Applied Sciences, 164 are in the area of Medical Sciences, 37 are in the area of Agricultural Sciences, 119 am in the area of Social Sciences and 26 are Universities/Colleges. DSIR has brought out Directory of Recognised Scientific & Industrial Research Organisations in November 1999.

The SIROs have employed qualified scientists and researchers and also established good infrastructural facilities for research. They have developed new processes, procedures, techniques and technologies and also filed several patents. They have also organised seminars/ symposiums/workshops and published research papers/ reports/books.

Fiscal Incentives for scientific research

Government have evolved, from time to time, fiscal incentives and support measures to encourage R&D in industry and increased utilisation of locally available R&D options for industrial development. The union budget for 1996-97 and 1997-98 has introduced a set of new incentives to encourage investments in R&D by industry.

Fiscal incentives and support measures presently available include: (a) Income tax relief on R&D expenditure; (b) Weighted Tax Deduction for sponsored research; (c) Weighted tax deduction on in-house R&D expenditure (d) Customs Duty Exemption on capital equipment, spares, accessories and consumables imported for R&D by approved institutions/ SIROs; (e) Excise duty waiver on indigenous items purchased by approved institutions/ SIROs for R&D; (f) Five year tax holiday for commercial R&D companies; (g) Excise duty waiver for 3 years on goods produced based on indigenously developed technologies and duly patented in any two of the countries out of India European Union (one country), USA and Japan; (h) Accelerated Depreciation Allowance on plant and machinery set-up based on indigenous technology (i) Price Control exemption on domestic R&D based bulk drugs; 0) Customs duty exemption on imports for R&D projects supported by Government.

Deprecciation allowance on plant and machinery set up based on indigenous technology

Government have introduced a system of allowing accelerated depreciation in respect of blocks of assets and rationalised the rate structure by reducing the number of rates as also by providing for depreciation at higher rates.

Secretary, Department of Scientific & Industrial Research, Ministry of Science and Technology, is the Prescribed Authority to certify expenditures where higher rate of depreciation is to be allowed for the plant and machinery using indigenous know-how. Guidelines have been issued for making applications for obtaining the aforesaid certificate. All such applications received are examined in the department, and discussions and technical visits to verify the claim are made to the plants by expert teams. Based on a detailed examination, certificates in deserving cases are issued for eligible expenditure.

During the year 1998, 11 certificates involving Rs. 2606 lakhs on cost of plant and machinery were issued by DSIR.

Customs duty examption on ggoods imported for use in government funded R&D projects

The Union budget for 1996-97 introduced the provision of customs duty exemption on specific goods imported for use in R&D projects funded partly by any Department of the Central Government and undertaken by the company in their in-house R&D unit recognised by DSIR. A certificate from the Ministry or Department, as the case may be, funding the research project stating the essentiality of the item/s in each case at the time of importation would make the item/s eligible for duty free import for that R&D programme by the company. During the period January-December 1998, 18 certificates for import of capital equipment and consumables/ materials for R&D projects supported by DSIR were issued.

Reference under section 35(33) of I.T. act 1961 regarding scientific research

In the implementation of various incentive schemes for the promotion of research and development, the Income Tax act inter alia provides that expenditures made on capital equipment and related to research activities are allowed to be written off 100% in the year in which the expenditures are incurred. the Government has however, provided that if a question arises under section 35 of IT Act 1961 as to whether and, if so, to what extent any activity constitutes or constituted or any asset is or was being used for scientific research the Central Board of Direct Taxes would refer the question to the Prescribed Authority. Director-General of Income Tax (Exemptions) in concurrence with Secretary, DSIR is the Prescribed Authority for deciding such cases. On receipt of the reference in DSK the department collects information/ background regarding the description of the activity claimed as scientific research, date of commencement of the relevant projects, date of completion of research work as also the results obtained from the specific project. After obtaining all these details, the matter is examined in DSIR. In case where it is considered necessary, a team of technical experts is constituted for on the spot appreciation of the research work done at the premises of the company. After receiving the technical assessment report from the visiting team, a discussion is also normally held so that the point of view of the Company is taken into account before arriving at a decision. After completing the processing of the case in the above fashion, the case file is placed before the Secretary, DSIR for giving a decision. The Secretary DSIR gives his decision by setting out a reasoned order duly signed by him which is communicated to Director General of Income Tax (Exemptions).

During the year recommendations of Secretary were sent to DG(ITE) in the case of M/s Indian Organics Ltd, Mumbai.

Approval of commercial R&D companies

In order to promote research and development activities in the commercial research and development companies the Union Budget for 1996-97 has proposed to provide for a five year tax holiday under section 80-1A of the Income Tax Act, to approved companies whose main objective is scientific and industrial research. This incentive is available to any company that has as its main objective, activities in the area of scientific and industrial research and development and which has been accorded approval by the Prescribed Authority. Secretary, Department of Scientific & Industrial Research is the Prescribed Authority for this purpose vide Gazette notification dated 26 December, 1996, issued by Deptt. of Revenue, Ministry of Finance.

The tax holiday is available to any company whether new or existing, which is accorded approval by the Prescribed Authority at any time before the first day of April 1998. The 100% deduction for a five-year period commences from the assessment year relevant to the previous year in which the approval by the Prescribed Authority is accorded to such a company.

The amendment has taken place from 1st April 1997 and will accordingly apply in relation to the assessment year 1997-98 and subsequent year.

The Department has approved two companies as commercial R&D companies during January-December 1998.

Excise duty waiver

The Union budget for 1996-97 introduced the provision of exemption of all goods falling under the Schedule to the Central Excise Tariff 1985 (5 of 1986) from the whole of the duty of excise leviable thereon provided such goods are manufactured by a wholly Indian owned company, such goods are designed and developed by such Indian company, the goods so designed and developed are patented by such Indian company in any two countries from amongst India, USA, Japan and any one country of the European Union, for a period of 3 years from the date of issuance of certificate to the effect by DSIR.

Customs duty exemption to recognised SIROs

All Scientific and Industrial Research Organisations recognised by DSIR are eligible for Customs Duty Exemption on the import of scientific equipment, instruments, spares, accessories as well as consumables for research and development activities and programmes.

The procedure for issuing the essentiality certificates to SIROs for obtaining the customs duty exemptions has been formalised. A Committee has been set-up in DSIR, which meets periodically, normally once in a fortnight to examine the requests. The recommendations of the Committee are put up to the Head of the RDI Scheme, for approval.

During the year around 700 essentiality certificates were issued for claiming customs duty exemption on import of scientific equipment, accessories and components, including consumable items. The value of scientific equipment instruments and the consumables was about Rs. 35 crores.

Some of the major equipment for which essentiality certificates were issued were:

Digital Dial gauge; Digital Pressure gauge; Digital Temperature Indicator; Mettler Electronic Analytical Balance; Polytron Aggregate; Atomic Absorption Spectrometer; Optical Design Software; ECV Crash System; VX1 front end system and accessories; Thermal plotter & its media with plotting software; Non-linear video editing DVD/VCD/CD player; Decoding accessories; Testing equipment for Ergonomics lab; Metallurgical microscope; CNC Wirecut EDM; CNC Vertical Machining Centre; Primary Reference Metal Standards; Multiproduct Calibrator; Universal Sampler; Special type of Silicon; Compact Capacitance Gauge; Triple output DC power supply; Pressure Transmitter; TRA differential pressure sensors; BOD-COD Analyser; HPLC with accessories; Thin Layer Chromatograph with accessories; Primary calibration samples, etc.

Excise duty exemption to recognised SIROs

All Scientific and Industrial Research Organisations (SIROs) recognised by DSIR are eligible for Excise Duty Exemption on the purchase of scientific and technical instruments, apparatus, equipment (including computers); accessories and spare parts thereof and consumables; computer software, Compact Disc- Read Only Memory

(CD-ROM), recorded magnetic tapes, micro films, microfiches; and prototypes for research and development activities and programmes.

This provision was introduced by Ministry of Finance (Deptt. of Revenue) vide notification No. 10/97-Central Excise dated 1 March 1997. The procedure for issuing essentiality certificates to SIROs for obtaining the Excise duty exemptions has been formalised. A Committee has been set up in DSIR to examine the applications received. The Committee normally meets periodically and essentiality certificates are issued with the approval of Head of RDI Scheme.

During the year 1998, 53 essentiality certificates for a total amount of Rs. 153.63 Lakhs were issued for claiming Excise Duty Exemptions.

Registration of public funded research institutions and others

The Union Budget for 1996-97 introduced rationalisation of customs duty exemption on import of equipment, spares and accessories and consumables for research purposes by public funded research institutions, universities, IITs, IISc, Bangalore; Regional Engineering Colleges, (other than a hospital) for availing the customs duty exemption. The pass book scheme which was hitherto operated by the Department of Science and Technology and the Ministry of Human Resources Development is superseded by a simple registration with the Department of Scientific and Industrial Research. The ceiling on the value of goods imported for R&D is also removed and the head of the public funded research institutions/organisations duly registered with DSIR can certify the R&D goods for duty free import as per the notification No. 51/96-Customs dated 23 July 1996.

The Union Budget for 1997-98 has introduced a provision of Central Excise Duty exemption for Public Funded Research Institutions and others. As per the

Government notification No. 10/97-Central Excise dated 1.3.1997, the Public Funded Research Institutions, universities, IITs, IISc, Bangalore, Regional Engineering Colleges, registered with DSIR are also eligible for Central Excise Duty Waiver on purchase of indigenously manufactured equipment, spare parts and accessories and consumables for scientific research purposes.

During the period January, 1998 - December, 1998, 175 registration certificates were issued to such public funded research institutions universities, IITs, IISc, Bangalore, Regional Engineering Colleges for availing customs duty exemption on import of scientific equipment, spares and accessories, consumable items and Central Excise Duty exemption on indigenous purchases for scientific research purposes.

4

Programme Aimed at Technological Self Reliance (PATSER)

The objectives of the scheme on "Programme Aimed at Technological Self Reliance (PATSER)" include:

(i) Supporting industry for technology absorption, development and demonstration.

(ii) Building indigenous capabilities for development and commercialisation of contemporary products and processes of high impact.

(iii) Involvement of national research organisations in joint projects with industry.

Activities

The activities under PATSER include the following:

Financial Support to Research, Development, Design and Engineering (RDDE) Projects of Industry:

The Department provides on a selective basis partial financial support to research, development, design, engineering (RDDE) projects to be proposed by industry in the following areas:

a) Development and demonstration of new or improved product and process technologies including those for specialised capital goods, for both domestic and export markets.

b) Absorption and Upgradation of imported technology.

The partial financial support by DSIR in the above areas primarily covers prototype development and pilot plant work, test and evaluation of products flowing from such R&D, user trials etc. Bulk of the cost of the project is met from industry's resources.

The Department under PATSER Scheme has so far supported about 75 R&D projects of Industrial units. These projects cover products and processes in various important industries such as metallurgy, electricals, electronics, instrumentation, mechanical engineering, earth moving and industrial machinery, chemicals and explosives.

During the year, a number of new R&D projects of industry were supported on partial financial support basis. The Department had invited, through advertisements in leading news papers, project proposals for technology absorption, development and demonstration from industrial units whose in- house R and D Units had been recognised by DSIR. Consequently, over 300 responses from industrial units seeking further details about the scheme, indicating their technology development projects were received by the Department. During the year, till December 1998,28 projects were submitted for consideration of the Technical Advisory Committee to PATSER for partial financial support by DSIR. Some more projects are likely to be considered by TAC in the period January - March, 1999.

As a new initiative during 1998-99, the Ministry of Science and Technology has launched a novel programme "Technopreneur Promotion Programme" (TePP) jointly operated by DSIR under its PATSER Scheme and DSIR under its Home Grown Technology Scheme to tap the vast innovative potential of the citizens of India

The progress of various projects under PATSER Scheme during the year is given below:

M/s. Litex Electricals Pvt. Ltd., Pune and Society for Applied Microwave Electronics Engineering and Research (SAMEER), Mumbai

The project of M/s Litex. Electricals Pvt. Ltd. for development of Xenon and Krypton filled lamps for laser pumping is being undertaken in association with SAMEER, Mumbai. This project involving DSIR support of Rs.8 lakhs out of total project cost of Rs.25 lakhs is in progress. The project has been completed.

M/s. CS Zircon, Kala Amb and Institute of Plasma Research (IPR), Ahmedabad

The project of M/s C.S. Zircon is for the development of Plasma based dissociation process to manufacture Zirconia, in collaboration with IPR, Ahmedabad, a research society under the Department of Science and Technology. This project, involving DSIR support of Rs.9.5 lakhs out of a total project cost of Rs.60 lakhs, has-been completed.

National Fertiliser Ltd. (NFL), New Delhi and Centre for Study of Man and Environment (CSME), Calcutta

The project for bench scale development and field testing of Zinc Polyphosphate based Slow release micronutrient fertilizers was successfully undertaken by CSME with DSIR support of Rs.1.25 lakhs out of a total project cost of Rs.2.50 lakhs. CSME has also been successful in undertaking repeat trials for residual effects with a further support by DSIR of Rs. 1.10 lakhs out of a total cost of Rs. 2.20 lakhs. NFL has supported the remaining costs of both the phases of this project. The project has been completed.

M/S. Central Electronics Ltd. (CEL), Sahibabad

The project for "Development of Hybrid (SPV-Diesel) Pilot power Plant was undertaken by M/s Central, Electronics Ltd. with DSIR's support of Rs. 14 lakhs out of the total project cost of Rs. 21 lakhs. The project which was initially targetted at meeting the requirements of Defence Radio Relay (RRD) and the Deptt. of Telecommunication.'s,

Repeater Station for Rural and Remote Telecommunications Networks was reviewed. In order to meet the enhanced technical requirements and specifications of DOT, the system was upscaled and its demonstration has been successfully completed at DOT Microwave Repeator Station at Manesar, with remote control facility at Sanchar Bhawan. The project pertaining to Defence application, however, was not considered techno-economically feasible to implement. The project has been completed

M/s Mishra Dhatu Nigam Ltd. (MIDHANI), Hyderabad

The project by MIDHANI is for welding of Molybdenum wire to make 20 kg coil. A special welding machine has already been developed in the project for this purpose Samples of welded wires have already been approved by user's both in India and abroad and more than 500 Kg of wires have already been prepared and delivered. DSIR support to this project is Rs. 10 lakhs out of a total project cost of Rs. 20 lakhs. The activities in the project have been completed.

M/s. Metallurgical and Engineering Consultants (1) Ltd. (MECON), Ranchi and M/s Durgapur Steel Plant (DSP), Durgapur

The project for development of Under Burden Probe for determination of temperature and chemical compositions of hot gases inside the stack of a blast furnace was undertaken by M/s MECON in association with Durgapur Steel Plant (DSP) with DSIR support of Rs. 30.00 lakhs out of *total project cost of Rs.82.00 lakhs. The underburden probe has been developed and installed on the blast furnace along with the related instrumentation. The project has been completed.

M/s T. Stanes and Company Limited, Coimbatore

The project of M/s T. Stanes & Company is for development of Digested Organic Supplement (DOrS) and its applications in a variety of crops involving a DSIR support of Rs.40.00 lakhs, out of a total project cost of

Rs.131.00 lakhs. The pilot plant has been installed at Madurai and production of DOrS has started. The product has been tested in green house as well as IARI's Centres located in several States. The project has been completed,

M/s Central Electronics Ltd. (CEL), Sahibabad and CMS Traffic System Pvt. Ltd., New Delhi

The project for the "Experimental Design and Development of SPV Powered Traffic Signalling. System" has been taken up jointly by M/s CEL, Sahibabad and CMS, New Delhi, with DSIR's support of Rs. 9.50 lakhs, out of the total project cost of Rs. 19.52 lakhs, The Delhi Traffic Police has also provided financial support of Rs. 2 lakhs for the project. The system has been successfully demonstrated to Delhi Traffic Police and the project has been completed.

M/s. Padmavathy Panel Boards Ltd., Bangalore

The project for upgradation of Rice Husk based plant and development of new variant of reinforced boards and particle board & fire check doors is being undertaken by M/s- Padmavathy Panel Boards Ltd., Bangalore in collaboration with NRDC, with DSIR support of Rs. 23.65 lakhs out of project cost of Rs. 95.00 lakhs for one year duration. The upgraded Rick Husk Board plant of 2000 TPD has been commissioned and development of fire check doors and new variants of reinforced boards have been successfully developed. The draft project completion report has been received. The project is expected to be completed by March, 1999.

M/s Triveni Structurals Ltd. (TSL), Naini

M/s TSL is undertaking a project for development of various types of 400 KV and 765 KV Self supporting and Guyed type transmission line towers, with a DSIR support of Rs 20 lakhs out of the total project cost of Rs 86 lakhs. Structural Engineering Research Centre (SERC), Madras is assisting the firm in design and testing of the towers. One prototype of 400 KV guyed wire single circuit 00-20 Transmission Tower has been developed and has successfully cleared the trials at SERC, Madras. Two more prototypes are under testing. The project is in progress.

M/s. Central Electronics Ltd. (CEL), Sahibabad

The project for "Development and Evaluation of Plasm Etching and Edge Grinding System for Edge Separation" was undertaken by M/s CEL, Sahibabad, with DSIR financial support of Rs. 50 lakhs out of the total project cost of Rs. 135 lakhs. The project is scheduled to be completed.

M/s. IBP Co. Ltd., Gurgaon

Four projects for (a) Development-of Site Mixed slurry (SMS) Explosives for deep bore-hole applications. (b) Adaptation and upgradation of Emulsion Explosive Technology (c) Development of Detonating Card for shaped charges used for perforation of wells in oil fields and (d) Development of Heat Resistant Explosives (with the assistance of CMRI, Dhanbad) were undertaken by M/s IBP, Gurgaon with DSIR support of Rs. 41.50 lakhs out of total project cost of Rs 137.00 lakhs. The project on Detonating Card for shaped charges has been completed and the firm has started selling the product to ONGC, The firm has filed an Indian patten" on the Detonating card. The field trials on Site mixed slurry have also been completed. The other two projects are in progress.

M/s. FACT, Cochin

The project for development of slow release fertilizers and their application on Paddy, Banana, sugar cane and Coconut crops is being undertaken by M/s FACT in association with Kerala Agricultural University, Thrisur and Tamilnadu Agricultural University, Coimbatore with a DSIR support of Rs. 12.00 lakhs out of a total project cost of Rs.46.00 lakhs. The sixth and final crop of paddy has been harvested and trial on other long duration crops such as sugarcane, banana, coconut are in progress.

M/s Mishra Dhatu Nigam Ltd. (MIDHANI), Hyderabad

MIDHANI has taken up a project to produce clean steel through filtration. Several filters have been identified for the project, and trials are being conducted on them. Trials have demonstrated the effectiveness of the filter in some type of steels. DSIR's support to the project is Rs. 37.00 lakhs out of a total project cost of Rs. 74.00 lakhs. The project is in progress.

M/s Mishra Dhatu Nigam Ltd. (MIDHANI), Hyderabad

The project for production of wires with high surface finish has been taken up by MIDHANII with a DSIR support of Rs. 12 lakhs and project cost of Rs. 36 lakhs. Such wires find extensive use in spark plugs and electrostatic precipitators. One batch of wires have already been produced and accepted by BHEL with some comments. Second improved batch is undergoing trials at BHEL.

Central Power Research Institute (CPRI), Bhopal and M/s G.K. Electricals, Bhopal

The joint project of CPRI and U/s G.K. Electricals, Bhopal is for development of 12 KV load break switches for use in Electrical Sub-Stations involving a DSIR support of Rs.5.5 lakhs out of total project cost of Rs.50.00 lakhs. Second prototype is under testing. The project is in progress.

M/s Semiconductor Complex Limited, (SCL), Chandigarh and C-DAC, Pune.

The joint project of M/s SCL and C-DAC is for development of ASIC (Application Specific Integrated Circuit) for Indian languages computing system GIST-II and the related card involving DSIR support of Rs. 30 lakhs out of total project cost of Rs. 50 lakhs. The project is in progress.

M/s Semiconductor Complex Limited, (SCL) Chandigarh and Electronic Research Development Centre, Thiruvananthapuram.

The joint project of M/s SCL and ER&DC is for

development of ASIC for microprocessor based power controller involving DSIR support of Its. 50.50 lakhs out of total project cost of Rs. 93 lakhs. The project is in progress.

M/s Semiconductor Complex Limited, (SCL), Chandigarh and Electronic Research & Development Centre, Thiruvananthapuram.

The joint project of M/s SCL and ER&DC is for development of ASIC and the related STD PCO machine involving DSIR support of Rs. 18.00 lakhs out of total project cost of Rs. 65 lakhs. The ASIC developed is under evaluation. The project is in progress.

M/s Semiconductor Complex Limited, (SCL), Chandigarh and M/s Indchem Research and Development Laboratory (IRDL), Madras.

The project for the development of ASIC for MPEG-2 (Motion Picture Export Group) Decoder was undertaken jointly by M/s SCL ad IRDL with DSIR support of Rs. 70 lakhs out of the total project cost of Rs. 225 lakhs. The project is in progress.

M/s Semiconductor Complex Ltd. (SCL), Chandigarh and M/s Bharat Heavy Electricals Ltd. (BHEL), Bangalore

The joint project of M/s SCL and M/s BHEL is for development of the Application Specific Integrated Circuit (ASIC) and ASIC based 3 Phase multifunctional electronic energy meter for industrial applications involving DSIR support of Rs 23.00 lakhs out of total project cost of Rs. 43.60 lakhs. The project is in progress. The ASIC design has boon completed and the ASIC has been sent for prototyping. The ASIC will be integrated with the rest of the meter.

M/s Bharat Earth Movers Ltd. (BEML), Bangalore

The project for development of Cut Crank Shaft used in their heavy duty engines was undertaken by M/s BEML with DSIR support of Rs. 27.00 lakhs out of total project cost of Rs.65.00 lakhs. The prototype of the S.G. Iron Crank

Shaft has been developed and will be fitted in a engine for testing. The prototype of Austempered Ductile Iron (ADI) Crank shift is under development. The project is in progress.

M/s Turbotech Precision Engineering Pvt Ltd. OWL) and National Aerospace Laboratories (NAL), Bangalore

The project being executed by M/s TPEL in collaboration with NAL, and Sakthi Sugars, Erode is for the development of low cost gas turbine (LCGT) generator set of 500 KW power class with multi fuel capability (biogas, piped natural gas and diesel fuel) involving DSIR support of Rs.73 lakhs out of total project of Rs. 238 lakhs. The sub-systems of the Gas Turbine system such as turbine, compressor, combustor and planetary gear box etc. have been successfully developed. The LCGT system is under testing at full 30.000 rpm speed at Turbotech's turbine testing centre, Nelamangla and full load test will be carried out shortly and thereafter the LCGT system for endurance testing at Sakthi Sugar will be undertaken. The project is in progress.

M/s Tamilnadu Petroproducts Limited (TPL), Madras and Indian Institute of Petroleum (HP), Dehradun.

The project for development of technology for Long chain (C10-C14) Alcohols by oxidation of n-Paraffin arising in the production of Linear Alkyl Benzene (LAB) with a DSIR support of Rs. 55 lakhs out of total project cost of Rs. 144 lakhs is being undertaken by M/s TPL, in collaboration with Indian Institute of Petroleum, Dehradun. Use of a novel catalysts system has given 40-45% conversion of n-paraffins into secondary alcohols, per pass, at a selectivity of about 95%. Work at UP Dehradun is completed. Basic engineering package is ready. TPL is now putting up pilot plant based on HP Dehradun technology. The project is in progress.

M/s Encon Thermal Engineers and Indian Institute of Petroleum (HP), Dehradun

The project of M/s Encon Thermal Engineers in collaboration with HP, Dehradun, is for development of Natural Gas Fired Industrial Gas Burners having a capacity of 50 and 100 cu. in. of natural gas per hour and involves financial support from DSIR and M/s Gas Authority of India Ltd. (GAIL), New Delhi of Rs. 11 lakhs each out of a total project cost of Rs.30 lakhs. Three types of burners have been designed and fabricated. LPG Storage and handling facility has been set up for trials of burners. The project is in progress.

M/s Electronic Corporation of India Ltd. (ECIL), Hyderabad and Central Road Research Institute (CRRI), New Delhi

The joint project of M/s ECIL, Hyderabad and CRRI, New Delhi is for the development of a microprocessor controlled Nuclear Moisture and Density Gauge with a DSIR support of Rs.18 lakhs out of a total project cost of Rs.28 lakhs. 5 prototypes of moisture and density gauges will be given to user agencies such as Border Road Organisation and State PWDs for user's trials in construction projects and based on the feed back of the performance of the prototypes, CRRI and M/s ECIL would modify the gauges, if required. The first prototype of Moisture and Density Gauge has been demonstrated. The second prototype is likely to be ready in May, 1999. The project is in progress.

M/s National Aluminium Company Limited (NALCO), Bhubaneswar

NALCO has taken up a project to develop technology for the production of Special Aluminas and Hydrates which are used in a variety of diverse applications such as grinding wheels, tooth paste, etc. DSIR is supporting the project with a financial grant of Rs. 100 lakhs. Customer evaluation of the product is under progress. The project is nearing completion.

M/s Central Electronics Ltd. (CEL), Sahibabad and Centre for Development of Advanced Computing (C-DAC), Pune

The joint project of M/s CEL and C-DAC is for "Development of a Solid State Interlocking (SSI) System for Railways" with DSIR support of Rs. 70.00 lakhs out of the total project cost of Rs. 95.00 lakhs. The project is in progress.

M/s Bharat Earth Movers Ltd. (BEML), Bangalore

The project of M/s BEML is for the design and development of 460 HP Wheel Dozer. This project was approved with a DSIR's support of Rs. 20 lakhs out of a total project cost of Rs. 85 lakhs. The prototype of the Wheel Dozer has been fabricated and is under testing. The project is progressing satisfactorily.

M/s JSL Industries Ltd., Vadodara

The project of M/s JSL Industries Ltd. Vadodara for upgradation of Air Circuit Breakers in collaboration with Electrical Research and Development Association (ERDA), Vadodara was approved with a DSIR support of Rs. 13.75 lakhs out of total project cost of Rs. 34 lakhs. Prototypes with 50 KV Short Circuit rating were successfully developed and tested. The project is in progress.

M/s INTRA Industries Pvt. Ltd., Pune

The project of M/s INTRA industries Pvt. Ltd., Pane for development of 14.5 KVA Inverter for Railways was approved with a DSIR support of Rs. 21.80 lakhs out of total project cost of Rs. 62 lakhs. The prototypes are under testing. The project is in progress.

M/s Central Electronics Ltd. (CEL), Sahibabad

M/s CEL has undertaken a project for "Upgradation of the Process Technology for the Production of Single Crystalline Silicon Solar Cells in the existing SPV Plant" with DSIR's support of Rs. 264 lakhs out of the total project cost of Rs.539 lakhs based on laboratory scale technology developed by Inter- University Micro

Electronic Central (IMEC), Belgium. The project is nearing completion.

M/s Central Electronics Ltd. (CEL), Sahibabad and Electronics Research & Development Centre (ER&DC), Thiruvananthapuram

The joint project of CEL and ER&DC is for "development and design of SPV Charger for Ni-Cd batteries using Smart charging technology" with DSIR's support of Rs. 24 lakhs (Phase 1) out of the total project cost of Rs. 71.80 lakhs. The SPV chargers will find applications for charging the batteries of man-pack/portable Radio sets of the Military and Para-military forces. The project is nearing completion.

Gujarat Narmada Valley Fertilisers Limited (GNFC), Bharuch, Gujarat and Engineers India Ltd., New Delhi

A project to develop the process for removal of Hydrogen sulphide and recovery of sulphur from sour gases was assigned to Gujarat Narmada Valley Fertilisers Limited (GNFC), Bharuch, Gujarat and Engineers India Ltd., New Delhi. The DSIR support for the project is Rs. 100 lakhs, out of total cost of project Rs. 207 lakhs. The catalyst for removal of Hydrogen sulphide and recovery of sulphur has been demonstrated at ONGC Complex at Hazira. The project is in progress.

ABR Organics Limited (ABROL), Hyderabad

The project for Technology upgradation of polyimide resins and their applications by M/s ABR Organics Limited (ABROL), Hyderabad has been taken up with DSIR support of Rs. 35 lakhs out of a total project cost of Rs. 150 lakhs. The project is in progress.

M/s Southern Petrochemical Industries Corporation Ltd., Chennai and Indian Institute of Chemical Technology, Hyderabad.

Southern Petrochemical Industries Corporation Ltd., Chennai, and Indian Institute of Chemical Technology Hyderabad have jointly undertaken a Project for development of Process for manufacture of Pyrazinamide using catalytic route. The project involves DSIR support of Rs. 195.00 lakhs in a total project cost of Rs. 466.00 lakhs. The project is in progress.

M/s Indus Natural Products Pvt. Ltd., Pune and National Chemical Laboratory, Pune

Joint project of M/s Indus Natural Products Pvt. Ltd., Pune and National Chemical Laboratory, Pune is for 'Development of Technology for L(+)Tartaric Acid, and Salts or Derivatives thereof, Pectin and Fruit Sugar from the Fruit of Tamarind with DSIR support of Rs. 16.5 lakhs out of total project cost of Rs. 33.00 lakhs. Tartaric acid finds extensive application in beverages, emulsifiers, pharmaceuticals, foods, electrochemical industry and development and purification of chiral compounds. Most common fruit from which tartaric acid is produced worldwide is grape, whereas in the present project tartaric acid is proposed to be manufactured from a totally new raw material-tamarind. The process has been developed by National Chemical Laboratory, Pune and will be scaled up to a pilot plant scale of 350 kg. raw material per batch basis. Blank trial run have been taken. The project is in progress.

M/s HMT Ltd., Bangalore

The project for the development of CNC Machining Centre is being undertaken by RMT Ltd., Bangalore and Pinjore with the aim of bringing out a new generation machine tool comparable to international standard. The DSIR's support is Rs. 75 lakhs out of the total project outlay of Rs. 197 lakhs. The machine has been displayed at IMTEX-98. The metal cutting trials are in progress.

M/s ACE Designers Ltd. and CMTI, Bangalore

The joint project for the development of PC Based CNC System is being undertaken by M/s ACE Designers Ltd., Bangalore in collaboration with Central Manufacturing Technology Institute, Bangalore with DSIR support of Rs.

35 lakhs, out of the total project cost of about Rs. 99 lakhs. The aim of the project is to develop a cost effective, advanced open architecture PC based CNC System for the machine tools. One PC Based CNC System has been interfaced with the lathe machine and its trial is in progress. Another prototype of the system is likely to be fitted with machining centre in January, 1999. The project is in progress.

M/s Innovation Communications Systems Pvt. Ltd. (ICS), Hyderabad

The project for "Development of Interactive Voice Response System with Multilingual Capability" was undertaken by M/s Innovation Communication with DSIR support of Rs. 7.00 lakhs out of total project cost of Rs. 23.80 lakhs. The project is planned to be completed.

M/s Webel Mediatronics Ltd. (A Govt. of West Bengal Undertaking), Calcutta.

The project for "Development of Computerised Braille Transcription System" was undertaken by M/s Webel with DSIR support of Rs. 16.00 lakhs out of the total project cost of Rs. 32.00 lakhs. The project is in progress.

M/s Enercon Systems Pvt. Ltd., Bangalore

The project for the "Development of Centralised Electrical Energy Management System" has been undertaken by M/s Enercon System with DSIR support of Rs. 20.00 lakhs out of the total project cost of Rs. 48.80 lakhs. The system was successfully demonstrated at Vasavadatta Cements plant at Sedam Karnataka and the project has been completed.

M/s National Aluminium Company Limited (NALCO), Bhubaneswar

NALCO has taken up a project to setup a plant for recovery of 1 T/annum of 5N purity Gallium from their sodium aluminate liquor. DSIR support to the project is Rs. 2.17 crores. The project is in progress.

M/s PMT Machine Tool Automatics Ltd., Pune

The project for the development and demonstration of 5-axis CNC internal grinding machine has been undertaken by PMT Machine Tools Automatics Ltd., Pune with DSIR support of Rs. 46 lakhs out of total project cost of Rs.98 lakhs. The project is in progress.

M/s Praj Industries Ltd., Punt

The project for "development and demonstration of energy efficient drying system", has been undertaken by M/s Praj industries Ltd., Pune with DSIR support of Rs. 24.00 lakhs Out of the total project cost of Rs. 49.50 lakhs. The project is in progress.

M/s Priya Bricks Pvt Ltd., Calcutta

The project for the "development and demonstration of stiff extrusion technology for extruding solid perforated & hollow building blocks " has been undertaken by M/s Priya Bricks Pvt. Ltd. with DSIR support of Rs. 45.00 lakhs out of the total project cost of Rs. 97.80 lakhs. The project is in progress.

M/s Delta Agro Chemicals Ltd., Serinarasannapalem, Krishna district, A.P.

The Project for the development of process for manufacture of furfuryl alcohol by hydrogenation of Furfural was undertaken by M/s. Delta Agro Chemicals Ltd., Serinarasanhapalem, Hanuman Junction, P.O. Krishna District (A.P.) with DSIR support of Rs. 18.5 lakhs out of a total project cost of Rs. 45.0 lakhs. The firm is engaged in manufacture of Furfural from agricultural wastes, such as rice husk, corn cobs, sugarcane bagasse, etc. The firm has proposed to put up a pilot plant to produce 250 Lt. per day of the product with the help of IICT Hyderabad in order to generate data required for further scaling up to commercial plant. Detailed engineering package for the pilot plant and assistance in the erection and commissioning and operation of the pilot plant and down stream processing will be rendered by IICT. Although this project is aimed at developing process for furfuryl alcohol the pilot plant will be designed in such a way that it can be used for any other catalytic process for similar nature in future. The, project is in progress.

M/s. General Exports & Credits Ltd., New Delhi

The project for development and demonstration of Azadirachtin—A Technical from neem seeds kernels and its formulations was undertaken by M/s. General Exports & Credits Ltd., New Delhi in collaboration with Dalmia Centre for Biotechnology (DCBT), Coimbatore and Indian Institute of Chemical Technology (IICT), Hyderabad, with DSIR support of Rs. 65.0 lakhs out of a total project cost of Rs. 248.97 lakhs. The project envisaged setting up of a pilot plant in which 300 kg/day neem seeds kernels will be processed to produce 100 gm. Azadirachtin-A of 60-70% purity per day in District Hardoi (Uttar Pradesh) based on lab scale technology developed by DCBT. IICT, Hyderabad has been entrusted with the task of designing and engineering of the pilot plant. National lab such as IARI centres will carry out field trials of pesticides. The project is in progress.

M/s. National Fertilizers Ltd., New Delhi and Ramam Centre for Applied and Interdisciplinary Sciences, Calcutta

The project for "pre-pilot plant trials of slow release zinc polyphosphate fertilizer" was undertaken by Raman Centre for Applied and Interdisciplinary Sciences (RCAIS), Calcutta in collaboration of M/s National Fertilizers Ltd. (NFL), New Delhi, with DSIR support of Rs. 4.15 lakhs out of a total project cost of Rs. 8.9 lakhs, M/s. NFL has extended its support of Rs. 4.765 lakhs to RCAIS. DSIR had extended its support for upscaling and field testing of this fertilizer in past which has been patented. DSIR had also supported study of residual effect of this fertilizer on various crops. The field trials of this fertilizer at three major national centres, bad shown encouraging results. However, the production of zinc polyphosphate had certain technical/engineering problems. In order to scale up at pilot plant, NFL and RCAIS have plans to have plant trials in some of the existing industrial plants, hoping that this trial will result in solving the problem being encountered at various stages of production of zinc polyphosphate fertilizer at lab scale. During this plant trials, the fertilizer produced could be used for trials to generate data for FCO clearance. After the success of these trials, pilot plant project would be taken up by NFL. The project is in progress.

Autopal Industries Ltd., Jaipur

The project for the development of Metal Halide Lamps was taken up by M/s Autopal with DSIR support of Rs. 50 lakhs out of total project cost of Rs. 145 lakhs. The project is in progress.

SM Electronics & Services Ltd., New Delhi

The project for development of Multilingual pager was undertaken by SM Electronics & Services Ltd., with CDAC, Pune with DSIR support of Rs. 36 lakhs out of total project cost of Rs. 80 lakhs. The project is in progress.

Bharat Earth Movers Ltd., Bangalore

The project for development of unified Electronic controller for off- high way Dump Trucks was undertaken by Bharat Earth Movers Ltd., Bangalore, with ER&DC, Thiruvananthapuram with DSIR support of Rs. 16.5 lakhs out of total project cost of Rs, 34 lakhs. The project is in progress.

Shree Pacetronix Ltd., Indore

The project for development of implantable Pacemaker with indigenous ASIC and programming unit was undertaken by Shree Pacetronix Ltd., Indore with Semi Conductor complex Ltd., Chandigarh with DSIR support of Rs. 40 lakhs out of total project cost of Rs. 90 lakhs. The project is in progress.

M/s. Usha India Ltd., (Electronics Division), Faridabad

The Project for "Design & Development and packaging of, high power converter grade Thyrister chips and devices; and optimization of related manufacturing technology" was undertaken by Ms. Usha India Ltd., (Electronics Division), Faridabad with DSIR financial support of Rs.40.00 lakhs out of the total project cost of Rs.147.00 lakhs. The project is in progress.

M/s. Sendconductor Complex Ltd., (SCL), Chandigarh and M/s. Bharti Telecom Ltd., (BTL), Gurgaon.

The project for the "development of telephone instrument based on the Single Chip telephone ICs" was undertaken by Ms. Semiconductor Complex Ltd., Chandigarh and Ms. Bharti Telecom Ltd., Gurgaon with DSIR support of Rs.35.00 lakhs out of the total project cost of Rs.89.00 lakhs. The project is in progress.

M/s. Karnataka Hybrid Micro Devices Ltd., Bangalore

The project for the "Development of Thick Film Hybrid Micro Electronic circuit Technology for Automobile underhood applications" M/s. undertaken by M/s. Karnataka Hybrid Micro Devices Ltd., with DSIR support of Rs. 38.00 lakhs out of total project cost of Rs.101.00 lakhs. The project is in progress.

M/s TCM Ltd. (TCML), Bangalore

The project for development of Technology for production of different grades of Barium Carbonate (heavy/ light, powder/ granules) has been taken up with DSIR support of Rs.30 lakhs out of a total project cost of Rs.140 lakhs.

M/s Targof Pure Drugs Ltd., Hyderabad

Targof Pure Drugs Ltd., Hyderabad have undertaken a Project for Development of Synthetic Route for manufacture of Bi-Naphthyl Crown Ethers. The project involves DSIR support of Rs. 40.00 lakhs in a total project cost of Rs. 133.50 lakhs. The project is in progress.

Customs duty exemption certificate

In pursuance to Customs Notification - No.50/ 96-Customs dated July 23, 1996 for Customs Duty Exemption on components, consumables, equipments etc. used in R&D projects supported by Government, 17 Essentiality certificates for nearly Rs.300 lakhs worth of components and consumables under technology development projects supported under "Programme Aimed at Technological Self Reliance "scheme of DSIR, have been issued.

Technopreneur Promotionn Programme (TePP)

As a new initiative during 1998-0,' the Ministry of Science and Technology has launched a novel programme "Technopreneur Promotion Programmes' (TePP) jointly operated by DSIR under its PATSER Scheme and DST under its Home Grown Technology Scheme to tap the vast innovative potential of the citizens of India. The activities under TePP will include providing financial support to individual innovators having original ideas and convert them into working models, prototypes, etc. It is planned that 30 projects would be supported during 1998-99 under TePP activities.

Expected. outputs and benefits

The completed technology development projects supported under PATSER Scheme have resulted in significant technological and commercial returns to the industries concerned such as cost reduction, higher quality, improved products and processes as well as foreign exchange savings, while building up the R&D capabilities of the industrial units. The on-going projects are expected to result in high commercial/societal impact and will lead to commercialisation and utilisation of 'state-of-the-art' technologies.

5

Scheme to Enhance the Efficacy of Transfer of Technology (SEETOT)

The "Scheme to Enhance the Efficacy of Transfer of Technology (SEETOT)" covers the following programmes:

a) National Register of Foreign Collaborations (NRFC)

b) Industrial Technology

c) Transfer and Trading in Technology (TATT)

d) Promotion and Support to consultancy Services (PSCS) which also includes the Consultancy Development Centre (CDC).

Activities and achievements of each of the above programmes are presented here. Although, Industrial Technology is not a part of the plan scheme, SEETOT, the information emanating out of the activities under Industrial Technology is mainly useful for SEETOT and hence it is covered here.

National register of foreign collabrations

Preamble

The "National Register of Foreign Collaborations (NRFC)", which is an ongoing plan scheme, continued its operations during the year 1998-99. It has completed a number of programmes that were targeted for the year.

Objectives and activities

The main objective of scheme is to facilitate acquisition and management of technology in the country, efficiently. The following major activities are carried out under NRFC & TM:

- Compilation and analysis of data on approved foreign collaborations.
- Undertake studies in select areas.
- Provide assistance in the effective transfer of technology process and efficient management of technology.
- Coordinate with Ministries and other organisations
- Organise interaction & awareness programs on technology related issues.

Activities undertaken, under the NRFC scheme can be put into following broad categories :

- Compilation and analysis of basic data on foreign collaborations (FCs) approved.
- Studies in selected areas.
- Organisation of Interaction meets to enhance effectiveness of technology transfer process.
- Programmes for enhancing technology management capabilities.
- Programmes for enhancing awareness of Intellectual Property Systems.

Foreign collabroation data compilation

The work of in-house compilation of primary data on foreign collaborations approved, continued during the year. The compilation for the year 1997 was brought out. It contained information such as names of Indian companies, the names of foreign collaborators, products covered under the collaborations, duration, nature etc. The compilation for the year 1998 is in progress.

Studies

A project to study the Market and Development Prospects of Fruits and Vegetables Processing industries in Eastern and North Eastern Regions and Andaman & Nicobar Islands was entrusted to West Bengal Consultancy Organisation Ltd., Calcutta. The main objective of the study was to analyse the growth, performance and bottlenecks of fruits and vegetables processing industries in the region; sources, availability and prices of various raw materials with reference to production and marketable surpluses of different types of fruits and vegetables in the region and identifying potential project opportunities with sources of appropriate technology for ready guidance to prospective entrepreneurs. The report has been finalised. The broad findings of the study are as given below.

India enjoys the first position in the world in production of fruits and second position in vegetables after China. World fruits production is estimated at around 370 million tonne, out of which, India accounts for about 8% (30 million tonne). On the other hand, in vegetables out of 456 million tonne of world production, India produces about 13% (59 million tonne). Inspite of such a high level of production in horticulture sector, only around 1% of the total fruits and vegetables are presently bring processed. However, the total installed capacity of fruits and vegetable processing industry has been increasing steadily and is estimated around 16.0 Lakh TPA, in Dec, 1995.

The export accounts for around 55% and the domestic consumption 45% of the output of processed fruits & vegetables, of which Defence is the largest consuming Sector. Export of processed fruits and vegetables has also been steadily increasing both in terms of quantity as well as value.

On present reckoning, it is estimated that the fruits and vegetable processing units in the state of West Bengal are 265, in the state of Bihar 22, in Orissa 17, and in the seven states, of North Eastern region, only 38. Although different, types of fruits and vegetable are available in the Eastern and North Eastern region, this region accounts for only 9% of total number of units that have obtained FPO licence in the country.

The total production of processed fruits and vegetables in this region for the year 1995 was 41.715 thousand tonne as against the national figure of 11.34 Lakh tonne during the same year. Lack of transport facility affects horticulture because fruits and vegetables are highly perishable, it is specially true for the North Eastern region. This problem is compounded: by the lack of an organised market network, due to which much of the produce is sold in the local market. Also because of inadequate storage facilities, a grower tends to involve in "distress sale!', not allowing a competitive climate in the market.

The processing units scattered all over the region suffer from the lack of technical knowledge. They are not equipped with well-trained technical staff. As a result of which the quality of finished products is inferior and fetches low return and most of the time they do not find the market.

Fruits/Vegetables either in fresh form or processed are perishable in nature. They require proper packaging. Proper packaging constitutes a major component of cost even to the extent of 60-65 percent of the cost of production depending upon the nature of the products. Packaging materials of proper quality are also not available in some of the states. High cost of packaging materials and its cost of transportation make the products uncompetitive in the market, at the same time, low cost substitute packaging material are yet to be developed in the country. To give the report a wider dessimination, a meet of industries, entrepreneurs & others was held, where the report was released.

A project to study the Status of Minor Forest Produce (MFP) Based Industries in the state of Madhya Pradesh is being taken up. This is being entrusted to Madhya Pradesh Consultancy Organisation Ltd, Bhopal. The main objective of the study is to gather information and analyse the occurrence and availability of commercially important MFP in each agro climatic zone of the state.

It would also analyse the present methods of collection, grading, pricing and marketing mechanism for the MFP and suggest how to improve its effectiveness and identify commercially viable enterprises based on available MFP. It would also assess the export & indigenous market potential for MFP based products, identify suitable technologies for manufacturing MFP based products and assess the viability of commercial plantation of MFP species, found suitable for commercial exploitation. The study would also identify potential project opportunities with sources of appropriate technology for ready guidance to prospective entrepreneurs.

A project to study the Status and Prospects of Electronics Industry in Eastern and north Eastern States is being taken up. This would be entrusted to West Bengal Consultancy Organisation Ltd, Calcutta. As the production of electronics goods in the region particularly the north Eastern region is very low, the main objective of the study is to analyse the present and future prospects of this industry in the region.

It would analyse the trend of growth of electronics industry in the region and identify the constraints if any and assess the growth opportunities in the major products groups, identify sources of technology and also the development efforts required. The study would also contain Project profiles including investment range on the identified opportunities for ready guidance of the prospective entrepreneurs.

A project to study the Essential and Medicinal Plant Species in the North Eastern Region -their present Status and Strategy for Development is being taken up. This study would be entrusted to the North Eastern Industrial and Technical Consultancy Organisation (NEITCO) Guwahati. The basic objective of the study is to collect information on essential and medicinal plant species, their present status with regard to their availability, production, commercial utilization etc. The study would cover identification and systemization of plants with potential medicinal and biocidal value, listing their uses, estimate the available quantity, their commercial utilization and estimation of the present level of technology being utilized for preparation of medicines from the herbs or plants and sources of improved technologies and equipments both indigenous and imported. The study would also suggest strategies for utilization of plants species for commercial purposes and for economic benefit of the region as a whole.

Technology management

The importance of technology management is increasingly being realised by industry, R&D organisations and others. Considering the need for enhancement of the awareness of the subject, knowledge and skills in this area, the DSIR has initiated a number of multifaceted programmes and activities on the subject. The programmes, and activities cover organisation of awareness programmes, undertaking studies, undertaking research reports, organising training programmes etc. These were taken in close association with industry, R&D organisations, institutes of management & technology , consultancy organisations, Government Departments and others.

Case studies on how technology has been managed in corporate settings had earlier been brought out in respect of two manufacturing organisations. Two more such studies are in progress. These studies cover several aspects such as strategy for, developing corporate plans for technology, its suitable integrations with business plans, R&D management, organisational structures, factors responsible for technological growth in the organisations, make or buy decisions on technology, methodologies for induction and implementation of new technologies etc. Such case studies have provided useful inputs to decision makers and reseachers apart from being very useful pedagocical tools, for academicians & trainers in management and technical institutes including those of industry and others.,

Managing technology in research organisations being also of considerable significance, two studies on the subject were brought out. This year two organisations which are oriented towards new technology development were taken up for study. The reports are being completed, These studies have carried out a holistic analysis of the organisational behavior based in numerous issues such as, decision making mechanism, organisational structure, formal and informal mechanism of information exchange, team work, motivation methods, user interaction, communication methods & others. These studies provide useful inputs to similar organisations, apart from researchers, academicians and others.

As bibliographies provide useful sources of information, two bibliographies were brought out during the year. One bibliography relates to books and is grouped under various broad categories such as Research and Development, Management of Innovation, Technology and Society, Science & Technology, Technology Forecasting, Managing Innovation, Technology Transfer, Technology Diffusion and Appropriate technology. The other bibliography is an annotated one covering recent anecdotes and papers on Technology Management published in reputed national and international journals. Again, this is grouped under different categories as the former one. These have been found very useful by the users.

Under the Distinguished Technologists Lecture Series of the DSIR, two Lectures were held during the year. Under this Series, leading technologists, scientists, managers from varied field of technology are being involved to deliver lectures on their experiences in managing technology in the organisations nurtured by them, One of the lecturers specifically covered the subject in a small/medium scale setting.

A module on Technology Management as part of MS Course run by the Consultancy Development Centre in association with Birla Institute of Technology & Sciences, Pilani was developed and implemented during the year. The course covered important subjects like, key issues in technology management, technology transfer, technology information, Intellectual Property Rights, Role of Consultants and others.

Assistance has been rendered to IIT Delhi in respect of a Module on Technology Transfer which is a part of a course on MBA with focus on Technology Management. The module has been conceptualized and relevant topics identified. A few sessions were also taken and Guest Lectures by experienced persons from industry & R&D organisations arranged. The IIT was also assisted i n the evaluation of the programmed.

The DSIR has been conferring awards to industrial organisations to recognise, the efforts of industry towards innovative research, technological development and commercialisation of research results. These are awarded in different sectors/areas of industry. With a view to carry out a comprehensive analysis of the studies of technology growth in these DSIR National R&D Award Winning Companies, a study has been undertaken. The study inter-alia covers the performance of award winning technologies and companies in the various segments over the years, especially with a view to assess the continuous technological upgradation, economic benefits, survival in a -competitive environment, factors leading to technological innovation, upgradation, growth or decline of the technologies awarded, impact of the technology on the total operations of the company, strategy of managing technology and other related issues, The report in the draft form has been prepared and is now under finalisation.

The DSIR has provided inputs to a Workshop on 'Training of Trainers in the field of Technology Management held at IIT Bombay. Specific Sessions were also taken.

Realizing the need for sustained joint efforts to enhance awareness of Technology Management issues and promote effective utilization of technology management methods, through a networking of the industrial needs, the academic and R&D inputs, a Core Group on the subject has been set up in which industry R&D and Department of Education and the AICTE are closely involved with the DSIR.

The main objective is to suggest strategies for enhancing the knowledge in, and skills in the practice of, Technology Management in educational and industrial systems; to meet the emerging needs of industry, R&D organisations and others in this discipline.

To achieve the above objective in the area of TM, the group is inter-alia working on:

a) Identification of thrust areas needing attention in the area of TM

b) Assessing the programmes and courses on TM currently being offered in the country

c) Identification of the state-of-art in the area of TM in select industrially advanced countries.

Interaction meets and awareness programmes

With a view to enhance awareness and knowledge in the field of technology management, programmes on the subject were organised. The basic objectives of these programmes have been to apprise organisations, managers, R&D personnel and others of the importance of managing technology efficiently and the intricacies involved there in. Various subjects such as technology strategy, issues in technology acquisition, R&D management and others are covered. During the year, 5 programmes were held as under:

For Shri Guru Gobind Singhji College of Engineering and Technology at Nanded on April 16, 1998.

For Mahratta Chamber of Commerce and Indu at Pune on May 13 1998.

For ADOR Thermal Engineering on 130, May 1998 at Pune.

For Institute of Entrepreneurship Development on September 22-25, 1998 at Bhubaneswar

For PSG Institute of Management, on August 28-30, 1998 at Coimbatore

Considering the importance of Intellectual Property Rights in the current scenario, three awareness programmes on the subject were organised. These were held at National Academy of Sciences (J&K Chapter) Jammu on 27 April 1998, Administrative Staff College of India on 27 June 1998 at Hyderabad, Consultancy Development Centre on 20 Nov 1998 at New Delhi. A two days Workshop on Patent Writing and Patenting was held at. Calcutta on 9-10 July 1998 in association with IIT Kharagpur. The workshop was designed to provide an in-depth information on several aspects involved in patent writing and patenting. Experts on the subject were the resource persons. Institute of Chartered Secretaries was also assisted in organising an awareness programme for their members. The basic objective of these, programmes has been to generate greater awareness of the issues relating to Intellectual Property Rights and to sensitize, industry R&D organisations, academia, consultancy organisations and others about the various issues involved in IPR, subjects such as Basic Issues and International Trends in IPR Systems & Procedures etc.

A Seminar cum Exhibition on Opportunities in the Agro Industry was organised on 5th & 6th Nov. 1998, at Calcutta with CH Eastern Region where in the Final report on Market and Development Prospects of Fruits &Vegetables processing Industry in the Eastern and North Eastern Region and Andaman and Nicobar Islands was released.

Industrial technology

The industrial technology deals with the proposals received from Secretariat for Industrial Approvals (SIA) for grant of Letter of Intent, foreign collaboration from Indian entrepreneurs/organisations, from NRIs and those willing to set up 100% export oriented project.

The broad activities are (i) receiving and examining proposals for grant of LOI, FC and import of CG, including those for 100% EOU and from NRIs (ii) participating in approval Committees/Boards such as Licensing Committees, Project Approval Board and Board of Approvals for 100% Export Oriented Units.

Industrial licensing

About 160 proposals forgrant of Letter of Intent/Carry-on-Business, Extension of Letter of Intent etc. were received during the year. The number of proposals have remained almost same as in the last year.

12 meetings of Licensing Committee were held by SIA during 1998. Almost at all the meetings were attended.

Foreign collaborations

During the year, the number of foreign collaborations and composite proposals exceeded 800. Of these, the department received around 100 proposals from Secretariat for Industrial Approvals as compared to 200 in the previous year. These excluded such proposals involving foreign investment, which were directly considered by the Foreign Investment Promotion Board.

During the year, the Department participated in the 11 meetings of the Project Approval Board and 11 meetings of the Board of Approvals for 100% Export Oriented Undertakings held by SIA.

Information/data processing

The Department has a database for Foreign Collaboration proposals and Composite applications since 1988. The data regarding Foreign Collaboration Proposals were updated for the year 1998.

The Department also maintained and updated the software for editing, preparing summary, processing and quick retrieval of the desired information. The software has been developed in-house for above mentioned proposals as well as approvals.

The Department also updated the software for editing, preparing summary, processing and quick retrieval of the information on proposals received under PATSER scheme. The software has been developed in-house for above mentioned proposals as well as approvals. Retrieval of information and updating of databases is continuously done with the help of the above softwares.

Internet

The Department is a subscribe to X400 Message Handling System of NICNET, the Network of National Informatics Centre. The E-Mail Address for the Department is dsir@x400.nicgw.nic.in. In the year under review, the Department also renewed its subscription to TCP/IP account of Videsh Sanchar Nigam Ltd. The E-Mail address for the Department is dsir@glasd101.vsnl.net.in. Another E-mail address dsir@vsnl.com has also been registered with VSNL.

Transfer and trading in technology

The TATT scheme mainly aims to promote and support activities towards the export of technologies, projects and services. The measures adopted include:

- Support to preparation of technology profiles of developing countries;
- Support to preparation of reports related to technology export capabilities and experiences in select industrial sectors;
- Publicity and dissemination of Indian capabilities through workshops, trade fairs, delegations and video films;
- Supporting demonstration of exportable technologies overseas as well as within India;
- Supporting Small and Medium Enterprises (SMEs) for value addition and export production;
- Facilitating linkages between R&D institutions and industry in hi-tech areas for technology exports.

Activities

The TATT scheme became operational during the year 1986-87 through a cell set-up in DSIR for this purpose. A number of programmes and projects aimed towards its objectives were completed during the 7th Five Year Plan. A re-organisation of schemes took place at the beginning of 8th Five Year Plan, when TATT scheme became a part of SEETOT programme and the Technical Advisory Committee was reconstituted. The thrust of the projects during 1985-1992 has been towards documenting our technological expertise and capabilities, preparation of technology profiles of select developing countries, and enhancing export efforts in the area of technology transfer through seminars/workshops, and video films. The focus during the 8th five year plan has been generally towards commercialisation of exportable technologies through setting up demonstration plants and export market development. Other activities undertaken related to compilation of data on technology exports and promotion of export of technology intensive services. Technical Advisory Committee was reconstituted during 1997-98 and fresh proposals for support under the scheme were considered during the Technology Advisory Committee meetings. Details of some of the projects/activities completed or in progress during the year under report are given below:

Compendium on technology exports from India

The work on bringing out a publication, providing ready information on exports of technologies including exports of turnkey and consultancy projects, consultancy exports and export of capital goods was continued during the year. A publication for 1995-96 was brought out in-house and disseminated to concerned organisations. The work related to bringing out the compendium for the years 1996-97 and 1997-98 was awarded to Indian Institute to Foreign Trade, New Delhi. A number of organisations including companies, export agencies and R&D institutions were contacted by IIFT for soliciting information on exports of technologies and services during 1996-97 and 1997-98. The information obtained was being compiled for bringing out the Compendium.

A study on capabilities for export of non-convention technology intensive consultancy services from India.

A study on export potential of non-conventional technology intensive consultancy services was carried out through IIFT. The study covers six areas, viz. technical education & training, hospitals and specialised health services, printing services, maintenance services, standardisation and quality assurance services and satellite mapping. A draft report on the study was discussed in a seminar during February 1998, and the study-report was subsequently printed in a book form during the year. The publication highlights our capabilities to provide technology intensive services in six sectors and also includes profiles of service providers in each of the six sectors. It also contains an analysis of the WTO provisions on the general agreement on trade in services and recommends the potential areas where India can take advantage to tap the available opportunities.

Export market development for solar photo-voltaic technology and systems

Support to Central Electronics Ltd., Sahibabad was continued to conduct a market survey in select countries for supply, installation and commissioning of sample Solar Photovoltaic Systems for demonstration purposes followed by transfer of technology for manufacturing SPV modules and systems. The project covers visits of CEL experts to the target countries to find out the potential and applications for SPV systems and technology and precise specifications of the equipment required in those countries, preparation of market promotion material such as brochures, pamphlets and video films, manufacturing of sample SPV systems based on the precise specifications, supply and commissioning of SPV systems, training of engineers from the target countries, preparation and handing over of technology transfer documentation etc. The sample SPV systems being supplied include SPV stand alone domestic lighting system SPV stand alone street lighting system, SPV community room system, SPV system for primary health centre, SPV shallow well water pumping system, SPV deep well water pumping system, SPV lantern and portable manpack SPV battery chargers. The project has helped CEL to generate substantial export earnings to the tune of around Rs. 8 crores during 1996-

98 in the form of know-how fees, royalty and sale of SPV modules systems and components. Publicity material such as brochures and video film have been prepared. Sample SPV systems have been supplied in Uganda, Bangladesh, Turkmenistan, Myanmar and few other African countries.

Task force for promoting technology exports from India

The above task force was constituted in June 1997 with the following terms of reference.

- Examine need and relevance of technology exports and technology intensive exports.
- Drawing Lessons from past experiences in technology exports.
- Review of present policy measures for technology exports in India.
- Strategy for enhancing India's contribution in the global technological markets.
- Recommending Mechanisms and Support Systems for speedy implementation of policies and boosting technology exports.

Based upon interactions with industry representatives during meetings at New Delhi, Bangalore and Mumbai, discussions with other export promotion agencies, meetings of the task force members and guidance of Chairman of the Task Force, Shri N. Vittal, a report of the Task Force for Promoting Technology Exports from India was prepared. The report was presented to the then Hon'ble Minister of Science & Technology Prof. Y.K. Alagh on January 13, 1998.

The report suggests -a target of Rs. 800 crores; (about 50% per cent of technology payments made by India) for technology exports by the year 2002 as a short term goal and a target of 2% share of global technology exports as a long term goal.

Follow-up work for implementing the recommendations made in Task Force Report were continued during the year. Proposal to setup an institutional mechanism for promoting technology exports in association with Confederation of Indian Industry wag at an advanced stage.

Technology exports pavilion in the India international trade fair November, 1998

A pavilion on technology exports was set up at India International Trade Fair November, 1998 in association with India Trade Promotion Organisation. Around 200 sq. mtrs. of floor space was made available in Pragati Maidan to participating companies and R&D Institutions, free of cost, to exhibit their technological capabilities. Twelve companies and organisations participated in the pavilion, which generated fairly good response from the visitors. Some of the companies also received enquiries for supply of technologies and services.

Seminar on technologies from India

A Seminar on Technologies from India was organised in association with India Trade Promotion Organisation in Pragati Maidan, N. Delhi, on Nov. 25, 1998. The Seminar was organised with a view to disseminate Indian capabilities for export of technologies and technology intensive products and services and to provide a platform for interaction between exporters and potential foreign customers of such technologies and technology intensive products. The seminar covered 3 sectors namely, Drugs & Pharmaceuticals, Chemicals & Petrochemicals and Food Processing & Packaging. It was attended by over 150 delegates, including around 40 foreign diplomats from some 15 developing countries in the SAARC, South East Asian, Middle East and African Region. Important recommendations emerging from the seminar were:

– Similar seminars may be organised more frequently

on a variety of subjects of common interest to developing countries.

- The focus should be on promotion of technologies appropriate to the economic and industrial development and social conditions prevalent in the host country.
- Collaborative arrangements may be evolved between different countries to promote technology development and exports for better exploitation of available resources and maximization of benefits.
- India should use its inherent advantage of a large pool of technically qualified manpower to promote technologies, which employ manpower efficiently, instead of focusing only on technologies based on automation.
- There is need for sustained efforts in building technology and technology intensive products exports. A mechanism may be evolved which would provide technological inputs on a continuous basis to industry, especially small scale industry
- The technology development efforts should be aimed at development of safer, cleaner and environment friendly technologies.
- The tremendous potential for export of technology for bulk drugs, which will be off-patent by 2002, in the SAARC region may be exploited.

Newsletter on technology exports

A quarterly Newsletter on Technology Exports was initiated during the year. The Newsletter is being compiled by M under the guidance of Editorial Board, comprising of representatives from DSIR, IIFT, CII, Exim Bank, L&T and Waterfalls Institute of Technology Transfer. Three issues of the Newsletter were brought out starting July 1998. The Newsletter includes a lead article and details on technology export related policies, global technology and India's technology developments, joint-ventures, India's achievements in technology exports, technology offers and requests etc. The Newsletter has been appreciated by industry, embassies/missions and other export promotion councils.

Feasibility study on export potential of Indian technical know-how in institution building and manpower training for construction industry in Bangladesh and Nepal

The above study was commissioned to NICMAR in April 1998. Two meetings of the Expert Advisory Committee took place to discuss the draft report on Nepal, prepared by NICMAR and also to review the general progress of work in respect of the above project. The report on Nepal has been finalised and work in respect of report on Bangladesh was in progress.

The study on Nepal has clearly brought out the potential for export of Indian know-how in manpower training and institution building in construction industry in Nepal and has outlined 5 main task&, viz., (i) upgrading the technical capabilities and managerial abilities of executives, (ii) training construction project managers, (iii) augmenting the supply .of trained construction engineers and technicians three-fold over next 10 years, (iv) establishing an Operators and Mechanics Training Centre (OMTC) in Nepal., & (v) training local workers in various construction trades.

Technical advisory committee

Second meeting of the Technical Advisory Committee for the TATT and the Consultancy Schemes of DSIR was held during the year. Two project proposals, namely, (i) Codification of Notifications on Technical Barriers to Trade issued by VM, and (ii) Directory of Exportable Technologies from India, were recommended under the TATT scheme by the Technical Advisory Committee. The projects were being sanctioned to the concerned agencies.

Promotion and support to consultancy services

The objectives of the Scheme include:

- The promote and strengthen consultancy capabilities for both domestic and export markets.
- Support to Consultancy Development Centre (CDC) and other promotional organisations related to consultancy.
- Human Resource Development including fellowships to bright and promising engineers as apprentices with eminent consultancy organisations, arrange training etc.
- Support R&D efforts of consultancy organisations and commercialisation of indigenous technologies..
- Organise Seminars, Workshops, etc. and document consultancy capabilities.
- Create awareness among users of consultancy.

Activities

Some of the programmes/activities carried out during the year till December, 1998, are briefly indicated below:

Documentation of consultancy capabilities and experience

36 reports on consultancy capabilities in specific industrial sectors as well as at state level have been printed so far under the scheme. These reports have been widely disseminated.

In addition to above, the following studies were at various stages of implementation/consideration.

(i) Study on Status of consultancy services in India

Precise information is not readily available on the overall consultancy capability scenario in the country To fill this gap, this study was taken up with the objective to compile information/data about the credentials and achievements of consultants including their profiles, through Consultancy Development Centre (CDC), New Delhi. The study is in progress. CDC has submitted draft report of the study prepared with the involvement of Tata Consultancy Services and Consulting Engineers Association of India (CEAI), which is being further, examined. The study is likely to be completed by March, 1999.

(ii) Study on policies and Incentives available to consultants in other countries.

With a view to have insights of various policies and incentives available to consultants in other countries for the promotion and development of consultancy profession, a study was commissioned to Consulting Engineers Association of India (CEAI). CEAI has submitted final draft report, which contains information of 47 developed and developing countries on various aspects related to policies and incentives available to consultants in these countries. The report is being examined and finalised.

(iii) Study on role of consultants in R&D and Innovation

With a view to enhance the interactions of R&D laboratories in CSIR system with consultants and widely disseminate their technological consultancy capabilities to industry, a study is under active consideration for NISTADS. The study is expected to explore nature and extent of involvement of external consultants in R&D and Innovation activities of CSIR labs. It will examine potential of R&D through consultancy for consultancy development in R&D organisations.

The study in nutshell will cover-specific technical areas, nature of services provided, Intellectual property generated, period of consultancy, Amount involved, Nature of clients, Export of R&D services, R&D collaborations and future prospects, etc. Information on issues related to the involvement of consultants in R&D and Innovations will be collected through a structured questionnaire as well as from field visits. The data will be analysed and report prepared.

Promotion of design engineering service centres and consultancy clinics

Though India has developed considerable consultancy capabilities in several areas, consultants need to develop design and engineering capabilities in specific industrial sectors towards meeting the challenges of globalization, and thus become more competitive. These centres would also be useful in commercialising and marketing of indigenous technologies. Also, consultants and consultancy services need to be utilised optimally not only by big and medium industries, but by the small-scale industries as well. Keeping these objectives in view DSIR has evolved programmes for promotion of Design and Engineering facilities in specific sectors, such as food processing, textile etc. and Consultancy Clinics to support SMEs particularly those located in clusters. The following centres/clinics are supported/under consideration.

(i) UPCIO-CFTRI Service Centre for Food Processing Industry at Kanpur

Keeping in view the large concentration of food grain production and food processing industries particularly the SMEs in the state of Uttar Pradesh, this centre is set up by U.P. Industrial Consultants Ltd., (UPICO), a technical and commercial consultancy Organisation of U.P. State and Financial Organisation, and CFTRI jointly to help the food processing industries in the North-Western region of the country. The centre is functional from an independent office at Kanpur and has submitted report for its first phase, which is being further, examined.

(ii) Consultancy Clinic for Textile Industry at Bhilwara

With a view to provide doorstep professional services for textile industry in particular and other industries in general, this consultancy clinic is set up by Rajasthan Consultancy Organisation Ltd. (RAJCON) at Bhilwara. The clinic has started operations, and clients have started availing the services of the clinic.

A similar proposal from Madhya Pradesh Consultancy Organisation Ltd. (MPCON) is under active consideration for consultancy clinic at Raipur in Madhya Pradesh.

Institutional programme support

DSIR has been supporting the capital and recurring needs of Consultancy Development Centre (CDC) establish to promote consultancy and implement programmes towards strengthening our consultancy capabilities.

Reports/publications/papers

A number of technical papers/reports relating to technology & consultancy, including the following were prepared and presented in various technical fora.

(i) Publication on "Consultancy Services in India, A critical study", in association with CDC, Allied Publishers Ltd., 1999.

(ii) A paper on "Role of consultants in commercialisation of technologies" was prepared and presented in the Interaction Meet on "Commercialisation of Technologies" organised by CDC/TDB at New Delhi.

(iii) A paper on "R&D in industry and technology exports" was prepared and presented at NISTADS training programme for IAS officers at New Delhi.

(iv) A paper on "Role of Consultants in Technology Management" was prepared and presented in An International Workshop on "Technology Management" organised by APCTT.

(v) A Publication on "Globalisation and Consultancy", Allied Publishers Ltd., New Delhi, 1998.

(vi) Valuation of Intangibles in Project Management, Second National Congress on Consultancy, New Delhi, 1511 January, 1999. Also, a publication through Allied Publishers Ltd., New Delhi; was brought out by CDC, with the help of DSIR.

Advisory services

Advisory services were made available to various Departments and Organisations in relation to their various programmes and activities. Following are examples of participation.

Committees:

(i) Governing Council, Executive Committee, Membership Committee, Accreditation of Consultants, Committee, Awards Committee for Excellence in consultancy, Task Force for Bylaws and CDPA committees of CDC.

(ii) Consultancy Committee of FIEO

(iii) Programme Committee of WASME

(iv) Boards of Directors of U.P. Industrial Consultants Ltd., Kanpur and Rajasthan Consultancy Organisation Ltd., Jaipur.

(v) Board of Governors of NICMAR, Bombay

(vi) Member of Advisory Board of Centre for International Management, New Delhi, from May 1998.

Seminars/workships/meetings

(i) Organising Committee of Seminar On "Consultancy in commercial applications of Radioisotopes Technology in process industries" organised by BARC and CDC at New Delhi.

(ii) Technical and organising committees meetings for Second National Consultancy Congress organised by CDC at New Delhi in January 1999.

(iii) Advisory Committee Meeting of TOKTEN, UNISTAR and TCDC Workshop on Management of Innovations from Concept to Commissioning.

(iv) International meet on "Consultancy for Commercialisation of Technologies" held at New Delhi.

(v) WASME seminar on "India - China Technological and Economic Cooperation" held at New Delhi.

(vi) Various Committees of IIFT, New Delhi.

(vii) Seminar on CE-Marketing for Europe and Certification requirement for exports organised by ITPO at New Delhi.

(viii) Seminar on 'Development of Domestic consulting services" organised by CDC and ADB at New Delhi.

(ix) Seminar on "emerging issues in World Trade Organisation" organised by IIFT at New Delhi.

(x) International Congress on "Environmental Technologies" organised by India Chapter of ICTP, Italy at Birla Science Centre, Hyderabad.

Consultancy development centre

CDC came into being as a registered society in January 1986, and is functioning from its office at India Habitat Centre Complex since May 1994. The centre is managed and guided by a governing Body consisting of representatives of consultancy organisations, R&D institutions, Government Departments, academic institutions, public sector units etc. CDC had a membership of 193 as on 31-3-1998, representing various types of consultancy organisations and individuals connected with the consultancy.

The CDC has concentrated mainly on development of human resources, providing computerised data/information services, and strengthening of technological and managerial consultancy capabilities through a scheme known as "Consultancy Development, Promotion and Assistance (CDPA)" Scheme. CDC is providing consultancy/training in ISO-9000 and 14000 Quality Management Systems, and has been awarded certificate for ISO-9002 by a Norwegian Company.

DSIR support

An amount of Rs.42 Lakhs was provided as grant during 1997-98, and a release of Rs.42 Lakhs is made till 15-1-99 during 1998-99. The capital assets at CDC include computer systems with peripherals and accessories as well as some software. This facility is used for collection, analysis and dissemination of data, for training of engineering graduates and for small consultants. It is estimated that these investments have resulted in useful activities for nurturing consultants and users of consultancy for better returns on investments and enhanced earnings of foreign exchange directly and indirectly, besides several other qualitative advantages bringing long term benefits to the country. The centre is equipped with Library facilities for consultants.

Technical Consultancy Development Programme for Asia and Pacific (TCDPAP)

In order to enhance technological and managerial capabilities as well as the export capabilities of consultants, interactions with international organisations - such as World Bank, Asian Development Bank, African Development Bank, International Trade Centre (ITC), UNIDO, ESCAP, APCTT, have been developed and programmes have been arranged for consultants at national and international levels which have proved to be useful to promote consultancy business.

CDC has been identified to be a nodal agency for Technical Consultancy Development Programme for Asia and the Pacific (TCDPAP) by ESCAP. CDC was again nominated to function as secretariat for TCDPAP upto 2000 AD during its Second Meeting of Advisory/ Promotional Committee. The first General Council meeting of TCDPAP held in October 1997 in Dhaka recommended that TCDPAP should be developed as an independent UN identity.

Activities

Some of the salient features of the activities carried out by CDC during 1998 are as under:

ISO certification for CDC

The ISO-9002 certificate awarded to CDC during 1997 by M/s Det Norske Veritas (DNV) for development and promotion of consultancy profession was recommended for renewal for a period of one year after surveillance audit by DNV.

MOU for ISO-14000 certification

CDC entered into a Memorandum of Understanding with Anglo American Environment Quality and Safety Certification services Ltd. (AAEQS) for Conducting Advanced Lead Auditors Course and Internal Auditors Course in ISO-14000 for CDC becoming a Certifying Agency in the area. Also, another MOU was signed between CDA and NQA Quality System Ltd. (NQAQSR) for ISO-9000 Consultancy.

Training

- During the year, CDC organised 8 short term specially structured training programmes on ISO-9000 Quality Management System and ISO-14000 Environmental Management System for consultants, construction and health care service R&D etc. to train various organisations in design, development and implementation of ISO-9000 and ISO-14000 systems.
- The 4th batch of MS Consultancy Management Programme in collaboration with BITS, Pilani commenced in August, 1998 with 17 students.

Consultancy in ISO-9000 QMS

During the year, CDC continued to provide consultancy in ISO-9000 Quality Management System to 8 organisations such as Gammon India Ltd., Central Road Research Institute, Intercontinental consultants and Technocrats Pvt. Ltd., Uttar Pradesh Industrial Consultants

Ltd., National Institute of Training for Highway Engineers, National Building Construction Corporation Ltd., U.P. State Bridge Corporation Ltd. (from January 1999), International Print-O-Pac Ltd. (from January 1999) for getting them ISO-9000 Certification and bring improvements in their functional areas, totaling to a professional fee of Rs.26.82 Lakhs so far, out of which Rs. 5.3 Lakhs are received by CDC by December 1998.

Study assignments

The centre completed a report on Consultancy Services in India, A critical study. Another study on status of consultancy services in India, on behalf of DSIR, was in progress.

Database and information services

The database of Consultants and Consultancy Organisations was augmented during the year. About 1400 profiles of Consultants/Consultancy Organisations were added.

Developmental services

Contact/interaction programmes

- During the year, CDC organised 8 contact/interaction programmes on various issues and themes related to consultancy profession such as Energy from waste as an Industry in India, Bio-mass Power Project in Gasifying, Consultancy Opportunities in Commercialising Technology, Development of Domestic Consulting Services, Consultany in Commercial Applications of Radioisotope Technology in Process Industry, Intellectual Property Rights and its implications for industry, R&D and Consultants, Information Technology for Consultants, Business Opportunities in Agricultural Consultancy.
- During the year, CDC had close interactions with the Technical Consultancy Organisations (TCOs) and organised interaction meets in collaboration with

them. They were also associated for augmentation of database pertaining to regional consultants.

- The centre continued with the scheme for R&D experts as Associates, to utilise their expertise in various developmental activities useful to consultants.
- The centre initiated a scheme for business developments for consultants through a fortnightly bulletin on business opportunities, which gives information on project opportunities likely to emerge in India and in global markets for consultants and professionals.

Internatinal cooperation

- The First Executive Committee meeting of TCDPAP was held in June, 1998 in Nepal, which was followed by a three days international workshop on Consultancy in next millennium. Delegates from 8 member countries participated in both the events. 200 delegates including 26 foreign participants attended the workshop. A total of 24 papers were presented during the workshop.
- The proceedings of the First General Council of the TCDPAP and the workshop on consultancy in infrastructure development held in Dhaka in October 1997 were brought out.
- The Government of India (Department of Science and Technology) had proposed that CDC could serve as the focal point for promoting Intra - Regional Consultancy contracts and utilization of local consultancy resources, among Science and Technology Policy Asian Network (STEPAN) Member Countries. This proposal was made in the STEPAN workshop on Development of Science & Technology Management held at Seoul, Republic of Korea September 2446,1997.

Publications/brochures of CDC

Brochure on consultancy business development

The brochure gives details of the facilities available at CDC for Business Development of consultancy services. It has been widely disseminated.

Brochure on MS post graduate consultancy management training programme

The brochure gives objectives, scope, implementation modalities and guidelines for the programme, The same has been widely disseminated to Consultants, academia and others.

Brochures on "Technical Consultancy Development Programme for Asia and Pacific (TCDPAP)"

The brochure gives information about the initiation and establishment of TCDPAP. It further highlights how consultants can avail facilities under this programme.

CDC newsletter-consultancy vision

4 issues of this Newsletter were brought out.

TCDPAP Focus-2 issues were brought out

National directory of consultants: This Directory contains profiles of 150 member consultants of CDC and a listing of another 800 consultants/ consultancy organisation.

Second national consultancy congress

The above Congress was held on 15-16 January, 1999 at New Delhi, with its theme as "Financing and Management of Projects". The Congress was attended by over 200 Indian and foreign consultants, exporters, policy makers, industry representatives, R&D personnel, and others relevant to consultancy. Five National Awards including three merit certificates for excellence in consultancy were given away in this Congress.

Linkage with international organisations

During the year, the Department continued to participate in the activities of various international organisations such as UNCTAD, WIPO, UNIDO, ESCAP and APCTT at various levels and forums on issues related to Technology Development and Technology Transfer in coordination with other concerned Ministries.

APCTT and ESCAP

The matter pertaining to the Asian and pacific Centre for Transfer of Technology (APCTT) under ESCAP were dealt with in cooperation with Ministry of Commerce. The Department of Scientific and Industrial Research continued to play the role of a focal point for the APCTT. DSIR helped in preparing a brief covering technological issues for the use of Indian delegation to the 54th Annual Session of ESCAP held in April 1998 at Bangkok.

Shri K.V. Srinivasan, Adviser, DSIR participated in the Fourteenth Technical Advisory Committee meeting of APCTT held during 24-25, November 1998 and the 13th session of the Governing Board of APCTT held during 26-27 November 1998 in Manila, Philippines. These meetings were attended by participants from Bangladesh, China, India, Islamic Republic of Iran, Republic of Korea, Nepal, Philippines, Sri Lanka, Thailand and Vietnam.

Senior officers of the department also participated in various workshops/seminars conducted by the APCTT during the year.

6

National Information System for Science and Technology

The increasing role of science and technology in the economic and social development of the country has generated a pressing demand for faster technology transfer to the industries. Apart from access to information generated within the country, it is also necessary to draw from the externally generated information to support internal efforts on research and development. Information centres that have come up to serve the needs of different industries and R & D units are therefore required to be coordinated and organized into an integrated system to avoid a haphazard growth and duplication of activities and in conformity with national and international standards.

The National Information System for Science & Technology (NISSAT) commenced its operations in 1977 with the objectives of organizing information support facilities for a customer base largely dominated by people engaged in research and academics. In tune with the changing global scenario and in pursuance of the national efforts in liberalization and globalization of the economy, NISSAT reoriented its programme activities continually in order to be useful to a wider base of clientele in diverse subjects. Besides establishing the internal linkages between the information industry, its promoters and users, NISSAT has been main efforts to establish a bridge between information resource developers and users in Indian and other countries.

Broad objectives

The broad objectives of NLSSAT are:

- Development of national information services
- Promotion of existing information systems & services
- Introduction of modern information handling tools & techniques
- Promotion of international cooperation in information
- Development of indigenous products & services
- Organization of skill development programmes
- Promotion of R & D in Information Science & Technology

Subject coverage

The NISSAT programme has the mandate to cover the entire spectrum of science and technology, However, during the process of programme implementation, special care is taken not to dwell upon subjects already being handled by other national programme like the BTIS, ENVIS or an agency like the ICAR.. NISSAT solicits the views of other programmes/agencies which are responsible for a subject under the allocation of their business. NISSAT requests for the expert views of institutions/individuals working on a given subject or its allied areas when required. As a proactive and Progressive step, NISSAT has taken the onus on itself to strengthen the library movement in the country through the introduction of modern information technology, tools and techniques.

As the boundaries between science and technology,

social sciences, arts and humanities are fast disappearing, emphasis on activities on one area can not subsist without the support for the other. Therefore, in due course, NISSAT would need to adopt the non-S &T subjects as well. Already, NISSAT does not differentiate between the S & T and non-S & T areas in the implementation of the library networks and manpower development programmes.

NISSAT is being implemented through several sub-programmes which include inter alia.-

- Development and maintenance of National Information Centres on specific subject areas
- Resource Sharing through Library Networks
- Facility for Information Access through Internet and National database access centres
- Programme on Coordinated Research Outputs - Analysis based on CDROM Databases
- Database Development Activities and R&D Studies
- Man Power Development Activities on Information Science & Promotion of Computer Applications in Institutions
- Publication of Information Today & Tomorrow

Nissat centres

Sectoral information centres

A sectoral information centre is established on a product, discipline or a mission. Sectoral Centres provide bibliographic as well as factual and numeric information to meet the various information needs of academicians, scientists, technologists, entrepreneurs, management executives and decision makers.

The Sectoral Centres are usually built around the existing information resources and facilities. They maintain extensive collections of published and unpublished documents in the from of books, periodicals, R&D reports, technical reports, standards, patents and trade literature in their subject areas.

A list of the NISSAT initiated National Information Centres in different Sectors is provided in the Table 1.

Table 1. The NISSAT cectoral information centres

	Subject areas	*Acronym*	*Host institution*
1.	Leather Technology	NICLAI	Central leather Institute, Chennai
2.	Food Technology	NICFOS	Central Food Technological Research Institute, Mysore
3.	Machine Tools Production and Engineering	NICMAP	Central Manufacturing Technology Institute Bangalore
4.	Drugs and Pharmaceuticals	NICDAP	Central Drug Research Institute Lucknow
5.	Textiles & Allied Subjects	NICTAS	Ahmedabad Textile Industry's Research Association Ahmedabad
6.	Chemicalls & Allied Industries	NICHEM	National Chemical Laboratory, Pune
7.	Management Sciences	NICMAN	Indian Institute of Management, Ahmeda bad
8.	Marine and Aquatic Sciences	NICMAS	National Institute of Oceanography, Goa
9.	Tea	NICMAT	Tea Board, Calcutta
10.	Advanced Ceramics* Ceramics Research	NICCAC	Central Glass & Institute, Calcutta
11.	Bibliometrics*	NCB	Indian National Scientific Documentation Centre New Delhi
12.	Crystallography*	NICRYS	University of Madras, Chennai
13.	CD-ROM*	NICDROM	National Aerospace Laboratory, Bangalore

– –

NISSAT supported sectoral information centres are well-equipped with modern information technologies. The mode of E-mail and Internet connectivity vary from one centre to another, but it is usually a combination of VSNL, ERNET and NICNET facilities. Given the high costs of leased lines, the centres are forced to use dial-up facilities. Only NICHEM, NICFOS, NICMAS have 64 Kbps lines through radio modems or VSATs.

Besides providing documents and preparing bibliographies on request, they offer selective dissemination of information (SDI), current awareness services (CAS), reprographic & micrographic services, industrial and technical enquiry services, technical translation and similar access-delivery services.

Some of the sectoral centres bring out serial publications of digests, indexing & abstracting materials and news highlights. Apart from publishing these in print form, the information is more often computerized.

The core activities of the NICLAI centre were focused on its development as a national centre for information on leather and allied industries. The areas of specialisation covered are leather science and technology, footware, leather goods, chemical engineering, colleges, polymers, leather economics, biochemistry, etc. The centre provides CDROM services using BIOSIS and document delivery services. The major database developed by the centre (Leather Science Abstracts), LECAT (Library Catalogue), PBCLRI (Publication of CLRI), PERHOL (List of periodical holdings of CLRI Library)

NICFOS centre is a clearing house for all types of information on food processing in the country and has initiated several information oriented programmes to fulfil the information needs of the food sector. The centre maintains seven databases on food technology. Some of the databases serve as supplement to the foreign database.

NICMAP is acting as a clearing house of information on machine tools and production engineering. NICMAP maintains about databases on bibliographical, statistical and product categories. The centre hosted its data on TIFACLINE of CMC for on-line accessing by users.

The centre has already selected Informatics and Silver platter to publish and market its product "Database on Manufacturing Technology and Machine Tools - Mtech". These apart, NICMAP provided consultancy to African Regional Centre for Engineering Design and Manufacturing (ARCEDEM), NIGERIA to evolve an information strategy for ARCEDEM and set up an information centre there. NICMAP also conducted sensitization programmes in different African countries to make them aware of the modem methods of information storage and retrieval.

NICDAP centre provides CDROM based services using Medline, Chemical Abstracts, Popline, Excerpta medica, International Pharmaceutical Abstracts, Biotechnology Abstracts, Drug Information, NUCSSI etc. The centre also provides on-line services using Datastar - Dialog and STN. The centre has INTERNET connectivity through RENIC.

The Services provided by the NICTAS centre includes literature searches, translation, reference service, E-mail facility, and CDROM services using TTD database and colour index The centre maintains six databases using UNIFY-RDBMS & custom made software. NICTAS continued the publication of TEXINCON and other state of art reports. The centre achieve self-sufficiency since 1994 and established an online database search centre.

NICHEM centre continued to perform well during the year 1998-99. More than 70% of its services are provided for industry, primarily chemical and pharmaceutical industry. The services provided by the centre includes repographic, document supply, translations, online search and patents. There has been a marked increase in the demand for patents and translation over the previous year. The centre also set up an internet facility to provide information to the clients, ordering of patents and journal articles, online searching etc.

The NICMAN Centre is providing services using ABI/Inform, Econlit, Social Science, Citation Index, Current Contents On Disc.-Behaviourial And Social Sciences. The centre developed a database consisting of records of current acquisition, articles and news items from Economics Times and Financial Express. The centre took initiatives in publishing its activities and tied up management development programme for extending information services to various programmes.

The centre has launched three information services such as information bulletin on management, current index on management and current contents in management & marketing. NICMAS centre maintains databases on Marine Science studies in Indian Ocean, Directory of Indian Marine Scientists and Contributions of NIO scientists.

An Indian National Oceanographic Internet Server (INOIS) established under NICMAS. The bibliographic databases available with NICMAS have been transferred into web format and published in INOIS server. The centre has developed a unique oceanographic search engine 'MANTHAN' on the web which would facilitate locating the oceanographic information/ data available on the web.

An Information Centre on Indian Tea would be established during 1998-99 to facilitate timely information on latest techniques and practices in India tea production, to access the latest market information on tea export, import etc and to provide a statistical database on India tea industry.

VAPIS: Value-Added Patent Information System

With the changing economic scenario in the country and the impending IPR regime, it is imperative to strengthen the patents information activities in India. The fierce competition faced by Indian industries, the necessity of the awareness of competitions innovations and the availability of foreign technology have made the patent information vital for the industry.

Considering the expert manpower available in the national R&D systems and the increasing need from industries for technical information, NISSAT established Value Added Patent Information System (VAPIS) at National Chemical Laboratory, Pune and Central Manufacturing Technology Institute at Bangalore to offer specialized, value added information services. The services are based on databases pertaining to US, European, World, Japanese and other patents available on CDROM. Separate subset of the database on Chemicals is located at NCL, Pune and on Engineering in CMTI, Bangalore. The information on patent and IPR legislations, etc of various countries are located at patent office of CSIR.

The main objective of the centre is to take advantage of the expertise available with the host institutions to add value to patent information and offer such services to industry. The addition of value to patent information is made by analysing contents of the patents. Value addition to patent information involved understanding the contents of patents, and adding to them details of technology options, technology gaps, and other items of crucial information.

The orientation of the centres would be towards market needs with a clear indication of activities, target clientele and revenue earning projections.

CD-ROM National Collection Centre

NISSAT has established a national collection of all CD-

ROM databases on India and about India at Foundation for Innovations and Technology Transfer at Indian Institute of Technology, Delhi in 1996.

A centre of this kind is deemed necessary to collect nationally produced documents on CD-ROM medium systematically as the Delivery of Books Act (1994) does not at present include provision to cover such products. However, the Centre buys the CD-ROM products instead of expecting free supplies by the CD-Producers.

The collection inter alia of the centre includes I products like:

Indian Patents Database	*Mtech*
Business India	Electronic Corporate
Health Asia Environment	Gandhi
Asia Directory	
Goa-the Pearl of Asia	Guru Nanak
Hindi English Dictionary	India Mystica
Invitation India,	Information interactive on Rajasthan
Karishma	Mythological Collections
Succhak	Taj Mahal
Karishma	Innoware Education
Kompass India	Yellow Pages

The centre prepared a Union list of CD-ROM databases acquired in various library/information centres in India.

Internet based activities

Web servers

NISSAT has moved a step ahead by establishing web sites/servers so far on:

- Indian Ocean Server, at NIO, Goa

- MYLIBNET at CFTRI, Mysore
- Indian Consultancy at CDC, New Delhi
- Indian S&T at the IISc., Bangalore.
- Website, on NISSAT
- Website on ISISCLEARING HOUSE

The Web server on Indian Ocean is a response to the recommendations made by the International Oceanographic Commission. It is also expected to help NIO to integrate its existing information activities for the provision of a one window information service. The NICFOS one is initially meant to facilitate the exchange of information among the libraries in Mysore under the MYLIBNET Programme and in due course organize information on Indian food industries.

The Indian Consultancy site hosts home-pages of consultancy organizations, their area of activities and also a mart for consultancy offers and those required. the S&T server project would be operational in 1998. It would include home-pages of R&D and academic institutions, information on materials and supplies, forthcoming events, employment opportunities, extra-mural support schemes of various agencies and so on.

Indian lisforum

In collaboration with the NCSI at IISc, NISSAT has set up an Electronic Mail Discussion Forum called LISFORUM for providers and users of information services in India. The facility provides an E-Mail based electronic forum for its participants to discuss issues of relevance to library and information services. The facility is available to users of ERNET and other networks that have connectivity to ERNET.

Information resource sharing

With a mandate to facilitate provision of broad based

information services in the country, NISSAT has taken initiatives for promoting resource sharing activities through Library Networks. These initiatives are aimed at ensuring better utilization of S&T information resources, minimization of functional load of information centres and encouragement of motivational factors to a large extent by better means of communication.

The NISSAT agenda for library networks is limited to the development of metropolitan systems, the logic being that libraries and library users in close geographical proximity can effectively utilize a library network. Given this, the goal of information/library networks is to interlink information resources in a metropolitan area such that users could access information irrespective of its location, format, medium, language, etc. Further, the development of such networks requires actions in several areas such as training, rationalization of acquisition of information resources, diffusion of standards, preparation of union lists, generation of database services apart from setting up hardware, software and communication facilities.

NISSAT strives further to develop self-sustaining information systems. With this end in view, NISSAT goes to the extent of setting up general infrastructural facilities like network service centres including hardware, software, manpower, organizational requirements and communication facilities. The participating institutions in a network have to arrange for their own terminal hardware, software, manpower and to take the responsibility of database development. Of course, NISSAT extends support for training, and common facilities like development of standards, preparation of union catalogues, data conversion and so on. Table 3 provides a list of Network Hosts and network services management bodies.

Table 3. NISSAT Sponsored Metropolitan Information/ Library Networks

Network	Host Site	Management
ADINET	INFLIBNET, Gujarat Univ. Campus, Ahmedabad INFLIBNET	Society drawing support from
CALIBNET	Regional Computer Centre, Jadavpur Univ. Campus, Calcutta	Society
MYLIBNET	CFTRI, Mysore Project	Institutional
PUNENET	Bio-Informatics Centre, Pune Univ., C-DAC and NCL, Pune	Institutional Project

Network activities like creation of OPAC bases, document delivery service facilities, inter library loan through local couriers (ILL), current awareness services (CAS), rationalization of periodicals acquisition, creation of Union fists of current subscriptions are taken up. With changed IT options, E-Mail, Remote login/ftp, Internet access services are offered to the participants. Network services centres also provide Online and CD-ROM based search services.

E-MAIL connectivity

NISSAT has established E-Mail connectivity with its information centre and library networks through ERNET. This connectivity greatly enhances the resource sharing capabilities and also the efficiency of user services.

Information technology applications

The demand for use of computers ranges from automation of routine management functions in libraries to information retrieval or analysis of global databases. Since the inception, NISSAT had accorded a high priority to all aspects of computer based bibliographic information processing. As a part of the programme, NISSAT acquired proven software packages like CDS/ISIS for bibliographic information processing & retrieval and IDAMS for statistical data processing. NISSAT subsequently obtained the official rights for distribution of the two packages in India from UNESCO.

As on date, there are about 1400 installations of CDS/ ISIS and 45 installations of IDAMS in India. The implementation of CDS/ISIS is monitored regularly through exchange of information, user's group meetings (seven such meetings have been held so far) and periodic surveys.

SANJAY is a package developed by NISSAT in collaboration with DESIDOC to help the libraries and information centres in India to improve their house-keeping and service functions through automation. The package is totally menu driven and can be used even by nonprofessionals. The package was released for marketing in September 1995, and till now it has an installation base of 40 sites.

These apart, NISSAT has collected several of small packages and utilities like Fangorn, CCF-MARC and vice-verse, dBASE to CDS/ISIS and vice-verse, GLOB for global replacement, NEWSDI from Indian institutions and abroad for distribution among Indian users.

NISSAT has entered into an agreement with t he MINISIS Resource Centre at the SNDT Women's University for marketing of the package and applications development.

Development of skilis in information science adn technology

Existing library and information science courses cannot keep pace with the rapid developments in the information field; there is a need to supplement these with continuing education programme at various levels. In view of the situation, NISSAT encourages and supports a variety of manpower development programmes which cover topics such as Application of computers in library and information centres, Use of personal computers & CDS/ ISIS, TQM in library services, Technical communication, Scientometrics, Computerized cataloguing, CDROM/ Online searching, Modern information access facilities to business and industry etc., Advanced Course on CDS/ISIS, Patent Information, Multimedia and Internet.

Research and development and survey studies

Sclentometrics and informetrics in India

In consultation with and active participation of the subject specialists, the NISSAT has formulated a plan of action for scientometric and informetric studies in India. As a first step in the, implementation of a programme of coordinated research, ten projects on National Mapping of Science using CA, Compendex, Inspec, SCI, Medline plus, BIOSIS, EMBASE, Georef, CAB, AGRICOLA, ISA database have been taken up. Table 5 provides the areas and institutions where the studies are being carded out:

Table 5 : Project areas under national mapping of science

Project Area	*PI Institution*
Agricultural	M.S. Swaminathan Foundation, Chennai Sciences
Biological	National Centre for Scientific Information, Sciences Bangalore
Chemistry	National Chemical Laboratory, Pune
Engineering	Documentation Research & Training Centre, Sciences Bangalore
Geo-Sciences	Regional Research Laboratory, Bhopal
Indian Science	Indian Association of Special Libraraies and Information Cenntres, Calcutta
Mathematical	MS Swaminathan Foundation, Chennai Sciences
Medical Science	Indian Council of Medical Research, New Delhi
Physics	National Physical Laboratory, New Delhi
Science & Technology	National Institute for Science, Technology Development Studies, New Delhi

NISSAT also promotes and supports research and development and survey studies. The list of such projects/ efforts is given in Table 6.

Table 6: Studies /surveys supported by NISSAT

Activity	PI Institution
Beyond Institutional Boundaries: A study of collaborative linkages of Indian Science through Bibliometric, indicators	NISTADS, New Delhi
Preparation of basic course materials for organizating a series of workshops on Patent Information for R&D and Business based on Case Studies	NISTADS, New Delhi
Indicators of Industrial Innovation	NISTADS New Delhi
Database and Annual Publication on Bibliornetric Indicators of Indian Science	NISTADS New Delhi
Holistic improvement of leather workers through information support in selected villages in Tamil Nadu	CLRI, Madras

Database development activities

In pursuance of its thrust on contents development, NISSAT encourages indigenous database development activities.

Besides library catalogues, union catalogues and lists, the activity could be on subjects in which a global database does not exist, or on subjects in which Indian elements are not properly represented. Table 7 indicates the various projects supported by NISSAT during the period of support.

Table 7: Indigenous database activities supported by NISSAT

Database activity	*PI Institution*
Database of Indian Chemical & Pharmaceutical Industries	NICCHEM, NCL
Directory of manufacture of various kinds of Ferrous and Non-Ferrous and Special Castings	IIF, New Delhi
INDAB: Database of Indian Databases, Abstracting and Indexing Services, and Directories	ISAC-NISSAT
Indian Sugar Industry	VDIS, Pune
Directory of Libraries and Information Centres in India	GGSS, Ahmedabad
Database on Indian Website Using MINISIS	SNDTWU Mumbai
Virus and Virology	NIV, Pune
Directory of Translators	INSDOC, New Delhi

International activities

The activities of ASTINFO/UNESCO (Regional Network for the Exchange of Information and Experiences in Asia and the Pacific/UNESCO) are closely coordinated with those of NISSAT the NISSAT Advisory Committee also functions as the National Advisory Committee of UNISIST and the National Advisory Group for ASTINFO.

UNESCO/ASTINFO often utilized NISSAT services for implementation of various programmes such as preparation of teaching aids for CDS/ISIS, CCF and MIS for libraries, course materials on marketing of information products and services and so on, apart from hosting of the ASTINFO Consultative Meeting in 1993. On several occassions, services of NISSAT were requisitioned for missions in countries like Bangladesh, Nepal and Malaysia. Recently, NISSAT has been given the responsibility to icing in establish a Clearing house on CDS/ISIS software and creation of database on library network experts in ASTINFO region A website is being established as apart of the programme.

NISSAT authored the section on South Asia in the World Information Report 1997. NISSAT also conducted a cross country analysis of the information scenario in Asia & Pacific Countries for the Study on the Information Infrastructure for Planning Information systems and Networks in Asia and Pacific Countries undertaken by UNESCO and the University of Library & Information Science Tsukuba.

Besides multi-lateral activities, NISSAT has also been providing inputs for bilateral cooperation. As a part of this programme NISSAT organized two Indo-Japan Workshops on Information in 1997.

Information today and tomorrow

Under the banner of ITT, two specific activities are undertaken

- A national meet of information industry, promoters and users, is held every year. The Information Today & Tomorrow meet, as it is popularly called, was held in Chennai during August 31 to September 3, 1998.
- NISSAT has been bringing out its *NISSAT Newsletter* - a quarterly newsletter since the beginning of the programme. Over the years, the format has undergone several revisions in keeping with the changing information scenario.

7

Public Enterprises

National Research Development Corporation

National Research Development Corporation (NRDC) is the principal organisation established by the Government to act as a link between scientific laboratories and industrial establishments for transferring technologies. It is a unique organisation in that it is the only public enterprise wholly dedicated to transfer of technologies from R&D laboratories to industry. What is more, its operations cover the entire spectrum of industrial technologies ranging from chemicals to metallurgy, mechanical engineering, electrical engineer, electronics, biotechnology etc.

The overall slow down of the industrial growth in the country, coupled with the intense competitiveness arising out of the several in-house technology transfer organisations/cells of various R&D organisations and liberalised industrial policy have placed the Corporation in a challenging situation during the year. Nevertheless, the overall performance of the Corporation for the year 1997-98 have been quite satisfactory. The Corporation's continued sincere endeavour and sustained marketing efforts have helped in maintaining its tract record of earning profits. The Corporation has earned Lumpsum

Premium and Royalty of Rs. 139. 11 lakhs and Gross Profit of Rs.30.68 lakhs during the, year 1997-98.

Profit

With aggressive marketing efforts with sincere and dedicated hard work of its executives and staff, the Corporation continued to earn a profit. During the year the Corporation has earned a gross profit of Rs.30.68 lakhs against Rs.26.28 lakhs in previous year.

The gross income of the Corporation from all sources, including premia and royalty, but excluding Grants-in-Aid, was Rs.245.23 lakhs as compared to Rs.291.72 lakhs in the previous year.

Processes assigned and licence agreements concluded

The corporation continued its efforts to widen its technology resource base by tapping new sources of technologies and nurturing the long term relationship with R&D Organisations in India and abroad. In this endeavour the Corporation signed an MOU with the Ministry of Food Processing Industries, New Delhi and Planter Energy Network, Madurai for the commercialisation of their technologies. During the year 38 new processes were assigned to the Corporation as compared to 24 in the previous year. Some of the commercially important processes assigned to the Corporation during the year were:

- Biodegradable plastic
- Powder hair dye (Henna based)
- Sutures from fish cat-gut
- Digested organic supplement
- Phorate formulation
- Defatting of groundnut without using chemicals & without losing its original shape & size.

Inspite of sluggish industrial environment and intensely

competitive scenario, during the year 34 licence agreements were signed as compared to 36 in the previous year.

Major technologies licensed

Some of the major technologies licensed by the Corporation during the year are:

- Biodegradable plastic
- Liposomal Amphotericine-B
- Vijetha (Silkworm bed Disinfectant)
- Silver Impregnated Graphite
- Rice Husk Particle Board
- NIM76 - A spermicidal formulation from neem oil
- Invert Sugar
- Glycol based hydraulic fluid (PEGCOL -89)
- Glass electrodes for pH, pK, pNa measuring
- Dental Varnish

Technology development projects

The Corporation has been promoting and financing mi collaboration with industry/R&D institutes, technology development projects for setting up pilot/semi commercial/ demonstration plants. The progress on major technology development projects is given below:

Completed Projects

Permanent marketing ink

The development work related to the project on improvement of permanent marking ink for election purposes at NPL, New Delhi in collaboration with M/s Mysore Paints & Varnish Ltd ., Mysore, at a total cost of Rs.6.5 lakhs has already been completed. However, testing/certification by the Election Commission is awaited.

On going projects

Thrombinase —a blood clot dissolving agent

Thrombinase, a novel blood clot dissolving agent has been isolated, identified and purified for the first time from a Bacillus species at Vector Control Research Centre, Pondicherry. However, the new drug needs to be evaluated through basic toxicological studies followed by clinical trials. The Corporation in collaboration with Malladi Research Centre, Chennai is carrying out joint development work at a cost of Rs.80 lakhs which is to be shared equally between the Corporation and the Company. The work on the project started in June 1996. A sum of Rs.15.75 lakhs has already been released. The work is progressing satisfactorily. The Corporation has filed patent applications for the process in India USA, EPO (Germany, Switzerland, Belgium and UK). The patent in USA has already been accepted. The Corporation has also initiated negotiations with a major Japanese Company for licensing of the Know-how and Patent Rights.

Projects supported by deparmtment of scientificand industrial research

DSIR has been supporting technology development projects under its "Programme Aimed at Technological Self Reliance (PATSER)" involving industry, research institutes and consultants. The Corporation has been identified as the agency to manage all matters connected with the intellectual property rights generated in these projects, as also to collect the royalty revenues accruing from the utilisation of the technology by the collaborating Company and also from third party licensing. A few of the major projects undertaken during the year under PATSER are:

- Development of Metal Halide Lamps including Arc Tube & Electronic Control Gear with M/s AUTOPAL Industries Ltd.
- Development SAARC Pagers with M/s S.M. Elect. Services

- Development of State-of-the-Art Machining Centre with M/s H.M.T, Bangalore
- Development Interactive Voice Response Systems With M/s Innovative Communication systems Pvt. Ltd.

Market surveys

Market surveys not only make the technology to be licensed more complete and credible but also help in assessing the realistic price at which the technology can be licensed. With this object in view, the Corporation continued to get market surveys prepared on commercially important technologies by commissioning professional market survey agencies for the purpose. During the year, market survey on the following items were completed:

- Intra Ocular Lenses
- Sericulture
- Biodegradable plastic
- Bio fertiliser
- Mini climbing crane

Invention promotion programme

The Corporation continued to promote and encourage inventive talent amongst scientists, engineers, industrial workers and students by awarding prizes to meritorious inventions and providing financial assistance for fabricating prototypes setting up pilot plants to prove such inventions.

During the year, the Corporation received 57 proposals for prize awards and 20 proposals for providing financial assistance.

The Corporation announced on Independence Day, cash awards amounting to Rs.2.5 lakhs for 6 inventions. On Republic Day (1998) cash awards amounting to Rs.1.45 lakhs for 4 inventions were announced.

World Intellectual Property Organisation (WIPO) Gold Medals have also been awarded to 3 inventions which have potential for wider use in developing countries.

Some of the meritorious inventions recognised through awards during the year were:

- Development of Process/Technology for manufacture of Detergent Grade Zeolite 'A' employing Sodium Aluminate Liquor from Alumina Refinery Plant
- Hydroxyapatite Coated Titanium Implant for Tooth Replacement
- Fluidised Abrasive Polishing Machine
- Acephate Technical

The Corporation also provided financial assistance to two inventors for fabricating prototypes/setting up pilot plants.

Patent assistance

Keeping in view the globalisation of economy, the significance of Intellectual Property Rights is increasing. With this end in view the Corporation is putting more emphasis on providing technical, legal and financial assistance to inventors in drawing up patent specifications, processing their patent applications etc. During the year the Corporation received 53 applications from individual inventors for such assistance. Assistance was granted to 30 inventors based on the patentability of the inventions involved and 71 patent applications were also filed on behalf of different R&D organisations.

Development and promotion of rural technology

The programme aims at the application of S&T for improving the standard of living of our rural people by increasing employment potential through the development and application of appropriate rural technologies utilising local resources. With this end in view, the Corporation continued the programme of Development and Promotion of Rural Technology as detailed below:

Development projects

On going projects

i) Pilot plant for the production-cum demonstration of euphorbia latex

India has a rich wealth of latex and resin bearing plants. One such wild plant Euphorbiaecea is commonly available in arid and semi-arid zones of our country The milky latex tapped from these plants can be utilised for industrial application. Paints, adhesives, corrosion and moisture resistant coatings can be produced from the latex. Latex from these plants mainly consists of resins, hydrocarbon and proteins.

Keeping in view the commercial potential of euphorbia plants (which is treated as waste at present), a pilot plant, at a cost of Rs.15 lakhs, having 30 litre per day latex processing capacity is being set up at Dehradun in association with ASHRAYA, A VOLUNTARY ORGANISATION working in Garhwal region where Royleana-euphorbiae is wildly grown. A sum of Rs.0.5 lakh has been released during the year. This will motivate people to set up cottage and small-scale industries in the rural belt of Himalayan region and will prove a boom to the unemployed youths.

ii) Design and development of direction finder to locate radio distress signals from fishermen at sea.

The Rural Electronics Group of the Electronic Research & Development Centre (ER&DC), Thiruvananthapuram of Department of Electronics has developed a sea-water proof, floatable, Radio Beacon for use of fishermen who go to sea in open boats without any form of safety equipment or means of communication. Keeping in view the usefulness of the device, the Corporation has provided a financial grant of Rs.2.3 lakhs to ER&DC for the design and development of a Direction Finder to work with the

Beacon, ER&DC has already made one prototype of the device. The Monitoring Committee has suggested some modifications, which are being carried out to get the desired accuracy in locating the distress signal and to withstand shock and sea spray, etc.

iii) Industrial resource survey of Nagaland

A study on Industrial Resources of Nagaland was carried out in collaboration with M/s Nagaland Sugar Mills Co. Ltd., Dimapur, at a total cost of Rs.5 lakhs, with an objective to identify the potential technologies and prepare the feasibility studies based on which industries can be set up in Nagaland. The survey report has already been submitted. An amount of Rs. 1.25 lakhs has been released.

Rural technology demonstration-cum-training centres

The methodology adopted by the Corporation is to demonstrate the utility of appropriate rural technologies and ensure their faster dissemination by setting up RTDT Centres in collaboration with voluntary agencies in various regions of the country. Pursuant to following this approach, some of the existing RTDT centres as detailed below have also been strengthened:

Installation of Solar Timber Seasoning Unit - A solar based timber seasoning unit has been set up at RTDT Centre, Kalika-Ranikhet (UP) with an objective to promote wood craft industry in UP hills. An expenditure amounting to Rs. 1 lakhs was incurred for the same. The demonstration facility will be utilised by local artisans in seasoning the local timber.

RTDT Centres located at Mendhar-Poonch (J&K), Udaipur (Rajasthan), Tirupathi (AP) and Kumily (Kerala) were strengthened with additional machineries and training programme arranged in their premises for the operation and maintenance of these machines.

Promotion of export of technology

The Corporation continued its efforts to export Indian

technologies and services to entrepreneurs both in the developed as well as the developing countries like USA, Germany, and countries in South East Asia, Africa and Latin America.

The Corporation has also been able to generate interest in parties from Germany, Indonesia, Malaysia, China and Japan in some of the corporation's technologies particularly for Rice Husk Particle Board, Disposable Blood Bags, Zeolite-A detergent grade and Thrombinase-a blood clot dissolving agent. The Corporation has signed a licence agreement with M/s P.T. Garama Dhananjaya, Jakarta, Indonesia for setting up three Rice Husk Particle Board Plants and received US$15,000 as part payment of the know how fees out of total contracted value US$90,000 for the first plant.

Foreign exchange exarnings

The foreign exchange earnings of the Corporation amounted to Rs.20.45 lakhs in 1997-98 as compared to Rs.1.21 lakhs during the previous year.

Publications

An important activity of the Corporation is to disseminate information on new processes to industry, entrepreneurs and the general public for the promotion and commercialisation of technologies. One of the means of doing so is through publications of various types. During the year, the Corporation continued to bring out the following regular publications:

– Awishkar - (Monthly in Hindi)
– Invention Intelligence - (Monthly in English)

The following special publications were also brought out by the Corporation during the year:

– NRDC at your Service
– NRDC technologies

– Corporate Brochure - from Minds to Global Markets

Sale of Dsir publications

The Department of Scientific & Industrial Research has entrusted NRDC with the marketing and sale of heir publications on Technology Status Studies/Tech. Evaluation Studies/Project Profiles/Consultancy and other Studies and Handbook of Foreign Collaboration Approvals (1981-90). During the year, the Corporation sold 259 reports valued at Rs.1.01 lakhs.

Exhibitions and publicity

Participation in exhibitions, seminars, workshops entrepreneurship development programmes etc. are of vital importance for the creation of awareness about the role of the Corporation in technology transfer. With this end in view, the Corporation participated in exhibitions; seminars and get-togethers organised by various agencies as detailed below:

i) ACHEME '97 International Exhibition -Frankfurt & A Preparatory Seminar at Rotterdam (5-1411 June, 1997)

ii) Delhi Book Fair, New Delhi (9-1711 August, 1997)

iii) IENA '97, Nuremberg, Germany (29th Oct.-2nd Nov., 1997)

iv) Made in India Exhibition, Amsterdam, Netherlands (1 -611 November, 1997)

v) Technopolis Foundation, Japan (9-160 November, 1997)

vi) IITF '97, New Delhi (14-27th November, 1997)

vii) NCSTCS Science since Independence, New Delhi (14-301 Nov., 1997)

viii) Techmart Africa '97, Mauritius (24-26th Nov. 1997)

ix) Techmart '97, Bangalore (3-81 Dec, 1997)

x) Swarozgar Mela '97, Jabalpur (20-23rd December, 1997)

xi) WISITEX '97, New Delhi (5-9th Feb., 1998)

xii) Indian Trade Exhibition, Mexico City (3-91 March, 1998)

Implementation of official language

The Corporation continued making efforts to implement the provisions of the Official language Act and Rules framed there under to ensure the continued use of Rajbhasha in its day to day working. Significant progress has been made in the field of correspondence, noting and drafting in Hindi. The Annual Report of the Corporation is being published in diglot form in both Hindi & English since 1986-87.7he Corporation also publishes a popular science and technology monthly in Hindi, entitled Awishkar. To popularise the use of Hindi, the Corporation celebrated the "HINDI PAKHWARK" from Sept. 14-29, 1997. During the Pakhwara different types of competitions like Hindi Essay writing, Hindi drafting & noting, Hindi Typing, Short Speech and Hindi Poetry were organised. Certificate and cash awards were given to winners. To promote Rajbhasha "The Comprehensive Glossary of Administrative Terms (Eng-Hindi) was distributed among all officers. Under the Hindi Incentive Scheme, Certificates and cash awards were also given to selected staff members for their use of Hindi in official work. One typist was sent for training in Hindi typing.

Central Electronic Limited

Central Electronics Limited (CEL) holds a unique position among the family of Public Sector Enterprises in Electronics, with its emphasis on indigenous technology inducted both from its in- house developments and from the country's National Laboratories, for its production programmes in diverse hi-technology areas of National Relevance. The activities of CEL are sharply focussed in three thrust areas:

(i) *Solar photovoltaic cells*—Modules and Systems for a variety of both Rural and Industrial applications.

(ii) *Selected electronic systems* - Equipment for Railway Signalling and Safety, Cathodic Protection Equipment for Oil Pipelines, Rural Automatic Exchanges (RAX) and Very Small Aperture Terminals (VSATS).

(iii) *Selected electronic components*—Professional (Soft) Ferrites, Electronic Ceramics, Piezo Electric Elements and Microwave Components.

CEL has been the pioneer in the country in the areas of Solar Photovoltaics, Ferrites and Piezo-Ceramics. Today, it enjoys an internationally recognised status of being among the, top few producers of Single Crystalline Silicon Solar Cells in the world.

Performance in 1997-98

Operating results

The production and sales achieved during the year as compared to the previous year are given below:

(Rs. in crores)

	1996-97 (Actuals)	*1997-98 (Actuals)*
PRODUCTION	61.38	80.21
SALES	60.57	67.00

The Company earned a net profit after tax of Rs. 45 lakhs as against Rs. 80 lakhs in the previous year. The profit for the year has come down since a provision for interim relief for the period from 1.1.1997 to 31.3.1998 amounting to Rs. 60 lakhs was made during the year.

Highlights of achievements in 1997-98

Solar Photo Voltaics (SPV)

In the Solar Photovoltaics Group, 2005.00 KWp of SPV Modules were produced and 1276.22 Kwp of SPV Modules were sold as against 1644.87 KWp and 1774.92 Kwp respectively in the previous year. A total of 4680 Nos. SPV Power Sources were supplied to DOT for its Rural Telecom Network as against 13000 SPV power sources supplied during the last year. A farther repeat order for 7000 Nos. of such systems was expected from DOT, however, the same could not be received by the end of the year resulting in increase in inventory required to execute the same.

33 Nos. of SPV power sources for the Very Low Power TV Transmitters were supplied to Doordarshan during the year. 10 Nos. of SPV Refrigerator Systems were supplied to Coir Board, Cochin.

In the 4th year of the National SPV Pump Programme of the Ministry of Non-conventional Energy Sources (MNES), the Company supplied 55 Nos. of SPV Pumps to various users through Indian Renewable Energy Development Agency (IREDA).

During the year, 1860 Nos. of SPV Lanterns as per the MNES specifications were supplied. The Company has also supplied 728.82 KWP (approx.) of SPV Modules to various customers including nodal agencies and Govt. Departments/ Public Sector Undertakings.

The Company supplied 50 Nos. Deep Well Water Pumping Systems during the year against the order for 200 pumps received from Deptt. of Rural Development (DRD). The work of site survey for the balance quantity was in progress during the year and the installation and commissioning of these systems is expected to be completed in 1998-99.

Exports

The Company has successfully executed export orders of 11.44 KWP of SPV Cells, Modules & Systems consisting of Domestic lights, Street Lights, Solar Water Pumping

Systems, Solar Lanterns, etc., worth Rs. 35 lakhs to various countries namely Costa Rica, Uganda, Oman, Bangladesh, Bhutan, Cuba, Zimbabwe, Hongkong and Belgium.

During the year the efforts for the promotion of exports of the company's SPV products particularly in the African Region received further thrust through fund support under the Transfer and Trading in Technology (TAIM Scheme of DSIR.

Electronic system

The System Group produced 11983 Nos. of Charge Controllers for the SPV power systems for the DOTs Rural Telecom Network. 209 Nos. of Universal Axle Counters were sold during the year. 6 Nos. of PTVs were also sold during the year. Against the order for 21 Nos. of VSATs, the Group produced and supplied 11 Nos. of VSATs using know-how from C-DOT to C-DOT/DST against orders received from them. For the balance quantity of 10 Nos. despatch clearance is awaited from DG, NCMRW - National Centre for Medium Range Weather Forecasting, DST, New Delhi.

The System Group has received a turnkey order worth Rs. 14.50 Crores; from the Gas Authority of India Limited against Global Tender, for the supply of Captive Power Generation and Cathodic Protection System for the HBJ Pipeline Project. This Project funded by the Asian Development Bank is a Deemed Export Project. The installation work on this project has been completed. Final commissioning and handing over is in progress. The company earned foreign exchange worth Rs. 11.79 crores on this project.

After successful turnkey installations of C.P. Systems for the Chakshu-Panipat Pipeline of IOCL, the company further received from IOCL an order worth Rs. 8.54 crores for a similar turnkey C.P. Project for the Barouni-Haldia Pipeline. The project is likely to be completed in the next financial year.

Components

In the Ferrites Plant, in addition to the normal mix of Ferrite Cores, 2011 Nos. of C-B and Microwave Ferrite Yokes and Rods were successfully completed and supplied for the Phase Shifter Assemblies.

The Group also supplied 24000 Nos. complete PZT Electric Systems to the Defence for their 84 mm. Carl Gustaf ammunition. A further order for 10000 Nos. of the same was also received which will be supplied in the next year.

The Microwave Electronics Division supplied 1000 Nos. of C-Band and 1050 of X-Band Phase Control Modules (PCM) against the order received from Electronics Research & Development Establishment (LRDE), Bangalore of Defence Research and Development Organisation (DRDO).

The Microwave Electronics Division has also supplied during the year, 2 Nos. of Direction Finding (DF) Systems, 3 Nos. of Microwave Sub-systems, like Down/Down-up Converter and Microwave Components like 20 Nos. of Power Dividers and 20 Nos. of Phase Correlators. In addition, orders for a number of Now Products for use in Electronic Warfare Systems namely Millimeter Wave Components, Detector Log Video Amplifier (DLVAs), Spiral & Biconical Antennas are under progress. MOU has been signed with LRDE, Bangalore, for the manufacture of Phased Arrays for Phased Array Radars for the Aakash Missile Programme of the Defence Research Development Organisation (DRDO).

Exports

The Component Group exported 22000 Nos. of Piezo Ceramic Tubes for the third successive year with likely further recurring export orders for 10000 Nos. for this component.

Other highlights of 1997-98

Visits of important dignitories

The Company remained an attraction point for various important International/National dignitories. As in the previous years, a number of VIPs visited the Company particularly the SPV Plant. These included foreign delegations from Syria, Burkinafaso, Republic of Benin, Tunisia, Kazakasthan, Zambia and Israel. The other notable visitors were:

Shri Swaran Singh Boparai, K.C, Secretary, MINES, R. Adm. SV Gopalachari, DG, Secretary, Naval (Hqrs.), Cmdr. SC Arora, Director General, DQA(N), Shri Virender P. Singh, Ambassador of India, Hawana (Cuba), DR. Anil K. Malhotra, Regional Energy Adviser, World Bank, Prof. A.K. Roy Choudhry, Director NPL, New Delhi, HE Dr. PV Joshi, Indian High Commissioner, Designate to Guyana, and others.

Voluntary retirement scheme

As part of continued efforts to meet its commitment in the Capital Restructuring proposal to reduce the manpower to bring down the fixed overhead costs, the company reintroduced the Voluntary Retirement Scheme during the year. The unspent grant of Rs.100 lakhs received during 1996-97 was utilised to relieve 11 employees, the balance amount will be utilised in the next year. The total manpower stood at 880 Nos. as on 31.3.1998 as against 950 before Capital Restructuring.

Memorandum Of Understanding (MOU)

The Company has been a regular signatory of MOU with the Government, since 1992-93. Based on the actual performance for the second consecutive year ending 31st March, 1998 the company has got 'Excellent' rating based on the MOU performance scoring for the year 1997-98.

technology absorption, adaptation and innovation

The Pilot Plant for the manufacture of Buried Contact

High Efficiency Solar Cells based on the laboratory know how taken from University of New South Wales (UNSW), Australia, has been put up and made operational. On this plant, special type of High Power and High Power Density modules were manufactured and supplied to ONGC and WBREDA, for offshore platforms and power plant applications.

Design and development

Solar photovoltaic group

The SPV-Diesel Hybrid Power Plant developed by CEL, with the fund support from DSIR under PATSER Schemes, was installed at Manesar Repeater Station of DOT for extensive field trials. It has been working satisfactorily without any failure and to the satisfaction of DOT. The project has now been closed after being duly certified by DOT on the satisfactory performance of the plant.

Another project funded under PATSER Scheme is the development of SPV Charger for Ni-Cd batteries using Smart Charging Technology. It is initially targeted for use by Army. First prototype of the same has been fabricated and laboratory trials are under way.

CEL had set up a pilot plant for the manufacture of Ultra High Efficiency (UHE) Crystalline Sillicon Solar Cells using the Buried Contact Technique know-how obtained from UNSW, Australia. An agreement was entered into between CEL and N.A.L, Bangalore for developing a fast electroless plating process for copper deposition for the above UHE solar cell production process. This will enhance the throughput of the production line, thus making the process commercially more cost effective. This pilot plant is being further expanded into a commercial plant of 1 MW capacity at CEL.

Component group

Professional ferrites

With the objective of achieving diversification in Ferrite

Division and to add high frequency Ferrite Components in the present range of Ferrites manufactured in the Ferrite Plant, a project has been taken up for development of Ni-Zn ferrite materials and components under S&T support from DSIR. This will result in the addition to the product portfolio of a new range of ferrite cores with higher value addition and catering to, among other things, the EMI/EMC applications which is an emerging market all over the world.

Microwave electronics

Upgradation of Technology of PCM's and Phased Arrays have been taken up with the development of Multi Channel driving system. The Discrete Circuit Model of the system has been successfully demonstrated to LRDE, Bangalore. The development of ASIC of the same is being negotiated with a foreign foundry.

Electronic systems

First prototype of Solid State Interlocking System for use by Railways was developed jointly by CEL & C-DAC, incorporating the latest features and revised specifications laid down by RDSO, Lucknow. The development is supported through the PATSER scheme of DSIR. Activities for engineering development and fabrication of the final prototype for submission to RDSO for extensive field trials and type approval were taken up during the year.

Role in national technology missions

Company's SPV group supplied about 4680 SPV Power Sources for the DOT's VHF Rural Telecommunication Network. The Group had also supplied 50 Nos. of Deepwell Water Pumping Systems for National Drinking Water Mission under the Deptt. of Rural Development.

Foreign exchange receipts and outgo

During the year 1997-98, your Company has spent Rs.3104 lakhs in foreign exchange as against Rs.1750 lakhs in the previous year towards the purchase of capital equipment, raw materials and components, travel etc.

The Company has earned foreign exchange of Rs. 1210 lakhs as against Rs. 267 lakhs in the previous year from export of its products.

Advertisements, entertainment expenses and expenditure on guest house

A total expenditure of Rs. 0.38 lakhs was incurred during the year on commercial advertisements as against Rs. 0.55 lakhs in the previous year. An amount of Rs. 1.69 lakhs was spent on entertainment as against Rs. 1.83 lakhs in the previous year. The Company has not invested any amount on construction or maintenance of a Guest House.

Engergy conservation

The Company being an electronic industry, its operations are not energy intensive. Therefore, the requirement to furnish information on conservation of energy/ energy consumption under rule 2(A) of Companies (Disclosure of Particulars in the Report of Board of Directors) Rules 1988 is not applicable to the Company.

Particulars of employees

In accordance with the Companies (particulars of employees) Rules 1975 read with Sub Section 2-A of Section 217 of the Companies Act, 1956 as amended in 1988, none of the employees of the Company either employed throughout the year or employed for a part of the year under review was in receipt of remuneration more than that minimum prescribed in the Rules.

Industrial relations

The Company had fairly cordial industrial relations during the year as a result of the Management's continuous dialogue with the recognised Workers Union and with the Officers/Executives Associations.

Employees participation in management continued through the forums of Shop Level and Plant Level Committees constituted for the purpose. 21 Meetings of the Shop Floor Committees and 13 of the Plant Level Committees of the different divisions of the Company were held during the year as against 12 and 4 respectively in the previous year. Other participative forums like Canteen Managing Committee, Safety Committee, IRC, Medical Committee, etc. also functioned actively.

Human reources development

In the face of global competition due to economic liberalisation programme of the Government and recognising the fact that in order to survive, the organisation has to be made a "Learning Organisation", increased emphasis was laid on the Training & Development of employees. Towards this end, all out efforts were made to impart training in the various facets of activities with the aim to broaden the skill and knowledge base of various categories of the employees.

601 Mandays Training was undertaken by organising in-house training programmes and 107 Mandays training by sponsoring employees to external training programmes for specialised courses during the year 1997-98.

Welfare of researved categories

All Government directives relating to the Reserved Categories such as, Scheduled Castes, Scheduled Tribes, the Physically Handicapped, Ex-Servicemen etc. continued to be implemented during the year. The total number of employees in these categories were 234 which represents about 26.59% of the total strength of the Company as on 31st March, 1998.

Use of Hindi

With a view to ensure the proper implementation of official language policy of Government of India and the directives received from time to time in this regard, Official Language Implementation Committee, Sub-Committee and branch of Kendriya Sachivalaya Hindi Parishad emphasized on progressive use of Hindi in the Company during the year. The employees continued to be trained in Prabodh, Praveen, Pragya Hindi courses, Hindi typewriting and Hindi Computer. Hindi week was organised from 14.9.1997 to 20.9.1997. The employees are being encouraged and motivated to work in Hindi. The work for writing notes, reports and letters etc. in Hindi is in progress.

8
Administration

The Department of Scientific & Industrial Research was created through a Presidential Notification of January 1985. The Administrative functions of recruitment of personnel, provision of general facilities, redressal of grievances of employees, parliament work and use of Hindi are being performed by the Department of Scientific and Industrial Research. Other house-keeping jobs are being performed by Department of Science & Technology., Activities related to promotions of scientific staff and officers (under the flexible complementing scheme) are also looked after by the Department.

Promotion of Hindi

DSIR made the following efforts for the use and promotion of Hindi in the official work and implementation of official language policy of the Government:

(a) The meetings of the Official Language Implementation Committee were held regularly in DSIR.

(b) The Quarterly Progress Report regarding use of Hindi in the Department was sent to the Department of, Official Language regularly and in time.

(c) Under Hindi Teaching Scheme, non-Hindi Knowing employees of the Department were nominated for

Prabodh, Praveen and Pragya courses. Employees of the Department were also nominated for basic training on computer.

(d) From 1st to 15th September 1998 combined Hindi Pakhwara was observed by the Department of Science and Technology and Department of Scientific and Industrial Research at Technology Bhavan. To promote the use of Hindi in the official work, essay, noting and drafting, debate, painting and quiz competitions were organised in the Department during this period and officials of the Department were given prizes. Hindi versions of Orders, Notifications, Letters, Standard Drafts, Annual Report and Performance Budget were provided.

The staff strength in the different groups in the Department of Scientific & Industrial Research as on 1. 1. 1998 is given below:

	Number of employees			
	General	SC	ST	Total
Group A (Gazetted)	37	5	1	43
Group B (Gazetted)	4	2	–	6
Group B (Non-Gazetted)	10	4	–	14
Group C (Non-Gazetted)	24	3	2	29
Group D (Non-Gazetted)	29	2	–	14

9

Infrastructure and Social Sector Prospects

The scenario around industry, infrastructure and social sector is not comfortable. According to a report published by Business Times Bureau of The Times of India on 18 January, 1997, 24 industries which have a weight of 50.37 per cent in the index of industrial production recorded a growth rate of only five per cent during April-November, 1996, down from 11 per cent during the corresponding period in the preceding year.

The growth rate in output of the infrastructure industries which have a weight of 28.77 per cent in the index of industrial production has also slumped to 3.3 per cent during the first eight months of 1996-97 as against 9.3 per cent in the previous corresponding period. Most of the State Electricity Boards are utterly mismanaged and are running at heavy losses. The power sector also could not be opened to privatization though it was officially decided long ago. The transport and communication sector also needs a thorough restructuring.

Most of the State transport organisation, run on heavy government subsidy, are incurring huge losses. Infrastructural facilities in the agricultural sector like irrigation and flood control measures are still at a very poor level. There are some areas where the farmers completely lack the basic knowledge of fertilizer and pesticide uses while extension services of government remain only on paper. Likewise, innovative ideas relating to small-scale industries and openings of self-employment opportunities are lacking among the educated unemployed who need proper consultancy services and basic training of entrepreneurship.

In the area of human resource development, the two pillars of literacy movement , viz Operation Blackboard and the Non-formal Education Scheme are floundering mainly due to casual attention of the implementing agencies. The adult literacy movement, for example, was not reoriented until six years after the mission began in 1988.

The recruitment of teachers for the literacy drive was in a shambles. Some vital aspects that need immediate attention now are the strengthening of post-literacy programmes to keep pace with the main drive, formulating a linkage with the formal school system and remedying the lack of vocational education and income generation schemes.

The unfulfilled promise of achieving 100 per cent literacy, renewed several times in the earlier decades, has once again been undertaken by the United Front government with a time-frame of AD 2000. So far, only 5.3 million have been made literate through adult literacy drive and as many as 44 million still remain to be covered.

One does not know how practicable will be the promise. Mere slogan of literacy mission, as has been done so far, is not going to transform the mission into a mass movement. It must be linked to improvement of quality of life, particularly with respect to improved health, nutrition, employment programme and, of course, social justice.

Under a shady family planning programme, INDIA is sitting on a population time bomb. According to the latest census, the country is going to be world's most populous nation by AD 2040 if determined efforts to reverse the growth trend are not made. It is fearful to think that the demography of India is adding every year to her size an additional population at the rate of 18 million, equivalent to the size of six Singapores.

Though during the last four and a half decades of planning the real national income increased by almost six times, the per capita real income could grow by only 2.4 times. Most of the benefits of India's growth and development are eaten up by population growth. Surprisingly enough, though the political class is well aware of the sensitive nature of the issue, especially after the excesses of emergency, the nation did not receive even a single imaginative suggestion of population control during these 20 years. What is more agonising is that there are many politicians who are not even averse to the unchecked growth of a deprived and dependent section which could be a good vote bank. If the country really wants to make progress with assured betterment of life, suitable programmes have to be so framed as to encourage control of births and small family norm at any cost.

Rapid creation of productive employment opportunities is the best way of reducing poverty.

The Economic Survey, 1995—96 reported Planning Commission estimates indicating a sharp increase in additional employment generated in the economy from 3 million in 1991—92 to over 7 million in 1994—95. The employment estimates for 1995—96 have not yet been finalised. However, there is little doubt that the high growth of the last few years would have led to a rapid expansion of employment opportunities.

The Common Minimum Programme (CMP), underpins strong commitment of the Government to the development of social sectors for achieving distributive justice. This commitment is reflected in the increase in Central Government Plan and non—Plan allocations for social services to a record high of 1.19 per cent of GDP in 1996—97 (BE). This ratio was 0.96 per cent in 1995—96. An additional amount of Rs. 2466 crore of Central assistance to States' and Union Territories' plans has also been allocated in the 1996—97 budget for expenditure on basic minimum services.

The Government has also accorded high priority to poverty alleviation programmes. The Central Plan allocations for social sectors and poverty alleviation programmes show highest growth of 85.6 per cent for education in 1996–97 over 1995–96 (BE). The outlay for elementary education has gone up by 247.8 per cent, mainly because of the programme of nutritional support to primary school students. The allocation for health was raised by 21.6 per cent and for rural development, encompassing the major programmes for poverty alleviation, by 12.1 per cent in 1996–97 over 1995–96 (BE).

The weaker sections especially scheduled castes/ scheduled tribes and women have been given importance in special programmes of poverty alleviation and employment as well as in several other programmes. The PDS has been steamlined recently in order to target the poorer sections of the population.

Population : According to Planning Commission estimates, population figures are expected to go up from 856 million in 1991-92 to 938 million in 1996-97, showing an annual average growth rate of 18 per cent . If the growth rate remains around two per cent, this figure will go up to 955 million, According to current indications, the actual figure will be in between these two figures since the death rate has fallen below even the 2000-2001 and in any case will be below the rate of around two per cent as estimated by the current UN projections, of around 1,042 million in that year.

If India is able to achieve a population growth rate of around 1.6 percent in the decade 2000-2001 to2010-2011, its population will reach 1,171 million, if the Planning Commission projections are used as a base. Even if this target is exceeded, the figure will be less than 1,224 million as estimated by the UN. These projections have not incorporated the detail of the 1991 census. The Registrar—General's Working Group on Population Projections set up conventionally by the Planning Commission, will have to firm up these alternative conjectural projections, in terms of underlying fertility, mortality and expected life span-behaviour, by age—group and rural-urban categories.

Land: The other major category needing examination on this kind of perspective is the land or resource base of the economy. The Planning Commission has correctly projected that the net area sown or arable land of the country will remain constant at 141 million hectares.

Growth in net area sown at around one per cent annually in the early period of planing fell to around 0.6 per cent and then to 0.3 per cent in subsequent decades and is now not growing at all. It is reasonable to assume that the exploitation of the geographical area of the country or the extensive land frontier has reached its limits. This is an important issue, the implications of which are not being realized with the urgency they deserve, since at a basic level resource constraints of a more severe kind faced by certain East Asian economies are now being approached in India. Organizations, communities, households and individuals will have to grasp this fact and live with it.

The intensive frontier for land use, however remains. It has been known for example that cropping intensity depends on irrigatin. Thus gross cropped area or harvested area has been shown in the past to be strongly determined statistically, in an econometric sense, by net irrigated area and irrigation intensity. This fundamental relationship can be used to project the intensive resource base of the economy.

Water management: Recognizing these problems the Finance Minister has been persuaded to introduce an Accelerated Irrigation Benefit Programme in the Annual Plan for this year. An outlay of Rs. 800 crore has ben provided for large irrigation project where substantial achievement can be expected—say in completing a section of the canal systems in the next two or three years and Rs. 100 crore for delivering water to the field in the next two agricultural years.

These programmes will be strictly monitored. More important, a blue ribbon commission has been set up with the following terms of reference:

- To prepare an Integrated Water Plan for development of water resources for drinking, irrigation, industrial, flood control and other uses;
- To suggest modalities for transfer of surplus water to water-deficit basins by interlinking of rivers for achieving the above objectives;
- To identify important ongoing projects as well as new projects which should be completed on a priority basis together with phasing;
- Identify a technological and interdisciplinary research plan for the water sector with a view to maximizing the benefits;

- To suggest physical and financial resource generation strategies for the water sector; and
- Any other related issue.

The projections assume a vastly improved performance on the land and water management frontiers. It needs to be remembered that the balance ground water reserves towards the later half of the nineties will be nore and more limited. A very dramatic effort will be needed to harvest and carefully use the available water. Otherwise, the projected increase in cropping intensity will simply not take place. Cropping intensity increased from around 1.3 in the early nineties. In the nixt two decades, this effort needs to be considerably strengthened, so that cropping intensity can increase from 1.3 to 1.5. Harvesting of rainwater, recycling water from agricultural drainage systems, more judicious use of water for cropping, will all be required, Non-agricultural use of water will have to be far more econmical.

Another way of looking at the severe land constraint is to see that a net area sown per person will go down from around 0.17 ha to around 0.10 ha. The gross area sown per person currently around 0.2 ha will, even if cropping intensity increases very rapidly, go down to around 0.15-0.18 ha.

It has been shown elsewhere that limited co-operation in waer use has been successful in many watershed projects in resolving the land constraint. The same is true of lower level surface irrigation systems. Community involvement is also important for judicous management of aquifer systems and ground water use.

In many cases, land management questions are equally important and are inextricably linked with water management, eg land shaping in hill slopes and on farm investment in irrigation commands.

The technology interface is important, both for land and water management and for cropping and non-crop farm systems that are optimal, in this class of issues. While a lot of research has been done and is available, the real issues are policy rules for fast replicability of existing knowledge and success stories. Community institutions have to be at the heart of this process. ICAR, its centres and sponsored institutions, have not easily participated in this process.

Work force: This kind of development is simply not possible if the functional literacy skills of the farm population arenot improved and if the peasant who works on the land, does not have rights to make improvements on it. There are a number of significant examples where based on local initiative, educational and training institutions led to knowledge-based growth in rural areas. These include the Charotar Vidya Mandal at Vallabh Vidyanagar (later Sardar Patel University), Dharamasthala Educational Trust (efforts of Veerendra Heggade) and many co-operative sponsored institutions in Maharashtra (for example the Pravara Ecucational Trust at Loni). Recognizing the importance of such efforts, the government of India has set up a National Council for Rural Institutes. The ICAR and its affiliates must be one of the major thrust institutions in this effort and its educational and extension wings must sponsor, acredit and support the effort.

BMSs: The government's Basic Minimum Services (BMSDs) Programme also has the same objective. It consists of the following programmes which need integration with our agricultural strategy:

- 100 per cent coverage of provision of safe drinking water in rural and urban areas.
- 100 per cent coverage of primary health service facilities in rural and urban areas.

- Universalization of primary education.
- Provision of public housing assistance to all shelterless poor families.
- Extension of mid day meal programme in primary school to all rural blocks and urban slums and desadvantaged sections.
- Provision of connectivity to all unconnected villages and habitations.
- Streamlining the public distribution system with the focus on the poor.

The major problems that confront India are poverty and unemployment. And both are interrelated. There is a lot of controversy regarding the estimates of poverty in the country. Estimates of Tendulkar and Jain show that rural poverty has increased from 37.5 per cent in 1990-91 to 39.7 per cent in 1993-94. On the other hand, urban poverty has declined from 35 per cent in 1990-91 to 30.9 per cent in 1993. The upshot of the argument is that even in 1993-94, around 40 per cent of the rural population (around 250 million) and 31 per cent of the urban population (around 65 million) were below the poverty line, or food insecure in terms of not having enough calories.

The continuance of poverty at such a colossal level has created great distortions in the economy. There are several reasons why poverty has persisted in rural areas. One obvious factor which has hurt the poor is the sharp increase in the prices of food grains. During the last five or six years, procurement prices of food grains have increased considerably recultural labourers. Secondly, the rural poor appear to have been left out of the gains of increased productivity in the agricultural sector. Thirdly, the rate of growth in employment in rural areas (both males and females), during the period 1987-88 to 1993-94 was significantly lower as comparesd to the urban areas as shown in . According to the 50th Round of the NSSO, while 'Open' unemployment at a little over 6.0 per cent, remained more or less unchanged. And casualization increased with a corresponding decline in self-employment, both in rural and urban areas. Casual wage employment increased from 31.2 per cent in 1987-88 to 33.5 per cent in 1993-94, while self-employment declined from 53.6 per cent to 51.9 per cent. Regular salaried employment also declined from 15.2 per cent to 14.7 per cent.

The census figures have given an alarming new for Indian planners again. The data paint a dismal picture both with regard to increase in population and unemployment. By 2040, India is set to become the world's most populous country with a population of 126 crores. And as far as unemployment situation is concerned, one-third of the populztion—300 million were estimated to be without work in 1994.

This implies that unless some effective steps are taken to control population, the rate of employment will increase in future.

The approach paper, however, recognizes that a sustained and long-lasting solution to gthe problem of poverty depends on the creation of adequate employment opportunities through a broad based programme of development and economic growth. Therefore, in the Ninth Plan, a great deal of emphasis has been given to agriculture and rural development. And agriculture has been delinked from rural development in order to emphasize the development of irrigation, watershed development, animal husbandry schemes, social forestry and so on.

Technology is the "in" thing for elite circles in industry as well as in agriculture for operational policies to be determined. This has implications—economic, social and political—which should not be missed in the wider context of the course and content of the entire economic and social development process.

There is, first of all, a high cost financing improvements in production and productivity of viable farmers and the marketing of surpluses from may be generated in the farm sector. The gains in agriculture too are monopolized in their entirety by the rich and party middle farmers who constitute hardly ten per cent of the farming population. The so-called incentive prices, guaranteed for the marketable surpluses, which under the system of public procurement have been scaled up even as production and productivity have risen, have distorted the structure of relative prices within agriculture and as between agriculture and non-agricultural sectors. Surpluses for investment in industry and for relief to the vulnerable sections of society, especially those which have no viable assets in land, have consequently eroded and processes of balanced economic and social growth have been blocked instead of receiving a boost from agricultural growth in the last three decades.

Precedence to Profit: It is interesting to note in this context the new ambitions which the beneficiaries of the new agricultural strategy have been nursing and have now acquired a critical importance after the structural adjustment based on market-oriented liberalization-globalization process was initiated in 1991. Important in this context too is the proposition which began to be advanced in influential quarters in the late half of the seventies that the "export principle" should apply as much to agriculture as to industry; more so to agriculture in which in recent years surpluses to effective demand in the domestic market have begun to appear from time to time and are creating their own set of problems.

This is an extension of the demand for the so-called principle of "parity of prices" between what the surplus farmer sells in the Indian market and what he buys. The idea is that price determination for agricultural produce should be governed relative to the highest price which can be fetched in the global market and not by any reference to a system or structure of relative prices of goods or labour (that is, wages) in the domestic market. There is, of course, at the same time a demand for protection against competitive prices. A logical further extension of this reasoning necessarily is that it is right economically to export agricultural surpluses rather than use them for satisfaction of the needs of those in the country who for want of adequate purchasing power are unable to provide a profitable market for increases in production. The commercial principle, after all, has a logic of its own had if applied to agricultural surpluses it must grant precedence to profit of the surplus producer rather than to the satisfaction of human wants.

Agriculture vs Industry—Distortion of Reality: Of special interest in this context again is the agriculture versus industry debate which began forcefully to be raised as commercial agriculture made headway. It is suggested by the votaries of higher priority for agriculture that India's development programmes and plans have been a failure because more resources have been pumped into industry, specially heavy industry, during the planning era and agriculture has been starved of funds and investment. It is argued that this resource allocation pattern should change and agriculture should have higher share in total financial outlays in development plans. It is, however, a distortion of reality to say, since after the launching of the new agricultural strategy in the mid-sixties, that agricultural development has suffered on account of greater priority for industry in the economic development process. The resource stringency has, on the contrary, been a far bigger constraint on industrial investment. The worst hit, of course, has been the social services sector. So far as the agricultural sector is concerned, the diversion of resources in favour of commercial farming has been considerable and impressive.

Rich Farmers Benefit Most: It is not at all enlightening to examine the allocation of resources in terms only of the budgetary allocations in the plans. There have been crash programmes for agricultural production outside the framework of the plans with their accent on additional non-Plan allocations.

Though the commercial banks have been oriented towards providing working capital needs of industry, agriculture began to claim a sizeable share in bank credit also. But the most important change has been a shift in the terms of trade in favour of agricultural sector through the policy of "incentive" procurement prices, especially of food grains. The huge income derived by surplus farmers on this account have been supplemented during the years of comparative shortages by black market prices extracted by the rich farmers in collusion with traders. The higher incomes originating in the agricultural sector have, moreover, been tax-free. The surplus farmers have been getting, in addition to subsidized supplies of various inputs, like irrigation, power and fertilizers.

The huge public investment in irrigation, power and fertilizers, therefore, does not give returns and has been showing big losses so that resources for additional investment on infrastructural facilities for the development of the agricultural as well as the industrial sector has had to be drawn from other than those who benefit from these subsidies.

Industry—Need for Growth at Faster Pace: It is indiputable, opf course, that strains in the economy cannot be relieved unlwss indian agriculture is able to produce adequate surpluses. The question, however, is whether it is at all possible to achieve this objective merely by budgetary allocation at the cost of further decay in social services and stagnation in industrial investment. The fact is that any scheme for the development of agriculture and uplift of the rural economy qas a whole cannot become viable and will not be possible to sustain unless industry and more specifically heavy industry grows at a rate faster than that of other segments of the economy,l including agriculture. This is borne out by elaborate input—output calculations and exercises in material balances and linkages that are involved in the growth process.

It was in the very initial stages of framing an economic development strategy in India that he question of the relative weight and pace of the development of heavy industry in relation to wage goods production, especially in the agricultural sector, was closely examined.

A galaxy of internationally renowed economists who assisted aIndian planners in drawing up the I and the II Five Year Plans during the fifties was unamious that heavy industry would have to be developed at a rate taster than the overall rate of development of the national economy. By simple calcuations with respect to material balances in a developing Indian economy, it was established that the desired rates of agricultural output and consumer goods production would require import of machinery and equipment on a scale which would be difficult to finance. The development of an indigenous heavy industry to meet this requirements was, therefore forced by the course of development of the Indian economy in the last three decades, particularly in respect of developments in the agricultural sector.

It may be noted that a high growth of even more than seven per cent can be achieved in India if the economy is geared up only in those sectors where production efforts are selectively concentrated to enhance goods and services mainly required by the top expenditure classes.

In such a case, even heavy taxation and substantial rise in price level could be absorbed by the consumers. However, the Indian economy cannot take such a step. A sustained growth of the economy has to give balanced attention to all the sections of society and particularly to the weaker and vulnerable groups of the people. So long the people were told that the poverty figures of India were declining at a fast rate. The way the statistical jugglery was used by the earlier Planning Commission and the earlier government to present a picture of fast declining poverty with the figures of the people below the poverty line coming down from 35 per cent in the 1980s to just 19 per cent in the mid 1990s, there should not have been poverty concentration in the country by now. Surprisingly, however, the present Planning Commission has rediscovered poverty and finds that the people living below the poverty line comprise almost half the population.

The modified version of the methodology for measuring poverty was suggested by the expert group of Lakdawall Committee as far back as in 1992 to unveil the ground reality. Poverty line is fixed at Rs. 264 for rural areas at 1992-93 prices. According to the new estimate, the number of people below the poverty line at the moment would not be less than 45 per cent of the total population.

It is important here to note that while the earlier method put the poverty rate at 29.9 per cent in 1987-88 and 203 per cent in 1992-93, the new method shows the figure at 39 per cent in both these years. What it means is that the liberalization and new economic reforms have not led to any improvement in the life-style of the masses.

If we go by the UNDP's Human Development Report and its "Capability Poverty Measure" which are put together by the National Council of Applied Economic Research, we also get the impression that the proportion of population who may be defined as poor on the basis of capability poverty measure would now be as high as 45 to 50 per cent of the population.

Thus, the fact remains that after half a century of freedom from colonial rule during which the net national product at factor cost of 1980-91 prices increased by 493 per cent from Rs. 40.454 crore in 1950-51 to more than 240,000 crore in 1955-56 and the real per capital income rose by 128 per cent from Rs. 1,127 in 1950-51 to Rs. 2,573 in 1995-96, almost half the population of the country still lives in poverty. What it indicates is that a total of 493 per cent growth during the decades of planning has remained incapable of reducing the gap between poverty and prosperity by any significant measure.

The benefit has mostly been eaten up by the high growth rate of population and the little improvement in real per capital income that could be achieved has made the rich section richer more than they have made the poor well off.

The confusion relating to earlier poverty figures centered round the limited definition under which the government did not take into account the components of poverty like morbidity, health status of people, education and skill-levels, frustration of the unemployed, etc.

The poverty ratio was defined purely in terms of

food intake while assuming the much needed education, health services and employment opportunities to be provided by government. Hence, the growth rate envisaged in the Ninth Plan draft must be qualified with an in-built mechanism structured to remove the earlier defects. Needless to say, the mechanism to deal with these shortcomings is to pursue economic policies that could promote a high labour-intensive growth with the combination of redistributive justice under high income generation and public investment in social infrastructure. Agrarian economy needs a thorough shake-up in the direction of redistributive justice since the gap between poverty and prosperity in the sector has gradually assumed a large dimension due to the wrong policy of discriminatory treatment in favour of the rich farmers. This is perhaps the key to a dent in rural poverty.

As the "Human Development Report" of UNDP, 1996 emphasizes, "it requires a combination of government and private sector initiatives to turn economic growth into human development. And investment in health and education along with growth-oriented redistributive economic policies could generate a 'virtuous cycle' of growth and development. "

An area of priority in the Ninth Plan is to improve project implementation and delivery mechanisms and to ensure that the intended benefits actually reach the people. Further, several social sector programmes are formulated without addressing the isssue of sustainability of benefits and most programmes run with ever-increasing government budgets and thus pre—empt resources which could find better alternative uses. The Ninth Plan must introduce necessary correctives to reverse many of the unsustainable trends in the implementation of poverty alleviation programmes. Just allotting higher outlay for rural development will mean nothing unless a major streamlining takes palce in the implementation and delivery systems.

The existion schemes whose delivery costs are disproportionately high or which fail to make the desired impact should be considered for reorientation and discontinuation.

It is necessary to shelve such schemes whose delivery cost exceeds, say 15 to 20 oer cent of the total cost of operating the programme. Monitoring and evaluation of programmes have to be made equally effective and purposeful. Therefore, the Centre, States and the grass roots level organizations/institutions would need to be involved to ensure the effectiveness of the system. It is encouraging that the Planning Commission would bring out compendium of evaluation studies and give wider publicity of the findings of research studies conducted and sponsored by it. This would be helpful for a meaningful public debate on issues involved.

An overall increase in the level of real wages of the unorgainzed workers will also help empowering them to be able to secure maximum advantage from the other developmental programmes of the government. The very concepts of democratic decentralozation and empowerment of the people imply a steady reducation in the paternalistic role of the State and increased emphasis on empowerment of the people themselves. It is hoped that during the Ninth Plan there will be much more attention on bringing about awareness among the unorganized workers as also on providing effective redressal mechanisms to enforce their rights.

The approach document of the Plan rightly observes that one of the most important weaknesses of the Indian social sector programmes has been is inabiligy to inform the target benefiviaries about the schemes that are available and to which they have a rightful clain. The Ninth Plan will, hopefully, stress the creation and deployment of an effective information dissemination system,and the necessary redressal mechanism for making the demands effective.

Finally, of course, there is no unique way to describe an ideal gorwth process. It can be hoped that the Ninth Plan will lay down foundations for a more progressive process of planning than has been the case so far. Growth involves a dynamic interaction of linked changes. The economic endocrine gland has to be clear as to how much other matters mingt have advanced. As such, it can also be argued that little attention is required to any particular rate of economic growth so long as it is positive.

Wouldn't it then make little sense to worry whether a baby will end up five or six feet tall when the real anxiety should be whether the baby can be safely brought through the problems of infancy, childhood and adolescence? The slower rate of growth, once under way, can pick-up speed and, of course, can slow down too. But the higher growth rate has the prospect of slowing down only. It is desirable to have a steady growth as it has more possibility of ending up with the fastest rate of growth of the economy just as the movement on a highway gives to the motorest the highest speed. The crux of planning is to find the turnpike and reach it. Also gorwth is no longer the guarantor of trickle down effects. To what extent these plan promises are taken care of in the Ninth Plan, can be anybody's guess.

The philosphy and practice of the policy of market-friendly liberalization, privatization and globalization has a logic of its own for planners and policy-markers. With profit maximization motive, to which private enterprise,

Indian and foreign responds rather than economic and social priorities which are of crucial importance in the process of planned development, there is bound to be a shift in the content and direction of the economic growth process.

Without the step-by-step removal of policy and administrative constraints on the play of market forces and pull of effective demand on the economy, investment flows, production structure and incomedistribution cannot conform to an order of meaningful and equitable socio-economic priorities. Any attempt to obfuscate this truth is a deception. The play of market forces cannot, of course, be denied. But the market mu;st be regulated to ubserve planned economic and social priorities.

The issue at stake in this context is the prime responsibility and obligation of the democratic State not only to direct healthy activity for economic growth and social development in all sectors, public private and co-operative, but also mobilize adequate resources, material, human and financial, for public investment.

There were defaults and lags in the planning process and the implementation of the polans inthe process under way for the last five years, the development role of Indian State is being attempted to be extinguished even as the content and direction of India's socio-economic development is increasingly determined and supervised by private terests, Indian and foreign, and the Indian State is asked and obliged to provide law and order and security to the vested interests entrenched in the socio-economic structure. The approach to the Ninth Plan as delineated by the Planning Commission and endorsed by the National Development Council has only made a laborious excercise to give a gloss of populism to amarket-driven growth path which is not amenable to authentic planning to subserve the needs and aspirations of themass of the people.

Hiding the facts: The shift to non-planning actually started, though rather gingerly, before the market-oriented policies overwhelmed real and meaningful planning. The charade of planning is still, however, kept up by the ruling elite for political-populist considerations. The planners are being used to give respectability to populist promises and gestures. The approach document on the Ninth Plan is, therefore, full of rhetoric on agricultural growth, productive employment, poverty eradication and self-reliance to hide the fact that economic policies being pursued by the government of the day are promoting growth objectives which far from helping the poor and the vulnerable mass of the people and give added strength to the claims and demands of the rich and powerful in society.

The high growth rate of seven per cent per annum with low domestic savings, drastic reduction in public investment and boost for private enterprise not only in organized industry and services sector but also agriculture is directly linked to a strategy in favour of giving commanding heights of the economy to foreign investors, especially multinational corporations and their collaborators among Indian big business. The ongoing structural adjustment programme for the economy launched in 1991 and the Common Minimum Programme (CMP) of the United Front government cannot really provide a sound basis for development planning. The CMP, after all, is a compromise between disparate political and ideological entities, a hotch—potch of contrary objectives and contradictory policies which do not add up and provide a basis for an integrated view and coherent strategy for meaningful development planning.

It is a bundle of preference of conflicting interests, economic, social and political which have only temporarily combined to run a coalition government.

Already, the differences in the interpretation and priorities of CMP have surfaced and look like becoming sharper and sharper.

The vested interests, Indian and foreign, in positions of vantage in the economy, society and polity, on their part, are eager to partake of the joys of "indicative planning" such as it has now become, to further stengthen their position. It is wrong really to make light of planning based supposedly on a division of labour as between public investment and private enterprise in socio-economic development process.

It is a grand deception to talk of reduction in poverty, increase of employment through agricultural growth and labour-intensive industry, vast expansion of the social infrastructure of education, health, and mass welfare when, side by side, private enterprise is relied upon to take care of investment for high profit-yielding production and distribution of goods and services to satisfy "effective" demand in the market. The Ninth Plan targets and projections, have, therefore, tended to be financial assumptions.

The challenges

The life and vitality of human beings depend crucially on certain vitamins and minerals that help in the efficient functioning of the brain, immune system, reproduction and energy metabolism. The body needs only small amounts of these nutrients, but it cannot synthesize them. They must be provided through diet. Deficiencies of even the small amounts required cause learning disabilities, impair work capacity and bring illness and death.

Micronutrient malnutrition (silent hunger) is most devastating for pre—school children and pregnant women but is also debilitating for all ages. And it is debilitating the national economy as well. The most important and well studied micro-nutrient deficiencies are vitamin A, Iodine and Iron. Virtually every developing country has deficiencies in the micro nutrients large enough to constitute a public health problem. Many developing countries have multiple deficiencies. Taken together micronutrient deficiencies affect a far greater number of people in the world than Protein-Energy malnutrition. 1.6 billion people live in areas where soils lack sufficient iodine, 655 million suffer from goitre, 26 million have had brain damage and 5.7 million cretinism.

Two billion pre-school children suffer from iron deficinet anaemia. 254 million pre-school children are affected by subclinical, severe and moderate deficiencies of Vitamin A.

In India, 167 millions are exposed to the risk of Iodine deficiency of which 54 million have goitre. Surveys conducted by DGHS indicate that 186 districts are IDD endemic area with goitre rates over 10 per cent. As regards Iron deficiency anaemia, multicentre study conducted by ICMR reveal that 87.5 per cent were anaemic. Deficiency of Vitamin A has long been known to be the largest preventable cause of blindness.

The main intervention strategies against micronutrient malnutrition are:

- Diet supplementation of vulnerable population.
- Dietary improvements.
- Fortification of common foods.

The richest sources of micronutrients are green leafy vegetable and fruits. India is rich in vegetable crops, some of which have good carotene content. Future programmes with respect to horticultural products must be directed towards identifying and propagating high micro-nutrient concentration varieties. People know when they are hungry but they have no natural hunger for vitamin. A, Iron, Iodine and other micronutrients. They do not know they need them and they often do not know what foods provide them.

Deficiency in soil nutrients reflect in the plants grown in the soil. One—half of all soils in all developing countries are deficient or low in available micronutrients. Soil depletion of S, Fe, Mn, Zn and Cu are due to intensive and indiscriminate irrigation and heavy use of high analysis chemical fertilisers. This gets reflected in the plants grown in these soils. Hence, in the national soil health care programme, we should ensure that both the macro-and micro-nutrient needs of soils are addressed.

The term Green Revolution was coined by Dr. William Gadd of USA in 1968, when our farmers brought about a quantum jump in wheat production by taking to semi-dwarf, non-lodging varieties with great enthusiasm and when similar progress appeared feasible in rice. Punjab took the lead because of the scientific and educational backstopping given by the Punjab Agricultural University on the one hand and on the other, by the presence of the essential pre-requisites for progress such as land consolidation and leveling, rural communication, rural electrification and above all, owner cultivation.

Twenty eight years after the term "Green Revolution" was coined, we are in a position to draw a balance sheet and chalk out a strategy for the future. Apart from erasing the "begging bowl" image of India, the most important gain has been the saving of forests and land, thanks to the productivity improvement associated with high yielding varieties. This year, Indian farmers harvested over 60 million tonnes of wheat, as compared to 6 million tonnes at the time of our Independence in 1947. Punjab farmers have raised the average yield of wheat to over 40 quintals per hectare. Likewise, Tamil Nadu farmers have raised the average yield of rice to over 50 quintals per hectare.

If the yield improvement associated with the Green Revolution in wheat and rice had not taken place, we will need another 70 million hectares to produce the wheat and rice we now harvest. Thus, the productivity inmprovement associated with the Green Revolution is best described as forest and land saving agriculture. The productivity improvement has taken place not only in wheat and rice but also in relation to milk and eggs. Only in the case of pulses, we are lagging behind.

The population of India is growing at a rate of 1.8 per cent per year. If this trend continues, our population will double itself in less than 40 years. Only Kerala, Tamil Nadu, Goa and Mizoram have so far achieved a demographic transition to low birth and death rates. Besides population increase, improved purchasing power among the poor will enhance the demand for food, since undernutrition and poverty go together. In contrast, per capita availability of arable land is shrinking. Water efficiency is still on the whole low and water disputes are growing.

In addition to the gradual decline in per capita availability of land and water, various forms of biotic and abiotic stresses are spreading. There is still a widespread mismatch between production and post-harvest technologies. In perishable commotities like fruits, vegetables, flowers, meat and other animal products, this mismatch is often severe, affecting the inyterests of both producers and consumers. This is why foreign experts frequently refer to the setting in of a fatigue of the Green Revolution. Lester Brown and Hal Kane in their book "Full House" released last year predict that at the current rate of population growth and environmental degradation coupled with an improvement in the consumption capacity of the poor, India will have to import annually over 40 million tonnes of food grains by the year 2030. This is four times the quantity we imported in 1966 i.e. before the onset of the Green Revolution.

We should examine this issue seriously and should not allow complacency overtake the farm sector, just because we now have over 30 million tonnes of food grains available with Government.

Industrial countries are responsible for much of the global environmental problems such as potential changes in temperature, precipitation, sea level and incidence of ultraviolet-B radiation. While further agricultural intensification in industrialised countries will be ecologically disastrous, the failure to achieve agricultural intensification and diversification in developing countries where farming provides most of the jobs will be socially disastrous.

This is because, agriculture including crop and animal husbandary, forestry and agro-forestry, fisheries and agro-industries provides livelihood to over 70 per cent of our population. The smaller the farm, the greater is the need for higher marketable surplus for increasing income. Eleven million new livelihoods will have to be created every year in India and these have to come largely from the farm and rural industries sectors. Importing food and other agricultural commodities will hence have the same impact as importing unemployment. Thus, what we need now is an environmentally sustainable and socially equitable green revolution or what may be termed as ever-green revolution.

Those who advocate going back to the old methods of farming ignore the fact that just a century ago when the population of undivided India was 281 million, famines claimed 30 million lives between 1870 and 1900.

The famine eradication strategy of India comprising the following steps is perhaps the most important achievement of independent India:

- Enhanced production and productivity.
- Better distribution through the public distribution system.
- Adequate grain reserves.
- Purchasing power enhancement through various employment generation and guarantee schemes.
- Special intervention programmes for children, pregnant and nursing mothers and old and infirm persons.

While famines have been prevented, widespread under-nutrition prevails among the economically underprivileged. Since non-food factors like health care, environmental hygiene and literacy play an important role in promoting sustainable food security of the level of the individual, we should redefine security.

Steps for achieveing sustainable food security are as under:

First sustained physical access to food will involve a transition from chemical and machnery intensive to ecological farming technologies.

Second, the emphasis on economic access underlines the need for promoting sustainable livelihoods through multiple income-earning opportunities.

Third, environmental access involves on the one hand attention to soil health care, water harvesting management and the conservation of forest and biodiversity, and on the other to sanitation, environment hygiene, primary health care and primary education.

If the political vision to implement this mission is forthcoming, population stabilisation can be more readily achieved. The prediction of Margins de Condorcet made in 1975 that population will stabilise itself, if children are born for happiness and not just for existence, will then come true.

The emphasis on the individual is important, since the household is not often a homogenous unit. Women and girl children tend to suffer more from under-nutrition than men and boys. UNDP's 1995 Human Development Report contains distressing data on the growing feminisation of poverty. To give operational content to such a concept of food security, we should initiate a Hunger-Free Area Programme (HFAP) consisting of the following components:

- Ensuring sustainable availability of food production over population growth through the development and dissemination of ecotechnologies, supported by appropriate packages of services and public policies. Ecotechnology involves the blending of the ecological prudence and technologies of the past, with the best in frontier technologies, particularly biotechnology, information technology, space technology, renewablre energy technology and management technology. Without ecotechnological empowerment, farm men and women will not be able to produce more food and other agricultural commodities on an environmentally sustainable basis from less land, water and energy resources.
- Sustain the productivity of the natural resource base, by conserving and improving the ecological foundations essential for continuous advances in crop and animal productivity.

— Ensure adequacy of household incomes through promotional social security, such as accessing assets, employment and organisational and marketing empowerment. Agricultural programmes should concurrently aim at more food, more jobs and more income. Integrated attention to farm and non-farm employment and value-addition to primary agricultural commodities will be necessary to enhance income and rural livelihood security.

— Provide entitlement to food through protective social security measures to the vulnerable groups, such as employment guarantee and food for nutrition programmes.

— Introduce a National Food and Livelihood Security Act for the purpose of paying integrated attention to:

- Conservation of lands, water, forests, biodiversity and the protection of the atmosphere.
- Enchancing productivity through ecotechnologies.
- Improving distribution in order to eliminate endemic hunger.
- Maintenance of adequate food security reserves.
- Strengthneing the techno-infrastructure for better post-harvest technology and expanding the coverage of sanitary and phytosanitary measures, and
- Efficient research, education, extension, marketing systems both to take full advantage of emerging opportunities in international trade and to ensure that research and extension designed to promote public good receive adequate support.

In 1993-94, the Planning Commission stated that only 18.96 per cent of the Indian people were below the poverty line. Now we are told that it is 40 per cent. A couple of shocking statistics, recently released by the National Council of Applied Economic Research (NCAER) provide a horrifying picture of where we are.

The first figure is that 39 per cent of India's population of nearly one billion remain under the poverty line, a number that has not changed in a decade. In real terms, this means a very large number of Indians have an earning capacity of a couple of chapatis. According to another survey by the NCAER, 37 per cent lof the country's rural population are landless and therefore unable to grow their own crop to put off hunger.

The second figure, less publicised but avilable from international agencies, is that food grains production is 1991 million tonnes in 1994-95 to 185 million tonnes in 1995-96 and in the case of wheat from 65.5 million tonnes to 62.6 million tonnes in same period. Unsurprisingly the worst shortfalls are in the politically volatile States of Uttar Pradesh and Bihar and yet the naked face of hunger continues to be maskedby the hypocrisy that India is a food grain exporter.

Apart from the rising poulation, agro-economists put forward a number of reasons for fall in food grain production, among them soil exhaustion and the larger number of landless that are concentrated in the States of UP, Bihar and eastern India. What they don't spell out is the endemic political instability and coruption these States, and the interminable cycle of fodder scams and caste wars, that are pushing the poor deeper into the poverty trap.

Economic reports do not point out that the agricultural ministry for many years has been managed by ministers, who only represent the narrow interests of wealthy landed farmers like themselves, and have no truck with the poor landless peasants.

The Ninth Plan will be an heir to the same hypocrisy despite agriculture being put on the top by all then nine objectives of the Plan.

Population time bomb: J. Gaur, a retired officer of Rajasthan government has a telling story about his visit to one of the villages of Dungarpur district. He was shocked to know from one of the poor schoolboys that he was served the family had ten members. This speaks volumes about our rural development and family planning programmes. The population clock outside the Capital's (Delhi) All-India Institute of Medical Sciences is galloping ahead but, for India's shoddy family planning programme, time has stood still.

The latest census data is proof, if any were needed, that we are sitting on a population time bomb. By 2040, India will be the world's most populous nation. In a situation where over 18 million—or six Singapores—are being added to the population every year, it can be of little comfort to learn that curde birth rates have declined from 34.7 per cent in 1991 or indeed that fertility levels have shown a negligible decrease of two per cent in that period. If the population has to stabilize at even a staggering 100 crore by 2001-2005, the average birth rate has to be reduced to two children per woman. But so far, only Kerala and Tamil Nadu have achieved this with Madhya Pradesh stated to do so only after 2060, Rajasthan by 2048, Bihar by 2039 and Uttar Pradesh by 2100. The government has confined itself to making tall claims about running a family planning campaign which is so "people oriented" that all targets have been removed.

The truth is that it is Central run and almost totally dependent on female sterilisation ignoring the variety of options which are available.

The desired goal of population as mentioned as one

of the objectives of the Ninth Plan could be achieved only through the willing co-operation of the population and specially of the rural people. The magic words are 'literacy' and 'healthcare'.

There is no "political will" as is evident from the fact that no political party has cared to emphasize the need for some concrete steps to restrict population growth in their election manifestoes. There is no mention of family planning even in the Common Minimum Programme of the United Front government.

Education : It should be a matter of deep concern for every thinking Indian that after 45 years of the so-called planning, the country does not have a comprehensive education policy. This is despite the constitutional objective to provite universal primary education and eradication of funding, enormous sums have been wasted on subsidies and populist schemes from which money is easily diverted into the pockets of corrupt politicians and officials. Even in education, priorities have been misplaced. While primary and vocational education, which would improve the skills of the work force, have been neglected, money has been spent on creating an army of inadequately unemployable at various levels. The crying need of the hour is not elaborate plans but the 'political will' to act and innovate.

Development—real criteria : The late S.K. Dey, a Minister of State in Nehru's Cabinet once visited Tamil Nadu. He met the late Kumarappa at Gandhi Niketan and with some pride of achievenment he claimed that the Community Development Programe was a grand success. Kumarappa was sharp to retort : "What is your scale for measuring the success of your projects? S.K. Dey answered by giving elaborate statistics of the miles of roads constructed, number of wells dug, school-buildings built, dispensaries opened, fertilizers distributed, improved seeds introduced, the manure pits constructed, and all the usual figures. Kumarappa looked doubtfully at S.K. Dey and said in a derisive voice, "this is your scale" and laughed. Pricked by Kumarappa's remarks, Dey asked, "what then is your scale of success?"

Kumarappa in a very emphatic tone said: "Mr Dey, before I cover an area with the Community Development Programme, I would select some six poor persons, count their ribs and if after three years (or five years) of implementing the C.D. Programme, there is some flesh to cover these ribs, thn I will call it a success". Dey was dismayed and implicitly accepted that his approach was defective. Kumarappa continued to say thay S.K. Dey was "trying to throw a silk shirt on a hungry person". The essentials of development are brought out in this one sentence. In other words, villages have developed and not the villagers.

Rich vocabulary : Kalia a poor villager at the time of India's Independence thought, he was poor. He was told he was not poor but needy. Then as to be called needy was self-defeating, he was addressed as deprived which was again changed to underprivileged. This term was also later changed to disadvantaged. Kalia said : "I have no dime or rupee yet but a rich vocabulary". He further said : "I have no idea of Five Year Plan". He was about 20 years of age at the time of India's Independence. Now he is about 70 years of age. In the last two-and -a-half decades, he was not able to eat chapatis with pulses. His earnings are so meagre that he is unable to afford prices to buy pulses for his family consisting of six members.

Against the per capita net availability of 501.9 gms of cereals the estimated consumption of cereals was of the order of 394 gms i.e. 78.6 per cent of the net availability. similarly in the case of pulses, per capita consumption was 28.05 gms. i.e. 75.8 per cent of net availability. Inequality in the consumption of foods among different income groups gets masked in the overall consumption estimates. Among the poor, nearly 80 per cent of consumption expenditure goes for food items. Recent surveys indicate:

- Percapita cereal consumption has declined over the years resulting in the aggregate energy intake of 1859 k.cal per capita as against 2200 k.cal recommended.
- 47.7 per cent of households have calorie inadequacy and 19.8 per cent of households have protein inadequacy. 19.5 per cent of households have both calorie and protein inadequacy.
- The exetent of moderate and severe growth retardation in preschool children varied from 34 per cent in Kerala to 72 per cent in Gujarat.
- 47 per cent of adults have body mass index value below 18.5 indicating large scale prevalance of chronic energy deficiency in the community.
- Haemoglobin levels among pregnant mothers reveal that as many as 87.5 per cent of mothers were anaemic.
- About 30 per cent of infants born had low birth weight.
- 167 million people are considered to be at risk for iodine deficiency disorders and 54 million have goitre.
- Preventable blindness due to Vitamin A deficiency still large.

Looking back the distance travelled and counting on various milestones towards food security, the country can be proud of some of the achievements so far. Yet the final milestone looks to be a long march. Shrinking arable land resources, soil degradation and depletion of nutrients from the soil, poor water management and unsustainable use of ground water, loss of momentum in the growth of food output, inefficient biological utilisation of the nutrients consumed due to poor environment and growing population are some of the problems the country faces in the march towards the final milestone of a hunger-free nation. The over-exploitation of the aquifer is also leading to the leaching of high levels of arsenic from natural underground sources into thousands of village wells in West Bengal. As estimated 200,000 people already have arsenic-induced skin lesions.

It is estimated that there are about 20 million species of poants, out of which 50,000 are edible. However, we are not using more than 200 plants as food, 80 per cent of our food supply however comes only from about eight species.

We are today laying much emphgasis on developing new varieties of these few plants. We should enlarge the food basket by including the excluded. Many nutritious grains fall under the classification "coarse grains". It is time we start referring to them as "nutritious grains" They are rich in micronutrients like Fe and Ca.

Seeing that between 75.0 and 80.0 per cent of the total expenditure at levels a little below the average is spent on food and its preparation, we might briefly examine the nutritional adequacy or otherwise of food at this level. In we show the per capita daily consumption of foodgrains and substitutes at different levels of expenditure.

As is to be expected, the consumption of foodgrains increases as we move from the poorest to the somewhat better. This occurs much more rapidly in rural area than in the urban area. In rural area, the per capita daily cosumption of foodgrains and substitutes reaches 616 grams for households with per capita monthly expenditure of Rs. 13-15 or per capita annual expenditure of Rs. 170.8. Calculating at the rate of 3.3 calories per gram of foodgrains (including substitutes), 616 grams of foodgrains give 2,033 calories per capita per day. As we have seen, this takes up nearly 60.0 per cent of the total consumer expenditure of these households. They spend another about 20.0 per cent on other items of food such as edible oil, ghee and butter, sugar and gur, and a little milk, meat and fish. The quantities of these items are rather small and they yield about 200 calories per capita per day.

Thus the entire food at this level seems to give about 2,250 calories per capita per day. Nutritional experts regard this as adequate under Indian conditions of climate, etc. It means that, in 1960-61, an annual per capita consumer expenditure of Rs. 170 was essential to give a diet adequate at least in respect of calories.

At consumer expenditure below this level, the diet was inadequate even in respect of calories. With reference to the population lying in monthly per capita expenditure classes Rs. 0-8, 8-11, 11-13 and half the population lying in the class Rs. 13-15 had per capita expenditure below this level. These classes add up to 33.123 per cent of the total rural population. Thus, in 1960-61, about one-third of the rural population lived on diets inadequate even in respect of calories.

Global action for sustainable food security

The commitment of the international community to ensure food and nutrition security to every child, woman and man on our planet has been reiterated at several international conferences held during this decade. Some of them are: World Summit for Children, New York (1990); International Conference on Nutrition (ICN, 1992),

Rome; UN Conference on Environment & Development (UNCED, 1992), Rio de Janeiro; World Conference on Human Rights (WCHR, 1993), Vienna ; 1994 International Conference on Population & Development, (1994) Cairo ; UN Conference on Social Development (1995), Copenhangen ; World Food Summit (1996), Rome.

Despite such high level political reaffirmation of the need to achieve speedily the goal of "Food for All", over 800 million human beings now suffer from hunger and malnutrition. Hidden hunger, arising from the deficiency of the essential micronutrients is widespread. Endemic hunger is now more due to the lack of adequate income at the household level than due to the lack of food in the market. Both poverty as well as non-food factors such as environmental hygiene, sanitation and lack of safe drinking water are becoming major contributors of food insecurity at the level of communities and individuals. A majority of the food insecure live in Asia.

There is also increasing concern about the earth's capacity to produce adequate food for the growing population. The increase in human population, now mostly confined to the developing countries, coupled with enhanced purchasing power leading to greater capability to buy food and increasing urbanisation will lead to a higher growth rate in demand for food as well as more diversified food products in the coming millennium.

Thus, on the one hand, there will be need for intensification and diversification of agriculture, particularly in the developing countries, on the other, the ecological foundations essential for sustainable advances in crop and animal productivity are getting eroded. This situation has led to the ringing of alarm bells by experts concerning the earth's capacity to produce adequate food to meet growing needs. Lester

Brown has concluded; "Constraints imposed by the earth's natural systems, the environmental degradation of land and water resources and the diminshing backlog of yield-raising agricultural technologies are slowing the growth in world food production, raising questions about the earth's population carrying capacity.

The earth's capacity to produce enough food to satisfy expanding demand is now emerging as the overriding environmental issue as the world approaches the 21st Century".

The year 1998 will mark the bicentenary of Malthus's essay on population. The onward march of science and technology, supported by appropriate public policies, has so far helped humankind to keep Malthusian forebodings on the population-food supply equation at bay. It is, however, becoming increasingly clear that without concerted national and global action to arrest environmental degradation, promote economic and gender equity and check population growth, the Malthusian spectre may still come true in the next century.

The Food and Agriculture Organisation of the United Nations (FAO) therefore, organised a World Food Summit in Rome from November 13 to 17, 1996.

At this Summit, a Rome Declaration on World Food Security and a World Food Summit Plan of Action were adopted.

The Declaration makes a commitment to reduce the number of undernourished people to half their present level no later than 2015. It also states:

"We will pusue participatory and sustainable food, agriculture, fisheries, forestry and rural development policies and practices in high and low potential areas which are essential to adequate and reliable food supplies"

"We will strive to ensure that food, agricultural trade and overall trade policies are conducive to fostering food security for all through a fair and market-oriented world trade system".

The Plan of Action includes the following seven commitments:

- Create an enabling political, social and economic environment designed to create the best conditions for the eradication of poverty, and for durable peace.
- Implement policies aimed at eradicating poverty and inequality and improving physical and economic access to sufficient, nutritionally adequate and safe food and its effective utilization.
- Pursue participatory and sustainable food, agriculture, fisheries, forestry and rural development policies and practices in high and low potential areas.
- Ensure that food, agricultural trade and overall trade policies are conducive to fostering food security for all.
- Prevent and be prepared for national disasters and man-made emergencies.
- Promote optimal allocation and use of public and private investments to foster human resources, sustianable food agriculture, fisheries and forestry systems, and rural development, in high and low potential areas.
- Implement, monitor and follow-up the Rome Plan of Action at all levels in cooperation with the international community.

The above plan of action integrates the principles of (a) conservation of the ecological foundations essential for sustainable advances in agricultural productivity and production, (b) sustainable production through ecotechnologies and (c) equity in acces to food through an appropriate blend of national and international action in the area of entitlements and employment. The Science Academies Summit held in Madras in July, 96, recommneded that all nations may provide an overall public policy support to action at these three levels through the enactment of a National Food and Livelihood Security Act designed to achieve the following objectives:

- That every individual has the physical, economic, social and enviormental access to balanced diet that includes the necessary macro-and micronutrients, safe drinking water, sanitation, environmental hygiene, primary health care and education so as to lead a healthy and productive life.
- That food originates from efficient and environmentally benign production technologies that conserve and enhance the natural resource base of crops, animal husbandry, forestry, inland and marine fisheries.

The Chief Minister of Tamil Nadu, India in his budget speech delivered on July 17, 1996 made the following announcement.

Feed the people who are hungary Educate the people to uplift the World"

To fulfil this dream of Mahakavi Bharatiyar, this Government will launch a new "Hunger Free Area Programme" with an aim to eradicate poverty induced hunger. A number of schemes are already under implementation to alleviate poverty and to cater to the nutrition requirements of different groups of the population.

Gaps in this coverage will be identified which can then be specifically targeted under the Hunger Free Area programme. Preovision has been made in the Budget for preparing a detailed strategy to implement this programme in association with Dr. M.S. Swaminathan.

Studies at MSSRF have shown that by adding a horizontal dimension to numerous vertically structured programmes and by promoting a coalition of all concerned with ending hunger and deprivation, it is now possible to provide opportunities for a healthy and productive life for all.

The problem of food and nutrition security at the level of the individual has to be viewed in 3 dimensions. First,, inadequate purchasing power leads to calorie-protein under-nutrition. Second, the lack of the needed quantity and variety of micronutrients and vitamins in the diet leads to several nutritional disorders including blingness caused by Vitamin A deficiency.

This kind of problem is referred to as "hidden hunger", a problem which affects today more than 2 billion people in the world. Third, lack of environmental hygiene and sanitation leads to a low biological absorption and retention of food, due to intestinal infection and diarrohea. Thus, both food and non-food factors assume importance in determining the nutrition secu;rity of an individual. Concurrent action at all these levels is necessary in a Hunger-Free Area Programme. The various steps involved in this process are described below:

- Step No. 1: Identify the basic underlying reasons for chronic under and malnutrition.
- Step No. 2: Collate information on available programmes and opportunities for the sustainable end of hunger.

- Step No. 3: Articulate the steps needed to provide the 'missing elements' in achieving the end of hunger.
- Step No. 4: Mobilise local level community action and commiotment for achieving the end of endemic hunger by the end of the Ninth Five Year Plan and enlist mass media support for this purpose.
- Step No.5: Assess the extent of (i) Financial resources required (ii) Technical resources for technological empowerment necessary (iii) Managerial and Organisational resources needed.
- Step No. 6: Foster the organization of a Grassroots level Coalition for Ending Hunger in each HFAP area comprising representatives of

— Elected representatives of the people.

— Government agencies.

— Civil society-non-governmental organizations, voluntary agencies, services organizations like Rotary clubs, Lions clubs, etc.

— Academia-Research, Training Instituitons and Universities.

— Corporate Sector.

— Financial Institutions and

— Mass Media.

The Coalition for Ending Hunger will be responsible for designing, implementing and monitoring the Hunger Free Area programme.

Grasroots level action

The challenge lies in converting HFAP from a concept into an operational programme. In such a programme, emphasis will have to be placed during the remaining years of this century on generating additional livelihood opportunities for those living below the poverty line in villages and towns. The increasing feminisation of poverty demands that priority attention be given to women and girl children. Based on these considerations, the following operational framework is suggested for a National Hunger-Free Area Programme.

This phase will relate tot he analysis of gaps and constraints. Under the Gap Analysis Programme, an inventory will be made of all the entitlements currently available to those living below the poverty line both through the Central and State Government programmes. The inventory will be suitably classified so as to differentiate social security and nutrition intervention programmes from those relating to employment generation.

Once the Entitlements Database is compiled detailed study based on random sampling techniques will be conducted in about 100 villages of a district to assess the extent to which the entitlements have actually reached the intended families. Within families, special studies will be conducted to ascertain the extent of male-female differences in access to entitlements. The gap between what the poor are entitled to and what they are actually receiving will be grouped according to gender and economic status (I.E., those having assets like land or livestock or fish pond or tress and those who do not own any productive asset).

Once the GAP Analysis is completed, a careful identification of the reasons for the gap and the contrainsts faced by the pooring getting their entitlements will be made. Such a gap and constraints analysis will be the starting how direct and imdirect opverty elimination programmes can be made to reach the unreached organisationfunctioning in the villages including under the GAP Analysis would be made together with an assessment of their effectiveness in serving as bridges between Government agencies and the poor. Discussions will be held with both voluntary organizations and men and women members of elected Panchayats and Nagarpalikas on how the gap can be ended and how the delivery systems of poverty in thier efficiency and impact.

This phase will be a strategic planning phase giving particular attention to the following:

(a) Steps needed to fill the gap between entitlements and actual delivery.

(b) Opportunities for mobilising human, financial resources in the concerned areas for improving the efficiency of delilvery of on-going programmes and for initiating new programmes to meet the unmet minimum needs of the population.

(c) Identification of methods of achieving synergy and convergence among all the programmes, whether governmental or non-governmental.

(d) Articulation of new livelihood opportunities based on both farm and non-farm occupations.

(e) Introduction of organisational and management methods which will ensure the oversight and effective participation of the primary stake holders in the implementation of programmes designed to strengthen the security of their livelihoods, and

(f) Identification of young women and men in the concerned villages for forming a Corps of Hunger Fighters. The young hunger fighters would undertake responsibilities such as creating awareness of entitlements, improving delivery systems and promoting environmental hygiene and garbage and sewage recycling.

The hunger fighters would be given a small honorarium for meeting their travel and other expenses and for compensating them for thier time. The members of the Corps of Hunger Fighters will be drawn from those who have a social or economic stake in living in their respective villages. There will be equal number of women and men in such a corps.

As a result of the work done during phases 1 and 2, awareness of the possibilities for ending hunger and deprivation, analaysis of methods of achieving the desired goals and an implementable action plan would have emerged. The Action Programme, to be effective, must emerge from discussions with the poor families and on the basis of their suggestions. The phase will therefore be opportune to establish a broad based local level Coalition for Ending Hunger and Deprivation. Such a Coalition for Ending Hunger could consist of representatives of local self-government institutions, government agencies responsible for fighting poverty and hunger, academic community, the civil society, corporate sector, women's and youth organisations, financial institutions and the mass media. Such a coalition will assign specific tasks to each member of the coalition in the areas of awareness generation, resource mobilisation task implementation, monitoring and evaluation. The Coalition will aim to add a horizontal dimension zto vertically structured government programmes. Coalition members will also help to develop methods of achieving gender equality and eliminating social evils like dowery and alcoholism.

During ths period, HFAP will be converted from a desirable concept to anb implementable local level action plan. Intensive efforts will be made to sensitise all sections of the community to the uncommon opportunities now available for achieving a sustainable end to hunger. The poor themselves will play an active role in both the planning and implementation phase. Many of the members of the grassroots level Corps of Hunger Fighters will come from landless labour families. The Corps of Hunger Fighters will include elected members of Panchayats and Nagarpalikas, so that they are able to serve as links between the elected bodies and the people. There should be a minimum of two members of the corps drawn form every village/town, so that they are able to play a role in improving environmental hygiene and sanitation as well as the health and nutrition secutity of the families living in their village/town.

Ours is a land of the young. Nearly 400 million women and men are below the age of 21. The nation's future depends upon the opportunity they get for a productive and healthy life. Youth can be attracted and retained in farming only if farming becomes and economically rewarding. This is where ecological agriculture, which is knowledge intensive, can prove to be a double advantage.

Our society is characterised by cultural, religious, linguistic and political pluralism. Political pluralism at the level of the central government provides an opportunity for elevating issues relating to hunger elimination and poverty alleviation to a level of overriding priority, transcending political frontiers and placing them at the top of the political agenda.

The world Conservation Strategy has recommended greater public participation in planning and decision-making concerning the use of living resources and proposed environmental education programmes and campaigns to build support for conservation. The Panchayati Raj is institutionalization of public participation in planning and decisison-making in rural India. The following issues can be listed for capacity building in Panchayati Raj for environment protection and improvement.

Through Panchayati raj institutions are not directly linked with the Indian federal system, they are closely related with State governments. Most State government departments, particularly departments of agriculture, education, public health, forests and finance have close functional relationship with PRIs.

The activities of State governments may be broadly analysed as general administration, technical assistance in the fields ofpersonnel, financial assistance, correction of errors, excesses and negligences. State governments provide administrative guidance and advice to PRIs n problems and issues. The 73rd Constitutional Amendment Act 1992 has strengthened the organizational aspects of PRIs. The success or failure of the object of environment protection through PRIs would largely depend on administrative ability, leadership and motivation of personnel. It becomes even more significant because of the fact that administrative capability is an important means of converting programme inputs into outputs with economy and efficiency. The administrative and transforming quality of the leadership would significantly determine the administrative capability of the Panchayati Raj. The administrative capability involves the ability to mobilize, allocate and combine the actions that are needed to achieve the objectives of environment protection.

India is one of the few countries of the Third World which has enshrined in its Constitution a commitment to environment protection and improvement. The environment law ia a new division of law. Even though it appears to be of recent origin and yet it not a sudden creation. Many provisions dealing with the environment are scattered in pieces and found in different enactments.

The Environment (Protection) Act 1986 was enacted with the objectives of protection, regulation of the discharge of environment pollutants; handling of hazardous substances; speedy response in the event of accidents threatening environment safety and health. The World Conservation Strategy has suggested reviewing and strengthening of legislation concerning living resources to ensure that it provides sufficiently for conservation, paying particular attention to enforcement as also to remove loop holes. The lack of proper co-ordination and co-operation among the administrative institutions is an important loophole. A greater degree of co-ordination and co-operation between Central, State and local governments is needed for the implementation of environmental programmes.

The other important weakness of the legislative enactments is its lack of recognition of the crucial role that the PRIs can play. The involvement of PRIs as the eyes and ears of the government in terms of grass roots monitoring of environmental quality, needs to be duly recognized. In due course, as experience is gained, particularly with regard to the respective roles of PRIs, enactment of new legislation for environment protection could be considered.

Though PRIs are not sound in their organization for technical tasks and do not have technical and professional experts, decentralization below the State level ensures technical expertise of a high order required for environment protection and improvement in rural India.

The Ashok Mehta Committee on Panchayati Raj has asserted that technical assistance and organization of a high order is necessary to sustain the momentum. The State governments have the requisite competence in this regard and the decentralization process at the district level is now under way. When the process of administrative decentralization is already taking place, analysis of the changes, and the ensuring emphasis on development point to the need for democratic management or rural development below the State level so that the entire programme can be effectively implemented, co-ordinated and supervised.

The inescapable conclusion is that the first point of decentralization should be at the district level. District heads of sufficient competence are already stationed here. Their capabilities ae also being upgraded. The district is also traditionally a unit of administration to which all are acclimatized. Further, it is the key planning unit for evolving the overall strategy, resource allocation including credit and the delineation of the different types of projects.

The establishement of a strong Panchayat tier at the district level appears to respond both to the organizational needs within district and the demands of emerging links with the State.

Despite the emphasis on the active role to be played by PRls, they were not, much effective in the past. A number of efforts were undertaken to bring forward the Constitution Amendment Bill 1992, to provide constitutional status to Panchayati Raj bodies and to strengthen them by making suitable provisions for this durability, continuity, adequate representation to all the sections of society and financial allocations.

The Act has empowered the State legislatures to authorize the Panchayats to levy, collect, and appropriate suitable local taxes and also provide for making grants-in-aid to the Panchayats from the Consolidated Fund of the State. In addition, a Finance Commission has to be constituted once in every five years to review the financial position of the Panchayats and make suitable recommendations to the State on the distribution of the funds between the State and the local bodies.

The Central Finance Commission shall also suggest measures necessary to augment the Consolidated Fund os a State to suppliment the resources of the PRIs in the State. Thus, a large amount of assured funds will flow to the PRIs involvement in environment protection and improvement.

In rural India, all the life support systems are now under serious stress and strain. Both human and animal population pressures have reached a level where the flora, fauna, soil and water and also atmospheric conditions are getting more and more depleted and pollutted. Consequently, in a predominantly agricultural country, the renewable base of land resources has been eroded and environmental degradation has taken place in the name of development. The Panchayati Raj institutions have existed for long in India, but these institutions have not been effective in environment protection and improvement. Against this backdrop, the 73rd Constitution Amendment Act assumes greater importance. Now it will no more be possible for any State government to fiddle with these institutions, as has been the case in the past. The continuation of these institutions will automatically result into strengthening of both horizontal and vertical linkage with the administration at different levels. This, in turn, will provide these institutions an opportunity to play their legitimater role in environment protection and improvement. Besides this, PRIs can play an educative role in environmental matters for younger generation as well as adults, with due consideration to the underpriviledged. This is essential in order to broaden the basis for an enlightened opinion and responsible conduct by individuals, enterprises and communities in protecting and improving the environment in its full human dimension.

Integrating environemntal considerations into development planning is not an easy task. Unless concern is backed by an ability to take ameliorative action, little can be achieved. India has been very conscious of this and has, over the past few decades, taken important steps to increase its capacity to handle environmental issues.

The initiatives have come equally from the Government, NGO's and individuals. Many collaborative and joint programmes exist today between the Government and the NGO's.

Environment and development problems are complex and there cannot be generalized and simplified solutions. Answers have to be found which are ecologically, economically and socio-culturally consistent in the particular milie. Given the size and diversity of a country like India, this task becomes extremely difficult.

Expertise is requied in framing appropriate policies and legislation, in planning, in creating mechanisms for implementation, in education and public awareness. India also needs to be above to bring its perspective to global forums and participate in evolving international treaties, protocols and conventions. Most importantly, with the increasing emphasis on decentralized decision—making and the stress on micro-planning, this capacity-building is taking on a greater urgency. Capability is required to enable decisions to be made in a decentralized manner—decisions which are not imported solutions, but are appropriate to the particular situation.

Addressing the plenary session of the UN Conference on Human Environment in Stockholm in 1972, Prime Minister Indira Gandhi and said, "Even though our industrial development is in its infancy and at its most difficult stage, we are taking various steps to deal with the incipient environmental imbalances, more so because of our concern for the human species, whic is also imperilled." It was at her initiative that a National Council Environmental Planning and Coordination (NECPC) was set up in 1972 to identify and investigate the problems of preserving or improving the human environment in the country, and to propose solution to environmental problems.

Another Empowered Committee, the Tiwari Committee, was set up in 1980 to review and recommend legislative measures and administrative machinery for ensuring environmental protection. On the recommendation of this Committee, the Department of Environment was set up in 1980 as the focal agency in the administrative structure of the Central Government for planning, promotion and coordination of environmental programmes. This department became part of the new Ministry of Environment and Forest in 1985.

The Ministry is the apex body under the Government of India for planning, promotion and coordination of environmental and forestry programmes. Its activities include conservation and survey of flora and fauna, prevention and control of pollution, afforestation and regeneration of degraded areas, impact assessment, forest conservation and research, and education and information. The National Wastelands Development Board and the Ganga Project Directorate are major components of the Ministry.

Most of the states have also set up their own Departments of Environment, Pollution Control Boards and other associated bodies. Various other ministries and departments, including those of Urban Development, Oceanography, Non-Conventional Energy Sources etc., at the state and central levels, are also concerned with different aspects of the environment. Greater coordination among these various agencies—government and non-government-would strengthen environmental efforts. State Governments are in the process of involving themselves seriously in environmental planning.

The Directory of Environmental NGOs, brought out by the World Wide Fund for Nature - India (WWF-I) in 1989, lists about 850 NGOs working in this field, but there are porbably at least four times this number. Their involvement is clearly seen. As the Secretary General of WWF-I says, "India's impressively large body of NGOs is becoming active on the environmental front because fo the increasingly clear nexus between meaningful, equitable, sustainable economic growth and the conservation of the environment.

For instance, the National Environmental Awareness Campaign promoted by the Ministry has successfully encouraged many NGOs whose primary concerns are rural development, appropriate technology, civil rights, women's development, tribal welfare etc. The interaction between NGOs and State Governments is largely confined to functional matters (clearance, information, advice etc.) whereas for financial and technical support various central departments and agencies have to be relied upon. However now there is a concerted effort by the Government to use their expertise for their own programmes."

NGOs range from clubs which encourage and assist in adventure travel, exploration, and dissemination of knowledge about an ecosystem to agencies which deal with various issues like creating gainful employment, wastelands development, afforestation, rehabilitation of tribals, and with preparation of educational materials and aids. They may be as small as groups of two or three persons, or as large as organizations with an eight-thousand-strong membership.

One of the most important signs of environmental awareness in India is the rise of people's movements which are challenging existing socio-political structures and development models, and are showing alternative paths. These have led not only to action at the grassroot level, but are also helping to shape developmental policies.

If Volunteer Service is as old as manking, its use as a tool in international development is relatively new. Within the United Nations, its importance was first officially recognised in 1961 in a resolution passed by the United Nations Economic and Social Council (ECOSOC).

In 1969 the subject came before ECOSOC again: this time the UN Secretary General was requested to explore the possibility of creating an international volunteer programme. The following year, Secretary General U.Thant, formally recommended that such a programme be launched: and on December 7, 1970 the Un General Assembly passed resolution 2659 (XXV) calling for the creation of the United Nations Volunteer (UNV) programme.

UNV is the world's unique multinational volunteer-sending organisation and has become one of the United Nations' foremost suppliers of middle and upper level specialist—professionals who work with national and international personnel in over a hundred developing countries in Africa, Asia, the Pacific, Central and Latin America, the Caribbean and the Arab States.

The most important objective of the programme, which came into operation in 1971 was to mobilise dedicated, skilled volunteers as an alternative source of technical cooperation, personnel capable of assisting developing countries in achieving these development objectives.

The aim of the programme is also to favour the development of domestic development services and to promote grassroots development activity based on a participatory process. Moreover, its objectives is to undertake operational activities promoting the active involvement of youth in development. Besides, it aimed at providing more people throughout the world with the opportunity to use their dedication and talents for the cause of development in countries other than their own and upon, returning home, to share their enhanced knowledge and experience with others.

The overall responsiblity for UNV was given to the United Nations Development Programme (UNDP). An executive coordinator directs UNV's activities and is responsible for promoting, managing and developing the programme.

UNV works closely with UN agencies involved in development and humanitarian cooperation, such as FAO, ILO, UNESCO, UNHCR, UNICEF, UNIDO, WFP and WHO. In their country of assignment, UNVs work in projects executed by the government by one or other UN agencies, or by the UN itself. In the respective country, UNC specialists and flied workers benefit from the general back stopping of the UNDP Resident Representative. The UNDP field office also provides logistic and administrative support for them, in most cases with the assistance of a UNV Programme officer.

There are more than 2000 qualified, experienced and motivated women and men of over 100 nationalities currently serving in developing countries as volunteer specialists and field workers. A further 6,000 who completed their assignments in UNV are themselves citizens of developing countries; one fifth coming from the industrialized world.

They work in technical, economic and social fields,

under three main headings—in technical cooperation with skills—short governments, with community based initiatives for self—reliance, humanitarian relief and rehabilitation. They are professionals who work on a peer basis. They listen and talk. They encourage and facilitate. They share and exchange ideas, skills and experience. They teach and train. They care.

The UNV programme involves a number of sectors: it maintains a roster covering 115 professional categories. Agriculture, health and education feature prominently, as do social conditions, community development, vocational training, industry, transport and population. Humanitarian relief and rehabilitation count for some 10% of assignments.

Over the years, they have served in more than 130 countries. Tiday, half are at work in Africa, a third in Asia and the Pacific, the remainder are to be found in the Arab States, the Caribbean, Central and South America, and with new programmes in Central and Eastern Europe. Nearly three quarters serve in the world's poorest nations—the least developed, the land locked and the Small Island economies.

Half work outside capital cities, frequently in remote towns and villages. This is in response to expressed needs, and it reflects the commitment which volunteers bring. Included here are the field workers serving at grassroots level within UNV's Participatory Development (or 'DDS'—Domestic Development Service) Programmes in Asia/Pacific and Africa. These are practitioners with excellent track records in village level community animation; they exchange skills and knowledge among countries of these regions.

The great majority of the finance comes from country and regional funds provided by UNDP. Other significant sources include the regular programme budgets of UN agencies, contributions from host governments, special purpose grants by donor governments, and the UNV Special Voluntary Fund. The average annual outlay on a UNV specialist assignment is some 20–25% that of comparable technical personnel working on market terms. Budgeting for field workers is based on local grass roots comparators.

Critical issues

Faith in & Use of Selection Procedure : The massive publicity and tremendous thrust given by the Government coupled with the increasing unemployment among educated youth caused in influx of seminal enthusiastic individuals to take up entrepreneurial career.

Enthusiasm creates a complex problem for the support agencies in the matter of choice of individuals to given necessary support for enterprise launching and management. There is always a danger by supporting those who are not genuinely interest but have been attracted to the support programme for many other reasons. The resources used for developing such persons by way of investment on training etc. often go waste. Besides being wastage of scarce resources, the wrong selection may also contribute to the volume of entrepreneurs facing closure and sickness.

Therefore, there is a need for choosing right type of people to be given support facilities. A three-tier system commonly used for selection purpose includes "the analysis of application blanks"; psychological tests and group planning exercises"; and "personal interview". Presently each of the above areas are given different weightage by different organisation. Also there is variation in selection of psychological tests, games and exercises for selection purposes. The standardising of such selection procedures requisites longitudinal studies spread overt long period of investigations. The administrators generally do not support such longitudinal studies. Since empirical evidences are lacking many organisations avoid conducting selection tests or apply a non-standard procedure as per their convenience (some time which). This erode the quality of EDP and may endanger even its credibility in the long run.

Inadequate Information : Industry specific information play vital role in selecting, designing and deciding the size of units, and market strategy. The inadequate information prevents entry into an Entrepreneurial venture. The lack of information also contribute considerably to the wrong decision resulting into sickness. Often the healthy units also have been reported stagnating format of appropriate information.

Problems are acute and the national organisation set up for collection, storage and dissemination of such informationm may require heavy reinforcement or even decentralisation at lower level. The existing network of industrial information is proving the major hurdle in accelerating the process of entrepreneurship develoment.

Transfer of Technology : Technology is fast changing. What is new technology today is likely to be obsolete in next five years. It is more true in case of the technology adopted by small entrepreneurs in general. With a change in technology, the unit loses its capabilities of competitiveness.

Subsequently, entrepreneurs are continuously worried about the product development in given period of time but their access to latest technology is very poor. Many of them do not have internal R&D and trade totally dependent on the technology/processes developed elsewhere. The urgency, however, is often not appreciated by research staff of technical institutes/

centres of excellence. This is one of the major hurdles in promoting Hi-Tech small industry. Mere physical proximity between researchers and industrialists may not necessarily eliminate the barriers which inhibit the meaning full interaction resulting into development and flow to technology. This issue requires continues attention an innovations in formulating strategy for the development quick flow and transfer of appropriate technology to the small entrepreneurs.

Effective Training : The human factor refers to the attitude, desire and motivation of individual, his capability to perceive the environment change and opportunities as well as his ability to solve the problem which an entrepreneurs is likely to fact.

The training is effective in developing all these aspects of human factor provided it is planned well with balanced emphasis on all aspects. An analysis of the development process that helps emergence of people opting for entrepreneurial career in the society and succeeding in setting and running self-employment activites, reveals that it follow a sequence of development in individual personality, capability and ability.

The first generation of entrepreneur requires to develop:

- Entrepreneurial quality/motivation;
- Capability for enterprise launching/motivation;
- Ability for enterprise management; and
- Sense of responsibility to the society that promote/ support them.

These aspects related to individual behaviour, abilities and capabilities follow the logical sequence of development which ultimately drive prospective entrepreneurs to actual entrepreneurial career.

The training has been the common component of most of entrepreneurial development programmes conducted by various organisations. Of course training conducted by these organisations vary in terms of their duration, content and methodology. Probably depending on the availability of faculty and orientation of the organising agencies, the emphasis shift towards one or the other. Training varies in methodology as well.

Of late, the efforts have been made to standardise such training by evolving 'Model Syllabi' for entrepreneurship development training at national level. But the issue related to standardisation of training in order to achieve the desired result is still alive to ensure the minimum standard.

Management Consultancy : The growth in number of small business is very rapid all over the world. But the percentage of small business unit facing closure or sickness are growing significantly. One of the every 12 units started in US is facing closure every year.

In India, according to the data available with the RBI, the number or sick units during 1982 was as high as 50,549 out of 10,44,405 units claiming 5.6% SSI units becoming sick. The Reserve Bank of India defines a unit as sick if "it has incurred cash loss for one year and in the judgment of the bank is likely to continue to incur such losses for the current year as well as the following year and which has imbalance in its financial structure such as, current ratio of less than 1:1 and worsening debt equity ratio (total outside liabilities to the net worth)".

According to the diagnostic study of a sample conducted by the Development Commissioner (SSI) India, the major causes of sickness are:

- 30% due to shortage of working capital/inadequacy and untimely assistance from the banks.

- 22% due to scarcity of raw-material.
- 13% due to lack of demand.
- 10% due to management deficiencies.

No account has been given for the remaining 25% except for the first case which explains for 30% sickness, the remaining factors can be broadly attributed to the management functions.

Even if certain percentage is assigned to environmental factors, beyond the control of the owner/ manager of small business, considerable percentage of sickness appears to emerge from management inadequacies. Moreover, against the great potential of further growth and graduating small business to medium & large industry, the majority of small business units beyond large are found stagnating with same level of operation.

The dominant factors may be the lack of management insight & competency. The great growth potential demand greater emphasis to devise content and methodology for management education, training and consultancy.

Most of the modern management techniques have been developed for the use of large business establishments. Theoretically and in principle these hold good also to small business management. But their scale of operation and the need of specialist for their application appear to be the major bottleneck in the use of such management techniques in small business management. This suggests testing and adaptation of such management practices.

Capital-A Critical Resource : The small entrepreneurs is up against considerable odds, when he goes out looking for funds either fixed or variable capital financing. This is not because the finances are not available or schemes have not formulated for meeting varieties of need for capital financing. India is probably one of those countries which have multiple schemes launched by various financial institutions under the leadership of IDBI. Although various schemes have been instituted, they are all functioning at a sub-optimal level.

The kind of venture capital support that is needed to nurture and sustain small technologically innovative and dynamic business is perhaps not present in most of the developing countries.

The another hurdle in raising capital financing by small entrepreneurs more often arise out of the comparison with medium and large industries. In a comparison to medium and large industries small entrepreneurs are often very helpess in providing assets and security which on paper, not required but in practices never ignored. Again for the purpose of industrial growth and rehabilitation of sick units the necessary funds should flow fast.

For sustaining entrepreneurship, the capital financing requires that the officials belonging to both industrial extension system and financial institutionms develop comprehensive understanding of health of industrial untis, posses diagnostic skill to assess the health and acquire counselling skill to influence needy SMI to implement remedial growth measures and above all develop favourably attitudes towards extension approach which is basically opposite to the concept of a donor.

Points of Caution : Entrepreneurship Development has been found a forceful movement to fight the acute problem of growing unemployment. When it has been attempted sincerely and systematically, it has yielded very rewarding results. In the past, many mistakes have been committed as a part of 'hit and miss' trial methods. The success is bound to be there provided we formulate strategy by understading the concept, process and techniques of developing entrepreneurship.

One area of caution is also necessary to understand the similarity and distinction between entrepreneurship and self-employment. All entrepreneurs are self-employed but all self-employed are not necessarily entrepreneurs. The tendency to ignore such differences may make the strategy weaker.

A diluted strategy for developing entrepreneurship may result in failure and consequently the task of piece-rate-workers. Both may be necessary and useful at different stages but should be attempted with clear-cut distinctions and omitting the confusion by titling the programme differently.

Middle-class families (middle-income group) seem to be the direct benefitciaries of EDPs. This group is important in terms of both number and influencing public opinions. In the course of developing entrepreneurship, the supply of inputs (including finance) plays a crucial role. Instead of treating such inputs as development requirements, there may be a tendency to use them as a means to earn favour. There may be temptation to politicize the whole movement.

The entrepreneurship movement which started in India, in mid sixties have proved its potential. Now the dynamics and methodology are clear, strategies are more or less standardised. The scope and coverage, however, is so vast and widespread that the movement requires active involvement and enthusiasm of all the government voluntary organisations and social reformer. Through entrepreneurship, it is possible to build new economic order with progressive socio-psychological make-up.

It is evident from the above discussion that the Panchayats have been denied the possibility of carrying out participatory planning for local development at the grass roots level. This vacuum has been filled by the voluntary efforts of the people with the participation of intellectuals and voluntary network organizations like the Kerala Sastra Sahitya Parishad, Bharat Vigyan Samithi. The results of their efforts have been remarkable. In the field of literacy, the "Erankulam model" is acclaimed across the world and replicated elsewhere in India.

The alphabet literacy has provided a sound base for a mass initiative in the field of environment protection, gender equality and women's empowerment. Thus social development in Kerala has been the contribution of an awakened and vigilant public.

Majumdar (1995) rightly observed that "The enlightened and politically conscious electorate in Kerala closely monitors the functioning of schools, including those in the rural areas. Here, cases of shirking on the part of teachers evoke strong collection protest (e.g. many such cases are immediately publicised through posters in public places), and as a corollary, elicit appropriate policy responses.

The expansion of literacy has given a sound base for participatory planning which has successfully been operationalised in Kalliasseri Panchayat in Kannur district of the State.

The Community Development Society (CDS), with its thrift and credit activities, has improved the lot of poor women in urban Kerala. The Alappuzha CDS is an example, where "poor women have mobilized up to Rs. 37 lakh from their own savings. In two years, the Alappuzha CDS has generated more than 4,000 jobs ensuring 100 per cent loan recovery and repayment to banks as on date". Due to this exemplary work, the Alappuzha model has received "We the People Award" in 1994 from the United Nations.

Although Kerala could not provide a successful model for participatory planning through Panchayats due to political instability, its people, with the help of dedicated voluntary organizations have offered one. The other States could benefit from its success stories in participatory planning.

Suggestive Framework

We have seen that Panchayats in Kerala have not become a viable and pulsating institution for ensuring participatory planning. The prime mover in this sphere has been the voluntary sector, But after the 73rd Constitutional Amendment which, among other things, has ensured regular elections to the Panchayats and reservation of seats as well as of posts of Chairpersons for the weaker sections at all the tiers, they have to assume this role. The elections to these institutions were also held last year.

The People's Campaign for the formulation of the Ninth Plan has also been launched in the State for making decentralized Planning the key input in preparing the State Plan. All these efforts on the part of the State government are in the right direction. But the main question is whether the Panchayats have really emerged as institutions of self-government (as envisaged in Article 243 G of the Constitution) to help materialize participatory planning.

As mentioned earlier, the two important dimensions of the people's participation are: who are the people and how would the participation occur. The answer to the first question is given by M.A. Oommen (1991) while discussing the formulation of a methodology for district planning with people's participation in Kannur district where he says, by people we mean those below the poverty line. The poor people, including other marginalized sections of society, have been statutorily given berth in Panchayats. The second question is also answered by constituting the Panchayats in the State.

But the most important question regarding realization of the objective of participatory planning is whether people enjoy autonomy in their actions.

In other words, whether the various provisions of the State Panchayat Act establish Panchayats as an Institution of Self-government (ISG), i.e. whether they have institutional existence, institutional capacity and financial viability. Therefore, the question discussed in this part of the paper is whether the various provisions of the Kerala Panchayat Act enable Panchayats to usher in participatory planning. And if not, what amendments need to be made.

Planning is not only an instrument of economic growth but it is accepted by all that it is an instrument of social integration. Indian society consists of many social groups both in caste, community and ethnic terms. During the national movement it was realized that political mobilization has to be done in the context of the castes and community terms. That is why Gandhi is known as a political fold. Their participation fold. Their participation in the political movement brought their economic and social needs into sharp focus. Any planning has to recognize their needs.

As such, the Indian Donstitution has recognized these social groups. They are socially and economically backward. They do not have access to modern education and social services. Planning as a concept was developed during the national movement. The democratic experiment of India has to take into account the needs of SCs/STs and the OBCs. It is mandatory.

New dimensions

Planning is an integral part of our political culture. Strengthening democracy is possible with planning,. Planning accepts the role of State in the market economy. The role of the State is to reduce the regional disparity. It is to reduce the income disparity between various sections of our society. Liberalization process has restricted the role of the State in the area of industrialization.

The private capital is today strong enough to stand on its own feet. Withdrawing the State from economic activities is a welcome step. But historical experience of the Third World countries show that the first decade of economic liberalization generated lot of economic distress. The approach paper to the Ninth Five Year Plan document has recognized this new development.

First, the regional disparity between poorer regions and richer areas has increased. Regional disparity has created already a lot of political mobilization on ethnic line.

Secondly, investment in agriculture has slowed down during this phase which sustains a majority of our people to earn their livelihood. Even after 50 years of industrialization, our agriculture is not self-sustaining. It needs State intervention for its growth.

The lack of agricultural growth has reduced the employment opportunities that is reflected in the rise of unemployment and underemployment in rural India and which has pushed them to overcrowd the cities. As a result, it has increased urban poverty. Both rural and urban poverty have a close relationship.

Thirdly, urban areas are facing the crisis, in terms of providing drinking water and sanitation where the urban poor are living.

Fourthly, the decade of economic liberalization has increased the number of poor, people below the poverty line. Who are these poor people in the rural areas and urban slums? They are nobody except the people from the SCs/STs and the lower OBCs. These social classes are today the worst victims of the economic process.

The approach paper to the Ninth Plan has looked into the factors explained in the above paragraphs. It demands the reorientation of the State role and definite thrust on the poverty alleviation and employment generation without which the poor are going to distrust the democratic system. Once alienation of these communities from the system starts growing, then the system itself is going to be vulnerable.

The Kerala Panchayat Act is full of provisions which empower the State government to interfere with impunity in the functioning of the Panchayats. These provisions have not created and enabling environment for participatory planning. They are as follows:

- Section 159 (1) of the Act empowers the State to remove the democratically elected Chairperson, and Vice-Chairpersons of the various Standing Committees on certain grounds.
- As per Section 161 (8) of the Act, the copies of the minutes of every meeting of a Panchayat shall be forwarded within 48 hours by the Secretary either to the government or its authorised officer. This is against the spirit of decentralization. What is the rationale for sending these minutes to the State authorities? This may be repealed as it will unnecessarily increase the burden of the secretary's work without any gain.

- Section 188 of the Act empowers the government and its officials to call for any record of Panchayats for verification, audit or examination. Section 190 empowers the government to direct the Panchayats to perform their responsibilities properly. The government can by an order fix a period for the performance of such duties. Similarly, Section 191 empowers the State government to cancel or suspend any resolution adopted by the Panchayat. The State government as per Section 193 can dismiss popularly elected Panchayats if they do not perform their duties properly.
- The Act empowers the State government to make rules and by-laws to carry out all or any purpose of this Act (Section 254). The State government, instead of making rules and bye-laws, may prepare model rules with flexibility which the Panchayats can modify keeping in view their requirements.
- The State government can delegate powers enjoyed by the VP, BP and DP to an authorized officer (Section 275). It means powers given to Panchayats by one hand can be taken back by another. Section 278 militates against Section 156 because as per the former, "executive functions of the President be construed as a reference to the Secretary of the village Panchayat," while as per the latter Section, the Chairperson is the executive head of the Panchayat. Thus Section 278 may have to be repealed.
- As per section 282, disputes between Panchayats will be referred to government officials. This Section should be amended to provide for referring disputes between Panchayats to the next higher tier of Panchayat.

Thus, a number of provisions in the Act are retrograde and reduce Panchayats to an agency of the State government. In order to ensure proper control with adequate safeguards over them, the following suggestions are made.

To establish an organic relation between and among the three tiers of the Panchayat Raj system for participatory planning, the VP should work under the direction of the BP and the BP should work under whose direction the DP. Now the question arises under whose direction the DP should work. Sometimes, due to political reasons, the upper tier of Panchayat may misuse its authority. The following measure is suggested to prevent such misuse.

A body under the chairpersonship of a person, qualified to be a judge of the High Court and comprising the representatives of the VP, BP and as members to be nominated by the government may be constituted. This body may handle all the cases relating to abuse accounts and other issues relating to decentralized governance.

The idea here is that Panchayats should in real sense emerge as an institution of self-government without any threat of political onslaught.

Participatory planning denotes people's involvement from initiation to the completion of the Plan. It is an indivisible concept as it encompasses people's participation in decision-making, implementation of the decision, sharing of the benefits and evaluation and monitoring of the plan. Thus, people's particulation has to be threaded like warp and woof in every stage of planning.

According to the Working Group on District Planning (1984), participatory planning has three dimensions: nature of the participation, participants and the way of participation.

The answers of the first two, i.e. the nature of the participation and who should participate, are based on the dictum "people plan and the government supports". The Panchayats are the institutions through which participation occurs. Thus, the whole concept of participatory planning depends on the extent of the autonomy of the people.

The objectives of the present paper are: (i) to review the role of the Panchayats in Kerala in a historical perspective with a view to examining the extent to which they have succeeded in ensuring people's participation in planning. (ii) to evaluate the role the community and the voluntary sectors have played in creating an environment for participatory planning in the State, and (iii) after critically reviewing the Kerala Panchayat Act, suggest changes in it so that it facilitates people's actions.

While examining the last question, a comparison of the Kerala Act with other State Acts has also been made.

The State of Kerala was formed in November 1956 by merging the Travancore, Cochin and Malabar regions to create a single State. Since its formation, the State has had a chequered history in the sphere of democratic decentralization. In April 1957, the first leftist government led by E.M.S. Namboodiripad was installed in the State. It introduced the Kerala Panchayat and District Council Bills in the Assembly. But these Bills could not become law as the government was dismissed on 31 July, 1959 by the Centre.

The succeeding government headed by Pattom Thanu Pillai, however, succeeded in enacting three Bills, the Kerala Panchayat Raj Act, 1960, the Kerala Municipalities Act, 1961. These Acts not only unified the laws in operation in the Malabar, Travancore and Cochin regions, but also enhanced the functional and financial autonomy of the local government institutions.

In 1964, the Kerala Panchayat Union Council and Zilla Parishad Bills, modelled on the recommendations of the Balwantray Mehta Committee report, were introduced in the State Assembly by the next government. These too could not be enacted due to the fall of the government.

In March 1967, the CPI-M government headed by E.M.S. Namboodiripad again introduced a Bill called the Kerala Panchayati Raj Bill 1967 in the Assembly which envisaged a two-tier system of Panchayati Raj at the village and the district levels and induction of an organic link between the two tiers by putting the Gram Panchayat under the supervision and control of Zilla Panchayat. This Bill was referred to a Select Committee which recommended substantial amendments in it. It enabled the district level institution to function as the district government. But it could also not become law as the State Assembly was dissolved in August 1970.

In 1971, the government headed by C. Achutha Menon came forward with the Karala District Administration Bill the Select Committee set up in 1968 to consider the 1967 Bill. This Bill also could not become law. In August 1978, the A.K. Antony Ministry introduced the Kerala District Administration Bill in the Assembly. But this Bill was passed by the Legislature during the Chief Ministership of the CPI leader P.K. Vasudevan Nair and got the Presidential assent in May 1980 when the office had passed into the hands of the CPI-M leader, E.K. Nayanar, who incidentally holds the reins at present. But this could also not be implemented as the Ministry fell in 1981. The government however, commissioned a study on the shortcomings in the Act. This study was undertaken by a senior IAS officer, V. Ramachandran.

In May 1982, a new government assumed office but

it did not demonstrate the necessary political will to strengthen Panchayati Raj in the State. In 1987, the Left Democratic Front (LDF) government led by E.K. Nayanar again came to power. It implemented, although not fully, the recommendations of the Ramachandran report on the measures to be taken in democratic decentralization at the district and lower levels, which was submitted in July, 1988.

This government also did very little for strengthening Panchayati Raj in the State, because at that time every political party was afraid of decentralization as V. Ramachandran (1995) had observed: "A fear has taken hold in the State that there was voodoo about decentralization in Kerala as every government, overcoming this fear showed political courage and announced elections to the District Councils in December, 1990. For the first time in the history of the State, District, Councils came into being in February 1991.

The provision of reservations for SCs, STs and women made in the Act enabled these marginalized sections of the society participate in the development process. The results of the elections held for the councils revealed that the share of SCs and STs in their total membership was 17 per cent. This was much higher than the ratio of their population in the State. The percentage of the SCs and STs in the total population in the State was 10.02 and 1.02, respectively. The LDF captured 13 out of the total 14 District Councils. The reservation for the marginalized sections of rural society in the District Councils gave them a Panchayat to enable them to participate in the system of decentralized governance and development.

But this welcome process could not be sustained for long as fresh elections to the State Assembly along with the parliamentary election were held in June 1991. In these elections, the LDF government law replaced by the United Democratic Front (UDF) regime led by K. Karunakaran. The first step this government took was to amend the District Administration Act, 1979. The amended Act made provision of appointing a junior officer as Secretary of the Council in place of the Collector who was its ex-officio Secretary under the original Act.

The State government was also empowered to amend, delete or add to the powers and functions devolved to the Councils. In nutshell, the District Council was reduced merely to an agency of the State government.

The village Panchayats (VP) in the State also have a poor track record. It only in 1963 that had their first elections with the second after a long spell of more than one and a half decade in 1979 and the third in 1988. After the expiry of the term of the elected representatives, the government officials have been made their administrators. The latest elections to the Panchayats (i.e. VP, BP, DP) were held last year after an amendment of the State's Panchayat Acts in accordance with the Constitution (73rd Amendment) Act, 1992.

It can be seen that the Panchayats in the State have not yet become vibrant institutions for enabling the people to participate in local development. The factors responsible for this plight of these institutions, among others are the vested interests, i.e. the political leaders and bureaucrats who have not been interested in parting with powers in favour of the Panchayats. The LDF, which wanted to make the Panchayats the fulcrum for participatory planning could not succeed fully as its governments had fallen for one reason or the other. Otherwise, an enlightened and articulate public coupled with land reforms could have made panchayats a sound base for people's involvement in planning.

That is why M.A. Oommen commented that "Kerala is probably on State where people's participation should be strong and successful given the level of literacy. However, the progress made, has been very poor"

Not giving membership to MPs and MLAs in Panchayats, not tampering with the VP and Block Panchayats (BPs) boundaries for the membership of the BPs and the District Panchayat, (DP) respectively and making the Chairpersons of the lower tier members of the immediate upper tier for establishing an organic link among them are welcome features of the State Act, which should also be emulated by other States.

But there are certain features of the Act which need to be amended as they are against the spirit of the Central Act and participatory planning. These are:

- In Chapter II of the Act, reorganization of the boundaries of the wards of Panchayats has been vested in the State government, which is against the provisions of Articles 243 k and 243 O of the Constitution. All functions pertaining to the delimitation of boundaries, including disputes between or among Panchayats, should be performed by the State Election Commission.
- A provision for reservation of OBCs should also be made in the Act to enable them to participate effectively in decentralized governance.
- The election of the Chairperson of the VP should be made direct as is the case in most States. In this way, the Chairperson will be able to draw authority from the people. Besides making Chairpersons accountable to the people, this will also strengthen the institution of the GS.
- To provide more space for weaker sections to participate in planning and development, the

reservation for SCs, STs, OBCs and women should be extended to include the post of Vice-Chairperson of different tiers. At present, Punjab is the only State where such a provision has been made at the intermediate and apex tiers. Kerala may do well to go one step further and provide reservation for these sections at all tiers of the Panchayats.

- As per Section 151 of the Act, if the government is satisfied that a Panchayat at any level cannot be constituted for certain reasons, like failure to elect the majority of the members, it can appoint an Administrative Committee consisting of at least the elected members and a President and Vice-President, or appoint a special officer for period not exceeding six months. This provision is against the spirit of the Constitution. If such an eventuality arises, only the elected representatives should govern the Panchayats for a specified period and not a special officer. Therefore, the provision of a special officer provided in this section should be deleted.

Devolving of adequate and clear-cut functions and powers to the Panchayats is very important for enabling them to function in a free environment.

Let us examine the scope of Kerala Panchayat Raj Act (KPRA) in this regard.

- Under Section 164 (2), a provision has been made for constituting a Ward Committee for each constituency with the purpose of informing the VP on the needs of the constituency. But the GS will also be held at the ward level only, which among others, will list out its needs as is also envisaged as the role of the Ward Committee. The VP may also constitute a vigilance Committee as suggested earlier in this paper. Keeping these provisions in view, constitution of the Ward Committee is dispensable.

- The District panchayats, Block Panchayats and Village Panchayats shall perform their functions under the financial and technical guidance of the State government [Sections 166 (2), 172 (2) 173 (2)]. This is wrong in principle and operationally difficult as it does not put Panchayats on a firm foundation. Through provisions of this nature, the government can meddle with the functioning of the democratically elected institutions and deprive the people of freedom of action which is essential for participatory planing.
- These provisions in the State Act may have to be suitably amended so that the VP takes help from the BP which, in turn, takes help from the DP and the DP from the State government, if it is required. The State may be benefited from the Panchayati Raj Acts of States like Gujarat, Assam, Manipur and Madhaya Pradesh which have enabling provisions for consultation among the three tires without much intervention from the State.
- Functions to be performed by different tiers of Panchayats have been listed in Schedules 3,4 and 5 of the Act. Looking at their distribution among the three tiers, an hour glass picture emerges, because they have been concentrated either at the lowest level or at the apex. This shows that in deciding the distribution, proper thought has not been given. For example, functions relating to education do not figure in the list for the BP, which thus emerges as a weak tier of the PR system and, therefore, does not provide sufficient scope for its members to play a role in participatory planning.

While participating in the Conference of Chief Ministers on basic minimum services 4-5, July, 1996 in Delhi, the Chief Minister of Kerala mentioned that less than one per cent of the total habitations in the State were fully covered as regards the availability of safe drinking water against the national coverage of 57 per cent. Shortage of clean drinking water is an important reason for the high morbidity in the State.

This is one of the basic needs and could be handled effectively at Panchayat level. But very little responsibility to this basic necessity has been devolved to the Panchayats. It is suggested that in order to conserve water resources, construction of check dams in the rivers should be entrusted to the Panchayats. If this function is given lock stock and barrel to the Panchayats, it being a basic requirement, will enthuse the people to participate in water management.

1 In inter-tier allocation of functions, the cardinal principle that what can be undertaken at a particular level should be entrusted to that level alone has been kept in mind. However, ample scope for improving the functional relationship between the three tiers is still there. Significantly, whatever functions have been allocated to the Panchayats in accordance with this principle have been taken away by Section 283, according to which the government may alter, amend or add to any of the entries made in the functions of the Panchayats. Hence this section should be repealed.

- To fully realize economic development and social justice, other functions like police powers and judicial powers should also be given to the Panchayats. Bihar, West Bengal, Punjab and Uttar Pradesh are the States which have given judicial functions to institutions at the grass roots level.

Recently, the Madhya Pradesh State Assembly has also passed a legislation for constituting Gram Nyayalayas to administer justice in rural areas. The Karnataka government also proposes to introduce an amendment to the State's Panchayat Act in the coming session of the Assembly for setting up Nyaya Panchayats.

The Kerala Panchayat Raj Act does not make provision for constituting Nyayalaya at grass roots levels for dispensing justice to the people. It is, therefore, suggested that police and judicial functions should be given to the Panchayats for meaningful decentralization.

Functional autonomy has not been given to the Panchayats, because provisions such as the schemes being contingent on the availability of resources and placing of performance of vital functions under the supervision and guidance of the government have circumscribed the role of participatory planning through the institutions.

For ushering in an era of participatory planning for Panchayats, the State government should amend all the Acts pertaining to the subjects in the XIth Schedule of the Central Act, take out all relevant portions from the existing Subjects Acts and incorporate them in the Panchayat Act through an amendment by the State legislature.

For enabling the people to participate effectively in planning and development of their areas through Panchayats, it is indispensable that these bodies should have their own officials. But this has not been provided for in the Kerala Panchayat Act.

- The secretaries of all the three tiers will be the government employees (Section 179) under the State Act. The power of transferring these employees is also vested in the government or in a prescribed authority if a resolution to that effect has been passed by the Panchayat by a simple majority. However, action on this resolution is not mandatory on the part of the government.

This provision is objectionable, because this does not entail autonomy of the people in their actions. What is the rationale behind insisting on a simple majority for a resolution for transferring an official? It is practised at the State and the Central levels? Hence this provision may have to be repealed.

- The Chairpersons of the Panchayats have been empowered to exercise supervision and control over the officials of the Panchayats and prepare their confidential reports (Section 156 (4) (b). It is a welcome feature of the Act. But provisions in the Kerala Munidipal Act [Section 14 (3) (b)] which say that Chairpersons prepare the confidential report of the Secretary as well as review the confidential reports prepared by the Secretaries in respect of their employees should also be made applicable to the Panchayats.
- An enabling provision for constituting a separate Service or Cadre [Section 179 (3)] has been made in the Act. Other States which have some such provisions are Karnataka [Section 196 (5) and Punjab (Section 26). But the provision in the Kerala Act is not substantial in nature as it has not been clearly specified as has been done in the Gujarat Panchayati Raj Act.

The provision under Section 179 (3) of the KPRA must be operationalized at once so that the Panchayats have their own officers and employees. Kerala may be benefited from Gujarat and Rajasthan Panchayati Raj Acts in which provisions for Panchayat cadre have already been incorporated. Under the Gujarat Panchayati Raj Act, there will be three cadres of Panchayat employees, namely the District cadre, the Taluk cadre and the Local cadre [Section 227 (3)]. For this purpose, a Gujarat Panchayat Service Selection Board shall be constituted. Besides this Board, a District Panchayat Service Selection Committee shall also be constituted at the district-level to recruit the primary education staff (Section 236).

In Rajasthan, a provision for establishing a District Establishment Committee under the chairpersonship of the President of the ZP has been made. This Committee shall make selections for the posts in different grades and categories for the Panchayats, prepare lists of the persons for promotion and deal with disciplinary matters affecting the officers and employee except officers of the State cadre.

Actually, a permanent solution of the cadre problem is to amend the Constitution, because the Panchayats after becoming local government must have their own employees as the State and the Centre have as per part XIV of the Constitution. But to begin with, the State government must invoke immediately the enabling provisions in the Panchayat Act.

The Gram Sabha (GS) is the comer-stone of participatory planning as it establishes direct democracy at the grass roots level, enabling the people to mobilize their collective wisdom for their development.

Thus, it is important to make this body strong and vibrant. But the Kerala Panchayat Raj Act, 1994 does not make it a strong body.

- As per Section 8 of the Act, the GS has been made a discussing and assisting body while it should have been made an approving and sanctioning authority for all programmes and schemes implemented by the VP, as it has been made in the Tamil Nadu and Punjab Acts.

- Meetings of the GS instead of being convened twice (Section 3) in a year, should be held quarterly as has been provided for in the Panchayat Acts of Madhya Pradesh and Bihar. The report of the Study Team on the position of the Gram Sabha in Panchayati Raj Movement (1963) had also recommended that its meetings be held more frequently, i.e. at least once in each quarter.

Moreover, to make sure that the meetings of the GS are held, provisions have been made in the Punjab and Haryana Panchayati Raj Acts that if a Chairperson, without genuine reasons, fails to hold two meetings he/she will automatically cease to function as Chairperson. A similar provision should also be included in the Kerala Act.

- The quorum for the GS (Section) is specified as not less than 50 members, while in most States it is one-tenth of the total number of the voters. However, in Tamil Nadu, the quroum for this body is specified as one-third of the total members. Keeping in view the educational and social development of Kerala where people are politically conscious, even fifty per cent of the total strength of the GS. An adequate representation of women in the quorum for the meeting should also be made mandatory for their effective participation.
- A provision for constituting a Vigilance Committee to oversee the functioning of the VP comprising members who are not members of the latter should be made in the State Act on the pattern of the Panchayati Raj Acts of Bihar, Manipur, Rajasthan and Tripura. In these Committees, adequate representation of SCs/STs and women should also be ensured.

- The presence of the village-level officials in the meetings of the GS is also very important for participatory planning. Therefore, it should also be made mandatory that the Secretary of the VP and officials of the development departments at decentralized level should attend all the meetings of the GS and assist it as has been provided for in the Panchayati Raj Acts of Haryana, Punjab and Rajasthan.
- To further strengthen the GS, the three-decade old suggestions of the Study Team on Gram Sabha in Panchayati Raj movement (1963), like holding the meetings during the period when villagers are not busy in agricultural activities, and organization of entertainment programmes immediately after the meetings, are worthy of consideration to ensure adequate attendance.

The introduction of PRIs was a revolutionary step to wards rural uplift in this country. Almost all the States have constituted Panchayati Raj bodies, with the exception of Bihar, Orissa, Lakshadweep. Pondicherry and the hill districts of Uttar Pradesh. The PRIs will function as effective institutions of local self-government and they would prepare plans for economic development and social justice and implement them. The PRIs will be the umbrella for integration of sectoral programmes.

During the Ninth Plan, CAPART will continue to provide projectized financial assistance to voluntary organizations which will have to play a more dynamic role in empowering the poor through advocacy, awareness generation and formation of self-help groups. Decentralized planning will be made more effective through greater involvement of panchayats as also the voluntary organizations and people's self-managed institutions.

In the preceding pages we have discussed the objectives, strategies and various programmes which have been given priority in the approach to Ninth Five Year Plan.

We all know that Rs. 30,000 crore had been earmarked for rural development in the Eighth Five Year Plan, even then we have not been able to achieve the desired success and the plan period is nearing completion. It has been proposed to spend RS. 90,000 crore on rural development during the Ninth Plan. But even then we cannot be sure that the whole objective and approach to the proposed plan will be moving smoothly and we shall be able to achieve our goals.

In this connection, it may be added that our policies in the past had hardly been in question so far as development objectives are concerned. At the implementation level there existed many bottlenecks which came in the way of proper implementation of the programme and achieving the real targets.

The co-ordination problem had been so much chronic and the gap between plan formulation and its implementation so vast that we failed to achieve our goals. No doubt, the approach paper to the Ninth Five Year Plan makes a laudable attempt but the question still remains the same. Now we have effective Panchayati Raj system in our country and it is hoped that they will be capable of meeting the challenges at the implementation stage. But the question is whether the bureaucracy and State-level politicians will actually allow these institutions to take up the challenging task?

While concluding we may say that if there is real political will to achieve the objectives of approach to the Ninth Plan and the Panchayati Raj institutions are given real powers to implement, the objectives could really be achieved. However, keeping in view the hung nature of our Parliament and survival of the government on within and outside support by various political parties, it is still doubtful whether we will be able to achieve the objectives.

A very pessimistic view suggests that it would be beyond the comprehension of the government. But an optimist student of rural development, may take a brighter view of the picture and hope that if not 100 per cent, at least 50 per cent of the objectives will be achieved.

Performance: In order to have more national generalisation, the past performance can be reviewed separately for two categories, i.e., (i) those efforts related to income generation and self-employment and (ii) others related to self-employment-cum-entrepreneurship category.

The first category covers the programmes/schemes under KVIC, TRYSEM, SEEUY and some other institutions exclusively devoted for self-employment. During 1985-86, KVIC, provided employment opportunities to 39.8 lakh persons whose earning amounted to Rs. 349.53 crores. In the total employment under KVIC Programme the share of SC/ST was about 29% and women's participation about 46%. Under TRYSEM Scheme 200,650 youths were to be trained during 1985-86. Out of this, 56,500 youth were trained and 41.845 were reported taking up self-employment.

The second category by and large, refers to SSI entrepreneurs. Under Indian context the two strategies, i.e., developing entrepreneurship and small industries are interwoven. Between 1973-74 and 1986-87, the number SSIs increased by over three folds generation by about two and half times. It is difficult to assess as to how much oif it is the outcome of planned efforts.

But programme wise SIDO conducted more than 1638 EDPs and trained 50,130 potential entrepreneurs during 1978-88. During 1970-86 they conducted 287 programme specially for 6,757 engineer entrepreneurs. IDBI sponsored 550 EDPs benefiting 15,369 entrepreneurs. 6 Since its inception NSTEDB sponsored 147 EDPs benefitting 3,090 potential science & technology entrepreneurs. 7 SBI conducted 125 EDPs during 1978-87 and trained 2,939 persons with success rate of 33 percent. NIESBUD masseurs sponsored 42 EDPs benefitting 1125 potential entrepreneurs. Besides such national bodies large number of programmes were conducted locally by other governmental and non-governmental organisations which have not been recorded systematically. As per one estimate about 1,250 full EDPs of 6 weeks duration are conducted every year benefitting more than 40,000 potential entrepreneurs.

Success Rate: Since entrepreneurship development presently pursued by variety of organisations/agencies with different types of approaches/strategies and also with varying degrees of resources for varied target groups, their rate of success (in terms of the ration of number of entrepreneurs who actually set up their enterprises to the number of persons trained/promoted) naturally show a very wide range of variation (8% of 80%).

Recently nationwide study by NIESBUD, however, reported 27.8% success rate as national average since there are experiences of higher rates of success there seems to be enough scope for further improvement in all aspects of EDPs starting from Identification & Selection of Potential Entrepreneurs; and Quality & Content of Training; Support Services; and Availability/accessibility to infrastructural facility.

Cost of Employment Generation : There are very

few, if any, published documents presenting quantitative and qualitative evaluation of EDPs. In the absence of uniform data for all reported programmes, it may be useful to consider cost of emploment generation from the typical programmes separately.

The cost of conducting full entrepreneurship development programmes include cost of initial campaign, identification & selection, 4-6 weeks training, and follow-up for about 4-6 months after the completion of training. These can be estimated from the existing pattern of expenditure. SISIs are conducting integrated EDP with an expenditure of Rs. 56,000/- for TCOs and other voluntary organisations who conduct EDPs sponsored by IDBI and other financial institutions; NSTEDB & NIESBUD, the cost comes in between Rs. 70-80 thousand. Under difficult areas and for special schemes such as women entrepreneurship the coast goes upto Rs. 100,000/-.

Considerig 30% as success rate and on an average 30 participants per programme the cost for promoting entrepreneurship comes in between Rs. 6000/- and Rs. 11,000/- (without establishment cost) per entrepreneurs who sets up an enterprise with an investment between few thousand to 35 lakhs. SBI Evaluation Study (1986) 10 further help us understand the pattern and size of investment and return by entrepreneurs promoted through such EDPs. The overall average investment by them was reported as Rs. 3.55 lakhs.

To be more precise maximum, i.e., 57.4% invested between 2-5 lakhs; and followed by those 27.9% who invested between 1-2 lakhs; and 8% invested upto Rs. 25,000/- and only 6% invested over Rs. 10 lakhs. In terms of benefits, out of such promoted entrepreneurs 83% sampled units reported making on an average a net profit of Rs. 48,200/- (about 4000/- per month) during 1985.

Another study that provided detailed information about cost/benefit refers to Assam Experiment-Self-Employment through entrepreneurship Motivation Training Centres during 1973-76.

With the total expenditure of Rs. 17.96 lack that included the cost of training of officers, all recurring and non-recurring expenditrue of 6 EMTCs in Assam 534 units started functioning (another 593 received financial sanction but not considered for calculating benefits here) and accordingly the cost for promoting each succeessful entrepreneur was reported having net profit between Rs. 300/- to Rs. 1500/- per month (during mid seventies).

Further the total amount raised and invested by these entrepreneurs in the area amount raised and invested by these entrepreneurs in the area amounted to Rs. 1.2 crores to which Govt. contributed only 12.26 lakhs as seed money. The evauation study further revealed that more than 90% units thus established provided employment to 1-2 persons besides the self-employed owner.

Another valuable and more recent information related to cost-benefit of a typical entrepreneurship development programme for self-employment (in SBI sector) is available with Rural Development Self-emploment Training Institute (RUDSETI), Gurgaon which has been set up jointly by a Trust and two nationalised banks since 1984.

RUDSETI trained 1,832 candidates and 1127 of them have already set up their enterprises, the total of cost on selection, two weeks training counselling and support activities comes to Rs. 795/- per successful self-employed entrepreneurs (this does not include the establishment cost).

In addition, the bank financing to these entrepreneurs on an average was reported as Rs. 18,214/-

per self-employed person, enterprises set up by these entrepreneurs represented 'business' enterprises 28.7% followed by 'industries' 19.6% and 11.6% 'service units'. It was further revealed that 68% of thus promoted entrepreneurs have started earning net profit between Rs. 500/- to Rs. 1500/- per month.

Like in other spheres, Indian women have proved their great potential as successful entrepreneurs. Some of Indian women entrepreneurs today lead the biggest shipping companies, trading and export houses, brewing industry, plastic & electronics establishment.

Garment and handicrafts exports are primarily in the hands of women entrepreneurs. However, such achievement by about 100,000 women entrepreneurs in India touches just the fringe of vast future potential promised to Indian women.

Out of the total 761 million people in India, female comprise 360.74 million representing 47.7% of the total population. There are 99.4 million women workforce (representing 28% of the female population), but as per 1981 census, there are only 150,000 self-employed women accounting for only 5.2% of the total self-employed persons in the country.

Majority of them are engaged in the unorganised sectors like agriculture, agrobased industries handicrafts, handlooms, and cottage based industries. Participation of women as industrial entrepreneurs, however, is comparatively a recent phenomena commencing from 70s onwards.

According to an estimate among 1.6 million SSI entrepreneurs in India during 1986-87, the total number of women entrepreneurs does not exceed 100,000.

Table 1 Indian women's status in entrepreneurial terms

Item	Percentage
Women % to total population	47.7
Women % to total Workplace	36.4
Women % to total Unemployed	40.0
Women % to total Self-employed	5.2
Women % to total SSI Entrepreneurs	7.5

In late 70s, it became conspicuous that women offer great potential as entrepreneurs. Accordingly, besides encouraging more women to join regular EFP, a number of special programmes and strategies were thought out to ensure women to take up entrepreneurship as their career.

During 1978-87, Small Industry Development Organisation (SIDO) with its network of Small Industries Service Institutes (SISI) spread throughout the country conducted 248 Courses exclusively for women benefitting 8,904 potential women entrepreneurs.

During 1986, Industrial Development Bank of India (IDBI) launched a special Scheme for Women Entrepreneurs according to which the training support and counselling is offered in a package.

The scheme emphasized the need to set up modern small scale units in electronics engineering, plastic and chemicals, etc. consistent with the knowledge, skills and personal background of trainees further suggests to include women entrepreneurs so far as possible and provide long lead time and the post-training escort services by the conducting agency until the projects taken up by women entrepreneurs generally reach their break-even stage. The success rate under this scheme has crossed the 50% mark of the national averag. Further, a this helped several new voluntary organisations in acquiring and improving their competencies and infrastructural facilities for conducting effective EDPs for Women.

In September, 1986 the Government of India set up a National Level Standing Committee for Women Entrepreneurs under the Chairmanship of the Minister of State for Youth Affairs, Sports, Women & Child Development. The Standing Committee made suitable recommendations & suggestions to the Government regarding the problem of entrepreneurship amongst women.

In view of the growing importance of women entrepreneurship, several nationalised banks opened special Cells for women entrepreneurs. Many State Financial Corporation have also developed special schemes for assisting the women entrepreneurs. Several entrepreneurs associations are very active in promoting and supporting the cause of entrepreneurship development. Most of them are now having a separate Women's Wing.

Only about a few year ago, an women entrepreneur, in India was visualised as a maker of pickles, papads, masala (spices) and other such household goods. But the recent EDPs have helped them in organising enterprises of complex type, bigger in size, with sophisticated technology involving higher managerial abilities.

As such, the number of women entrepreneurs is increasing very fast. In order to further accelerate the process, it may be necessary to develop more man-power undertaking training and support to women entrepreneurs. Presently, two National Institutions, NIESBUD and EDII are organising half-a-dozen trainers training programme producing not more than 150 trainers in a year. To this even another 100 are added by other newly established institutions such as ICEW in Ahmedabad and IED in Lucknow hardly meeting the 50% of the total requirement.

Usually, it has been observed in the West that economic independence to women will increase the incidence of breaking of 'family tie'. Economic prosperity through entrepreneurial pursuits by Indian women has proved just the contrary. More often, women entrepreneurs have succeed in evolving other family members such as husband, father, mother etc. into her entrepreneurial folds.

This is supported by the fact that majority of successful women entrepreneurs were married (85.5%), mostly between the age 36-45 year (56.2%) and most of them (81.7%) had children of about the age of 10 years. These empirical evidences raises a great of early entrepreneurisation of the whole society by promoting entrepreneurisation of the whole society by promoting entrepreneurship amongst women. Through women participation, the movement is bound to add momentum.

Introduced in 1959, the Panchayati Raj is considered a political and administrative innovation of far-reaching importance. Initially, people envinced keen interest in the Panchayati Raj system and their representatives participated actively in local affairs.

With passage of time, the initial enthusiasm and public participation gradually diminished. Again, after the enactment of the Constitution (73rd Amendment) Act 1992, there is a resurgence of rural local bodies in India. The objects of this amendment are:

- To place more powers in the hands of rural people to determine their own destiny and to build a society;
- To enhance the capabilities of rural people to frame planning from below;

- To decentralize execution of all kinds of development activities with the effective participation of the people; and
- To alter the administrative methods in rural area.

The Panchayati Raj is the embodiment of rural local government with a three-tier system—village, intermediate and district levels—interconnected to provide for a community in experience as well as programme formulation and its implementation. To this system has been given powers and authority of governance as well as of plan formulation and execution.

It has three roles to play simultaneously: (a) as a unit of rural local government; (b) as an instrument of community development; and (c) as an agency of the State government.

XI Schedule: The Constitution Amendment Act 1992 has specified 29 items in the Eleventh Schedule which may be entrusted to the Panchayats in additon to any other schemes for economic development and social justice which may also be entrusted to them by the State governments.

The following items from the Eleventh Schedule are important from environment protection and improvement point of view:

- Agriculture;
- Land immprovement, implementation of land reforms, and soil conservation;
- Minor irrigation, Water management and watershed development;
- Social forestry and farm forestry;
- Minor forest produce;
- Rural housing;
- Drinking water;
- Fuel and fooder;

- Non-conventional energy sources;
- Health and sanitation.

If we compare the jurisdiction of Panchayati Raj with the aims of World Conservation Strategy, we find that Panchayati Raj is fully incorporating the aims in the following manner:

- To maintain essential ecological processes and life-support systems (such as soil regeneration and protection, the recycling of nutrients and cleaning of water) for human survival and development.
- To ensure the sustainable utilization of species and ecosystems (notably fish and other wildlife, forests and grazing lands) which support millions of rural communities as well as major industries.

Decentralized planning: The role of PRIs is crucial for environment protection and improvement. Each tier is involved in the process of local planning about their jurisdiction. The plans are made at village Panchayat and then examined and compiled by the Panchayat at intermediate level (known as Block or Panchayat Samiti). After this, at district level as Zilla Pairshad) all plans from intermediae levels are considered. At the district level, there is a District Plan Committee which consolidates the plan looking to rational utilization of natural utilization of natural resources and environment conservation and forward it to the State Government. Such planning process takes care of local conditions, needs of the people, natural resources and geography of local areas.

The Panchayati Raj institutions have an effective role in the implementation of various policies and programmes contributing to environment protection and improvement, formulated by State and Central governments. In the Rajasthan Panchayati Raj Act, it is specifically mentioned that the State Government by its direction assigns the task of management and maintenance of forests in Panchayat area to Panchayat.

The PRIs also provide necessary assistance to the other agencies engaged in environment protection such as land allotment for forest and establishment of research centres. Besides this, the following roles of PRIs are also important:

- To create will and determination among the rural people to protect and improve the environment;
- To understand the local situation and to share the information about environment;
- To achieve integrated approach by co-ordinating the activities of various agencies interested in environment protection in rural areas;
- To provide a an open forum for discussion on environment protection;
- To give guidance and training to rural people; and
- To restrain the people from those activites which are harmful to environment, if necessary by imposing penalty and fine.

Key to success

Development is the primary concern and responsibility of the people. They must prepare the plan and implement the same. This is much more true with the introduction of Panchayati Raj. The voluntary organizations may also be actively involved in this task. People are the primary concern. It is their confidence and credibility that needs to be obtained. It is mutual trust between government and the people that will repose faith in each other.

There are three basic principles of people-centred development. First, sovereignty resides with the people. Second, to exercise their sovereignty and assume responsibility for their own development and that of their communities, people must control their own resources, have access to relevant information, and have the means to hold the officials of government and voluntary organizations accountable. Third, those who would assist people with their development must recognize that it is they who are participating in support of the people's agenda, not vice-versa. The value of the outsider's contribution will be measured in terms of the enhanced capacity of the people to determine their own future.

The Gandhian model of development requires active involvement and participation of man building his own "destiny". This is possible if some of us belonging to the so-called rich and middle class voluntarily, instead of dfrifting toward consumerism, are willing to sacrifice and share our pleasures in the interests of the downtrodden of our society.

For rural India, time is running out and it must adopt strategies and methods to transform the socio-economic life of people to suit Indian ingenuity and culture. Integrated development sets forth a strategy of working with rural people—a strategy, in which participation by all is both the means and end itself.

In sum, the real wealth of a country lies in "human capital" and if you create conditions where human capital can flourish without being squashed by government controls, you can beat the rest of the countries of the Ninth Plan has to be very positive in building up "social capital" and infrastructure. Our social achievements are not outstanding despite our fifty years of Independence.

Our literacy rate is 52 per cent; infant mortality 74 per thousand; access to sanitation is available to only 16 per cent of the people. Though life expectancy has gone up to 62, the fertility rate is still 3.3 which would double India's population in the next century. Just as the proof of the pudding is in the eating, similarly the success of the Ninth Plan will depend on as to how far it has raised "human capotal" of India.

We have to shift the paradigm of development from a right centred-economy to a duty motivated economy, from self-centredness to the love of our fellowmen, if we want to succeed in our planned development of rural society.

Even though India is one of the few Third World countries which has constitutionalized protection and improvement of environment, the various enactment suffer from several lacunae including the non-recognition of the crucial role that PRIs can play in the endeavour. The involvement of PRIs as the watch-dog of environmental protection at the grass roots level needs to be duty recognized. The Constitution (73rd Amendment) Act 1992 now provides these institutions an opportunity to play their legitimate role. Environment protection represents one of the more recent and yet one of the more profound aspects new public affairs dimension in public administration. Environmental issues have aroused too much intellectual and academic interest both in developing and underdeveloped nations. They include envioronmental degradation, deforestation and desertification, atmospheric pollution and imbalances as well as disertifications in ecology resulting from the way natural resources—land, water, forests, minerals, etc are harnessed for fulfilment of human needs.

The UN Conference on Human Environment in 1972 proclaimed that the defence and improvement of human environment both natural and man-made had become an imperative good for mankind, to be pursued together with fundamental goals of peace and worldwide economic and social development. The achievement of these goals was the responsibility of citizens, communities, enterprises and institutions at every level. Later on, the World Conservation Strategy (1980) and the Brundthland Report also noted the irreversible destruction of ecosystems of the poor countries and the implicit threat to the world security and the consequent political instability and social problems. The problem of environmental crises of the developing countries is different from that of the developed countries.

The establishment of viable community-based institutions for environment protection was suggested with full legal, administrative and technical support. These institutions should be empowered to plan, to work out the modality and to implement the various measures for environment protection and conservation. The Panchayati Raj as an institution of local rural government is the excellent model for it in rural India.

Among the developing countries, india is also facing environmental problems and crises. The enormous increase in population is the most potent cause for acceleration of the overutilization of productive resources and downgrading the quality of environment.

India has a domesticated animal population of nearly 500 million. Considering that only 3.5 per cent of the land area are under grass, the population is supported by the forest and agriculture residues which are thereby diverted from agricultural land. Out of the total cultivable land, 175 million ha are degraded needing special treatment to restore productivity.

Of the 75 million ha designated as forest land, only 35 million ha are close forest. Despite all efforts, India has continued to lose forest cover. The deforestation causes loss in bivodiversity. Over 1,500 species of plants and animals are on the endangered list. Levels of air and water pollution are much beyond acceptable limits. These challenges disturb the environment equilibrium and the life of mankind.

The basic aim of our National Forest Policy must be to ensure environmental stability and maintenance of ecological balance including atmospheric which are vital for the sustenance of all forms of life—human, animal and plant. Rural India has different kinds of environmental crises compared to other countries. The rapid growth of rural population has placed inexorable burden on farm as well as on other land resources, on forests, on water resources and worsened the quality of life of the rural poor in respect of housing, health, ecological surroundings and other essentials.

Constitution & environmental protection: The Un Declaration on Human Environment in 1972 signalled India to initiate positive steps in the direction towards environment improvement.

The Constitution of India has conceptualized its thinking on environment in the form of the Directive Principles of State Policy in favour of protection and improvement of environment, and safeguarding of forests and wildlife (Article 48A), a fundamental duty to protect and improve the natural environment including forests, lakes, rivers and wildlife and to have compassion for living creatures [Article 51A(g)], and a subject in the Consurrent List in its Seventh Schedule (Item 17A and 17B). Both the Directive principles and Fundamental Duty are non-justiciable, but these provide the necessary constitutional sanction if the State intends to adopt a law in the matter.

Administrative control: The other component of the infrastructure for environment improvement and protection is provided by the existing legislation. There are 30 major enactments such as Water Cess Act, Forest Act, Forest Conservation Act, Wildlife Protection Act, Environment Protection Act, of Union and State Governments. Administrative actions—regulatory, negotiational and persuasive—under these enactments are mainly taken by the Central and State administrative organizations—the Central Ministry of Environment and Forests, the Central Pollution Control Board and the State Departments of Environment and State Pollution Control Boards.

Besides this, there also exist the other administrative mechanisms concerned with the implementation of policies on environment. The Panchayati Raj institutions have also become important instruments in rural India for environment protection and improvement.